PENGUIN

Live. Fight. Survive.

Born in Watford, Shaun Pinner served for nine years with the British Army's Royal Anglian Regiment, latterly as part of 24 Airmobile Brigade on operations for the UN in Bosnia. He joined the Ukrainian military in 2018 as the country rebuilt its armed forces following the annexation of Crimea. He was deployed to a forward position with the Air Assault Company, 1st Battalion, 36th Brigade, Ukrainian Marines when Russia invaded in February 2022. Captured after the siege of Mariupol, he spent the next six months as a prisoner of war. Following his release in September 2022, Shaun was awarded Ukraine's Order of Courage by President Volodymyr Zelenskyy. He has since travelled extensively, briefing NATO forces on his experiences. He is currently living in Ukraine with his wife, Larysa.

Live
Fight
Survive

One Soldier's Extraordinary Story
of the War against Russia

SHAUN PINNER

WITH MATT ALLEN

PENGUIN BOOKS

PENGUIN BOOKS

UK | USA | Canada | Ireland | Australia
India | New Zealand | South Africa

Penguin Books is part of the Penguin Random House group of companies
whose addresses can be found at global.penguinrandomhouse.com.

First published by Penguin Michael Joseph 2023
Published in Penguin Books 2024
001

Printed and bound in Great Britain by Clays Ltd, Elcograf S.p.A.

The authorized representative in the EEA is Penguin Random House Ireland,
Morrison Chambers, 32 Nassau Street, Dublin D02 YH68

A CIP catalogue record for this book is available from the British Library

ISBN: 978–1–405–95977–3

www.greenpenguin.co.uk

I'd like to dedicate the book to the brave fighters of the Armed Forces of Ukraine for the continuing defence of its sovereignty, to my colleagues and friends still in captivity and to those who paid the ultimate sacrifice.

Слава Україні

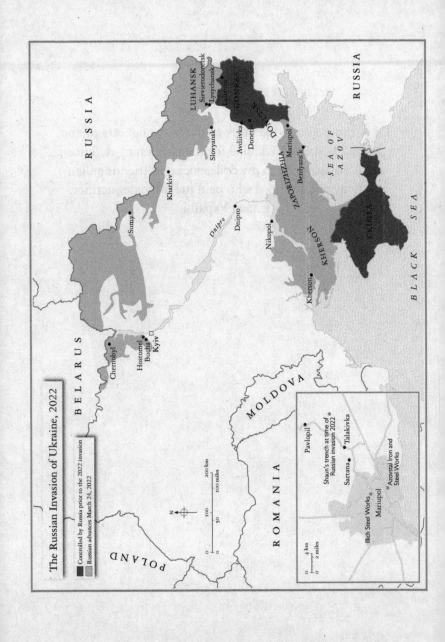

The Russian Invasion of Ukraine, 2022

- Controlled by Russia prior to the 2022 invasion
- Russian advances March 24, 2022

POLAND

BELARUS

RUSSIA

Chernobyl
Hostomel
Bucha
Kyiv

Sumy

Kharkiv

Slovyansk

LUHANSK
Sievierodonetsk
Lysychansk

DONBAS

Avdiivka
Donetsk

DONETSK

Dnipro

Dnipro

Nikopol

ZAPORIZHZHIA

Mariupol
Berdyans'k

SEA OF AZOV

Kherson

KHERSON

CRIMEA

BLACK SEA

RUSSIA

MOLDOVA

ROMANIA

N

0   50   100   200 km
0   50   100   200 miles

Pavlopil

Shaun's trench at time of
Russian invasion 2022

Talakivka

Sartana

Illich Steel Works

Mariupol

Azovstal Iron and
Steel Works

0   4 km
0   2 miles

FOREWORD

Shaun Pinner and I served together in another eastern European war zone, in the Balkans in 1994. Back then he was a Royal Anglian infantryman just out of his teens and not long out of training, but it was already obvious he was exactly the sort of man you would want standing beside you when the bullets were flying. That's what his comrades in the Ukrainian Marines found out as they fought back against blistering Russian assaults, as did those who shared captivity with him in a menacing black site, struggling to survive months of brutal imprisonment. Shaun's military training and combat experience, as well as his stoicism, care for his fellow man and, not least, his British soldier's unyielding sense of humour, kept him and those around him going despite beatings, torture and growing hopelessness. When I saw him shortly after his release under a deal struck by the Crown Prince of Saudi Arabia, it was the same old Shaun despite all the horrors he had been through. I was mesmerized as he told, with both his words and his eyes, a visceral story of close battle, seizure by the enemy, incarceration and kangaroo trial complete with death sentence. He now shares it all so graphically in these pages, a war story unlike any other, which will both chill and inspire everyone who reads it. His experiences help us understand the tragic conflict in Ukraine, with a fascinating real-time glimpse into the minds of those doing Putin's malignant bidding and the brave men fighting to defend their country's freedom. But above all, this book is an unforgettable insight into how an ordinary human being can find the strength to live, fight and survive unbroken despite pulverising battlefield bombardments and a sinister prison regime intent on shattering the spirit.

Colonel Richard Kemp CBE
Former Commanding Officer,
1st Battalion, The Royal Anglian Regiment

AUTHOR'S NOTE

Some of the dialogue that takes place in this book was conducted in a mixture of Russian, Ukrainian and English. Some interviews, interrogations and legal meetings were conducted through translators – either official language experts or friends who could speak better Russian than me. Rather than detailing exactly how certain conversations happened, I have reproduced the meaning faithfully throughout.

PROLOGUE

DATE: 13 APRIL 2022
LOCATION: AN FSB BLACK SITE,
RUSSIAN-OCCUPIED DONETSK

The torturer's mask was a worry.

A gossamer-thin balaclava, the type worn by an old-school bank robber, it had two eyeholes and a gaping space for the mouth. Even though I was hooded and close to blacking out after several hours of physical abuse at the hands of Russian special forces operators, I'd briefly spotted it while being pushed into what I guessed was an interrogation room. The wearer was a beast: an intimidating bloke who looked like he lived in a gym, all while feasting on a diet of 'roids and raw meat. From what I could tell, his skin was pale and his brown eyes were bloodshot. Through the contours of the mask I'd noticed the silhouette of a broad nose and small chin. The rest was a mystery, other than the fact that everybody around him seemed eager to please, which meant one thing: the fucker was from the secret police or maybe even the Federal Security Service, or FSB – Vladimir Putin's rebranded version of the KGB. As a group they were known to specialise in torture, intimidation and cold-blooded murder.

Great. That's me done for, then, I thought.

Everything about the past twelve hours in captivity had told me I was in serious trouble. The Russian military clearly gave zero shits about the Geneva Convention, and I had already been beaten, stabbed in the leg and electrocuted. In an attempt to stop the pain, I had handed over a few basic, inconsequential details about my life, stuff that anyone with a phone could have found on social media. Snippet Number One explained who I was: a forty-eight-year-old, former British soldier from Watford with previous stints in Northern Ireland and Bosnia. Snippet Number Two gave away the bare minimum about what I was doing: helping Ukraine's 36th Marine Brigade, First Battalion defend the city of Mariupol in the south-east of the country. And, finally, snippet Number Three revealed my *why*: I had grown to love the place while living there with my wife for the best part of three years. Ukraine was my home and I was determined to protect its borders from a Russian land grab. At the time, I'd hoped those details would save me from further torture. It clearly hadn't worked out that way.

There's a chilling reality that kicks in when someone is being smashed about by the highly skilled thugs Mother Russia tends to employ as interrogators. Keeping quiet is not an option, and at some point the captive has to give up a little information to stay alive – about who they are, where they're from and what they're fighting for. Sidestepping a question or acting snarky will only end in a beating, or a punishment so dehumanising that it leaves a deep emotional scar. The trick is to give up just enough intel without overplaying the hand. In my case, I didn't intend to reveal anything that would identify the lads from my platoon, many of whom were still on the run, or their intended destination.

For a while, I'd been fairly pleased with my performance, but now that a possible FSB agent was scrutinising my story, there was a worrying reality to consider. It was probably more convenient for the Russians to kill a prisoner of little value than to incarcerate them and Mr Balaclava's appearance was a sure sign that my arrival had been deemed a priority. The enemy must have thought I had important intelligence to share, whether I wanted to or not. Meanwhile, the fact I'd been taken to a 'black site' – an off-the-grid interrogation facility where, presumably, a lot of bad stuff happened – meant I could expect plenty of hurt and stress. I looked down and shuddered. Through the gap in my hood, I noticed I'd been sitting on a medical trolley.

This is going to be bad, I thought, wanting to puke, realising that all I could do was accept the suffering coming my way.

I pictured Mr Balaclava pacing the room, circling me, as if picking a moment to strike. *Left, right. Backwards, forwards.* Every now and then I heard the squeak of shoe leather and jerked my head, flinching at an imagined punch. *But nothing came.* Around me, several people laughed loudly and swore in Russian.

I focused on my next breath. Even if I'd been able to see, there was no effective way of defending myself. I'd been bound tightly at the wrists with loops of masking tape, and the attack might come from anywhere. (Masking tape was cheap, readily available, and painfully effective when hooked around a prisoner's limbs in a figure-of-eight shape.) There was also the realisation that my mind was playing tricks on me. At one point, the hairs on the back of my neck prickled. I could have sworn Mr Balaclava was breathing close by, and it was hard not to catastrophise. As the seconds passed like minutes, the worst-case scenarios played out in real time. I pictured a rope tightening around my throat, then a jawline of teeth cascading to the floor like smashed piano keys. *Jesus, were they going to waterboard me?* My mind galloped. Every muscle, bone and ligament in my body was braced for agony.

And then Mr Balaclava spoke in English.

'Don't worry, Shaun Pinner,' he said. 'You will find discomfort and pain in this place. But you will be OK . . .'

Bloody hell. *Was that supposed to be reassuring?* I guessed not, because as far as the Russians were concerned, I'd involved myself in a war that wasn't really mine to fight, and that made me fair game. Then I noticed *why* his voice was so bloody unnerving. *There was no emotion.*

Zero anger. *Don't worry, Shaun . . .*

No frustration, tension or anxiety. *You will find discomfort and pain . . .*

His timbre was deep, almost soothing, like a dentist chatting to a nervous root-canal patient. *But you will be OK . . .*

The penny dropped. Mr Balaclava sounded like a Buddhist monk because he was in complete control. Me? I was the caged lab rat, exposed and vulnerable and highly likely to suffer, especially if I said the wrong thing. Death was probably going to feel like a merciful release at some point in the very near future.

My torturer spoke again. He had moved even closer.

'The Russians used to break the legs and arms of my ancestors when they dared to invade the Motherland . . .' he said.

Oh, God. I wanted to edge back on the table, to protect my limbs, but it was impossible to wriggle away. *What ancestors? Who was this bloke?* I pictured Mr Balaclava wielding an iron bar or baseball bat. He was probably sizing up my legs, deciding which kneecap to hobble. *Left? Or right?* I wondered whether I was ever going to walk again.

'. . . However, you will not experience that here.'

My head spun. *How was I supposed to react now?* I knew that composure was everything in these situations, but putting the theory into practice was harder than most people realised. At the same time, pushing back or reacting to provocation would only crank up my chances of getting seriously injured or killed. What I said next would be vitally important.

'Look, I—'

'Do you know where you are?' said Mr Balaclava suddenly.

I shook my head. *Not a bloody clue.*

'You are in the city of Donetsk.'

My heart sank. Talk about being dropped into the lion's den. I had been transported deep into Russian-occupied Ukraine.

'So this is what is going to happen,' he continued. 'We are going to give you some food. But first we are going to stitch up your injury.'

I felt another someone, a medic maybe – *hopefully* – prodding at the stab wound in my leg. Every push and pinch was hell.

'And we are going to give you an injection, too.'

'No. I don't want that—'

'Don't worry. It is for the pain.'

There was no point in pleading, because whatever happened next was beyond my control. The needle plunged into my neck and my mind blurred and darkened at the edges. As I faded away, Mr Balaclava talked me to sleep.

'You have had a bad day, Shaun,' he said, calmly.

My eyes drooped.

'But now you can get some rest . . .'

I had no idea whether I was going to open them again.

PART ONE

Where the Warriors Go

PART ONE

Where the Crawdads Sing

When the invasion kicked off on 24 February 2022, I was right at the bloody front of it, running up and down the lines of a muddy trench in the freezing cold, diving into cover from artillery fire while trying my best not to get ripped apart by a bullet or mortar blast. That opening day in the conflict between Ukraine and Russia was some of the hardest fighting I had experienced as a soldier, and the enemy threw everything they could at us in an attempt to bludgeon our forces into submission. My guess was that they wanted to steamroller their way across the country in a couple of days. Miraculously, we held firm.

At this point, you're probably wondering how a bloke from Watford ended up scrapping with the Ukrainian Marines in the first place. Well, the answer lies in a weird combination of the love of military service and the love of a good woman. And without the first, it's unlikely the second would have happened at all. Growing up, I'd always wanted to be a soldier in some capacity, which was the fault of my grandad – a World War II veteran with the photos to match the stories. My dad's passing when I was nine years old instilled plenty of resilience, and when Mum later moaned about my being in front of the computer all day as a teenager, I looked into the military life. For a while I quite fancied the Royal Navy, but eventually I joined the Royal Anglian Regiment. Thrust into basic training at the Bassingbourn Barracks in Cambridgeshire in 1991, at the age of seventeen, I soon learned everything a soldier needed to know about combat survival. By the sound of things, war was hell, but I was fit and up for it.

Before long I was serving in Northern Ireland, which was an eye-opening way to earn your dough, and my role was multi-layered. At times, I supported the Royal Ulster Constabulary in both covert and overt operations during the bloody conflict with the Provisional IRA. I also provided security from snipers for bomb-disposal experts as they defused explosive booby traps. But mainly I monitored terrorist activity by watching people of interest from under-cover positions. For the most part, I was able to avoid too much contact or drama, though everything changed with the Shankill Road bombing in 1993. The attack was apparently an assassination plot gone wrong. Two members of the IRA had delivered a bomb to a fish and chip shop with the claimed intention of murdering the leaders of the loyalist Ulster Defence Association. The device went off early and ten people were killed, including one of the bombers and two kids. Many more were injured. I was one of the first on the scene and helped to set up the cordon around the site. When I arrived, the ground was still smouldering.

I experienced a powerful sense of duty and camaraderie in Northern Ireland, and I loved it. Everyone had my back, as I had theirs, and at times it was as if I'd joined another family. We trained, fought and drank together – the bond was essential given the risks were so high. One day, while sitting in the canteen in the Grosvenor Road RUC station, a Provisional IRA car drove past and opened fire at the two officers on duty outside. After hearing the commotion, we sprinted into the street and chased after the vehicle. Friendly rounds ripped past us, striking the car and setting it ablaze, but by the time we'd caught up, the enemy had scarpered.

The job wasn't done though. Someone shouted out that the car might have been booby-trapped with a secondary explosive device and the terrorists were luring us in with what was known as a 'come-on'. We approached cautiously and once we'd checked the scene over safely and returned to the station, I burned with adrenaline for hours.

During my nine years of service with the Royal Anglian Regiment, I was assigned to the 24 Airmobile Brigade (in 1993 and 1994), a quick reaction force that operated in Bosnia following the violent fragmentation of Yugoslavia. My role required me to move to any part of the country at any time, and when it was explained that I'd possibly have to help rescue downed pilots from the UN peacekeeping mission, which included personnel from the UK and France, among others, I was stoked.

As part of my training, I had to undertake a six-week Survival, Evasion, Resistance and Escape (SERE) course, in case I was unfortunate enough to be captured behind enemy lines. This work sent me to Washington State, in the Pacific Northwest of the USA, where I was schooled in how to think on my feet and how to survive in the wild by living off the land, snaring all sorts of animals. We were trained to build shelters that were difficult to detect with the naked eye, and in a series of escape-and-evasion assessments, I had to go on the run with a small team, moving from grid to grid, all while evading a highly motivated hunter team. Having eventually been captured, I was hooded and interrogated, and the treatment I received felt terrifyingly realistic – I learned as much as I'd wanted to know about how to handle tactical questioning, physical intimidation, stress positions and the various phases of capture. Nobody was given special treatment and everyone suffered. In fact, the work was so intense that some of the team caught mild hypothermia after crawling around in the snow for a few days. Having negotiated these challenges, I came through the test in good shape.

Luckily, I never had to put those skills into practice during my army career, though I witnessed the grim reality of war close up. In Bosnia, there was evidence of ethnic cleansing and rape by Bosnian Serb forces, and while on leave in Croatia, I heard the historic city of Dubrovnik being bombed to pieces. The explosions sounded like rolling thunder, even though I was miles away at the time. Later, I met a local kid some of the lads had nicknamed Harry, after the spivvy Flash Harry character from those old *St Trinian's* films. He was only about twelve years old, but he had the salesman skills of an arms dealer: he offered to sell me a grenade for 200 dollars and an AK-47 for 900. Although he was Bosnian, he spoke in an American accent he'd picked up from watching MTV. It was a sad indication of how conflict could wreck a kid's life.

When I left the military in 1999, my world fell apart. For two years I slogged it out in a manufacturing plant, making mono blocks for driveways, but my marriage was failing and I felt awful. Work was shit, life was shit – *everything was shit*. After working for a hazardous waste management company in Bedford and Nottingham for several years, I started my own business in the same industry in 2014, turning over around £200,000 a year. I'd briefly found a sense of purpose again, but the feeling was short-lived. Another relationship broke up, my mojo went with it and I became nostalgic for the camaraderie and adventure of military life. It turned out that with a business to run I felt bloody unhappy, maybe even depressed, but with nothing more than a rucksack on my back, I could lead a happy life. Something had to change. I was in my early forties at the time and my son was buggering off to university to find his drinking legs. There certainly wasn't a lot to hang about for in England, so when some mates told me about their lives working in the contract soldiering game in 2016, I took an interest. Typically for a group of former squaddies, they had created a self-deprecating name for themselves – Minimum Wage Mercs – but, in reality, they were nothing of the sort: these lads were professionals and committed to the work they were doing. In Syria, they scrapped alongside the People's Protection Units, also known as YPG International, a group of Kurds and foreign fighters who were helping the Syrian Democratic Forces (SDF) in a campaign against ISIS. But it wasn't the money that interested me, it was the realisation I could do some good in the world again, and when I agreed to sign up, the move proved life-changing.

For starters, we were smuggled into Syria via a network of safe houses, which was a first. I then experienced a different style of conflict from the kind I'd been used to. Most days were spent working in twelve-hour shifts, providing security for the tactical medical unit as my team patrolled the civilian areas behind enemy lines, all while looking for hostile gunmen that might have broken through. Sometimes we experienced contact, sometimes we didn't, and I soon discovered that the war was a fairly lopsided affair. ISIS, while heavily funded and highly motivated, didn't have the mortars, artillery or air support. *But we did.*

I then worked with a platoon of foreigners helping to build training infrastructure by constructing shooting ranges and improving communications. It was made up of Americans, Germans, English, Kurds and, of course, Brits striving to liberate the city of Raqqa and the work opened me up to a whole new military career. Some of it I connected with, some of it I didn't, and the positives were found in the fact that I had joined a force for good. In many ways, the YPG represented a very modern ideal within the region: its aim was to promote multicultural equality and rights for women. The YPG even referred to itself as the women's revolution, which was something I could get behind. We were also working to stop a barbaric enemy looking to inflict maximum pain on innocent civilians. When a town or village was liberated from ISIS control, we'd often find evidence of mass rape and torture. Given there was a $250,000 bounty on the head of every Western fighter, avoiding capture was a priority.

I soon realised that most of the people I was working alongside could be divided into one of three categories: runaways, killers or believers. I fitted best in the first bracket because I craved adventure, brotherhood and purpose. I certainly hadn't been getting that at a waste management company in Bedford. Mainly, I was scrapping alongside people with a similar world view, lads who wanted to help defeat an enemy that was wreaking havoc on a vulnerable civilian population. The downside of joining such a diverse group was the others it attracted: the anarchists and communists. Many were untrained and either overly religious or intensely political, and the different groups sometimes squabbled amongst themselves. For all the good we did in Syria, I knew that being part of such a messy set-up didn't work for me. I preferred structure and discipline.

When I was later asked to help out in Ukraine in late 2017, I thought, *Why the hell not?* I knew a lot of experienced soldiers who were travelling there from the UK, the USA, Europe and Australia, and they were defending the country from an aggressive Russian army who were causing trouble on the border. Though I hadn't witnessed first-hand how ruthless Putin's forces could be while serving in Syria, I knew they were considered a highly trained, heavily tooled-up mob of thugs and killers – and I was eager to push them back. When it was suggested that I help to train the Azov Assault Brigade, a Mariupol-based wing of the Ukrainian National Guard, I jumped at the chance. At that time, Azov were legit, an official wing of the national military. Also, Mariupol was an up-and-coming city perched on the Sea of Azov, with one or two cracking beaches nearby. Given that Bedford hadn't exactly turned into a tropical paradise during my absence, I took the plunge.

My brief on arriving in Ukraine in 2018 was fairly straight-forward. The higher-ups in the Ukrainian military, fearing another large-scale Russian attack in the wake of the 2014 annexation of Crimea (more on which later), were keen to learn from their Western counterparts. My previous experience and knowledge put me in the top one per cent of military assets in Ukraine, and from 2018 to 2020 I trained the men and women of the Azov brigade, specialising mainly in sniper skills, fieldcraft, surveillance and reconnaissance. I shared my knowledge of map-reading and navigation, and how to master basic shooting techniques without the use of too much technology. One thing I'd noticed was that a lot of troops were using the GPS on their phones for navigation, which was a massive red flag. A mobile was a treasure trove of intelligence and, if picked up by the enemy, any locational data could be used against an individual or team.

At this point it's probably best if I explain the political affiliations of Azov, because in 2022 the group became the focal point of some wildly exaggerated, Kremlin-backed propaganda during the early weeks of the war. The smoke-screen for Putin's initial bombardments of cities such as Mariupol was that he was engaging in a specialist military operation in order to de-Nazify Ukraine. Certainly, in its early days, Azov had been vilified for carrying an association with neo-Nazism and far-right symbolism, a lot of which had to do with their past connections to extreme football-hooliganism culture. I heard one original member describing the 2014 incarnation of Azov as being 'a bunch of ultras with guts'. However, the group I'd signed up with was a completely different animal and those unpleasant elements had disappeared.

As far as I was concerned, Russia was talking bollocks. While working with Azov, I don't recall anyone forcing their ideology on me, whether they were on the far left or the far right, and I worked with people from all sorts of cultures. Within my company, there were Jewish, Islamic and Muslim lads; blokes from Crimea, others who were Tatars. Yes, I saw one or two debatable tattoos, symbols inspired by the Nordic gods, but I'm not entirely sure what they meant and I never witnessed or overheard any racism. That's not to say it didn't exist, though. One or two people might have held some suspect views, but in that respect Azov was no differ-ent from any army, navy or air force. Sadly, in such a large group of people there will always be a few manky apples.

At that time, the Ukrainian military was one of the big-gest employers in the area. Unemployment was high in the regions around Mariupol, especially in its outlying villages, and there were plenty of willing men and women looking for work. I could understand the appeal: Azov gave its troops a sense of purpose, there was unity and everybody got to work out daily and learn new, transferable skills in organisation and leadership. Also, the military provided food and a steady income. All of the people I came into contact with during my early days working in the city had bought into the 'brand' and the idea of fighting for a democratic and free Ukraine. That was good enough for me. When joining an army, I wanted to stand alongside people who were up for the good fight, soldiers who knew their stuff and weren't going to scarper in tough times. Whenever I walked through Mariupol, the fighters in Azov were treated like heroes.

There was plenty for them to fight for. Like a lot of foreign fighters in Ukraine, I soon came to understand the country's complicated political situation, its weird relationship with Russia and the long-running Donbas War in the east of the country. For years the Putin regime had reportedly held designs on reclaiming former Soviet Union states, including the independent Ukraine, and the idea of them taking the country by force had been amplified when Crimea – a peninsula in the south – was invaded and annexed in 2014. That same year, forces sympathetic to Putin took over several government buildings in Donetsk and Luhansk, claiming the two regions of the Donbas as independent republics. A similar uprising was attempted in Mariupol, but it failed to gather momentum.

The Ukrainian government, understandably annoyed at these land grabs, began to resist, and both groups became locked in a long-running 'static' conflict in the Donbas, where two armies, their soldiers hunkered down in trenches and tunnels, lobbed artillery at one another. Not even a couple of peace treaties and dozens of ceasefires could slow the violence. Russia backed the separatists, known as the Donetsk People's Republic (DPR) and the Luhansk

People's Republic (LPR), with covert military support, and it was later estimated that 14,000 people on both sides were killed between 2014 and 2021. Around 3,400 of them were civilians.

From the Kremlin's perspective, Ukraine had plenty worth fighting for: it had vast natural resources such as coal and steel, and the most fertile farmland in Europe. Its reserves of sunflower seeds and grain made it a serious agricultural power. I'd certainly never seen so many golden flowers until I'd made it through my first Ukrainian summer. The fields glowed. Strategically, the country was positioned on the border of several eastern European and NATO countries and Russia's gas pipelines ran across its land. In Odesa it had a port with access to the Black Sea. Within the country, the population spoke both Russian and Ukrainian, but most importantly, all of it had once belonged to the Soviet Union, of which Putin was an unashamed fanboy.

On the forefront of all this was Mariupol, an industrial, coastal city perched on the land that stood between the Russian-occupied regions of Luhansk and Donetsk and Russian-occupied Crimea. Essentially the city and its sur-rounding settlements were a vital blockade when preventing Russia from taking eastern Ukraine. Success for Putin here would only mark the beginning, though. By snatching the city and its surrounding territories, the Russian military could then make a strong start in landlocking the entire country. When the Donbas War had first kicked off, a series of rocket strikes on the city killed thirty people in 2015, but Mariupol had held firm.

From a financial perspective, the city was also an export powerhouse and home to a number of steel and iron works that were positioned to service ports across the Middle East, among other places, making it a vital cog in Ukraine's overall economy. But it was playing a part in the country's changing identity too. Mariupol was transforming. Its bustling squares, coffee shops and restaurants were more in line with a fancy European city, and the popular bakery Lviv Croissant had opened a branch, which was a sure sign of progress. McDonald's was rumoured to be returning and the nearby beaches were some of the best in the region. A tourist could grab a spot on the sand, put down a towel and not see another person. It was just about everything Putin hated, which is why he wanted to send it all back to the Dark Ages. Defending it was a must.

Suddenly, I had a cause to get behind, but to help Ukraine defend its territories, I first had to prove myself as a soldier by passing a basic selection test. One element of this induction was the completion of a three-kilometre run in under fifteen minutes. During my younger years I'd have breezed through it, but I was approaching my mid forties and my body wasn't as supple as it once was. At times, I wondered whether my knees would hold out under the pressure. In the end I came top of my selection group after nailing a series of shooting tests with a Kalashnikov AK-74 assault rifle. But the pressure on me remained high. In my first few weeks of up-skilling the group, I was told my work would have to be next-level because (1) I was British, and (2) because of (1), everybody would be copying my actions. Luckily, I still had the will and desire to prove myself.

And this is where the love of a good woman comes into the story. It was September 2018 when I first met Larysa. I'd been working with the Azov Brigade for around three or four months and the connection was like a lightning bolt. The pair of us had been friends for a little while and at first there had been nothing romantic or even flirtatious between us, but I fancied her. Larysa was beautiful. Even better, she had heart and was up for the scrap. When we were introduced, Larysa had been working with a civilian organisation that specialised in locating and deactivating landmines planted in Ukraine by Putin's forces. On her days off, she often took part in protests against Mariupol's steelworks and the pollution they brought to the area. I thought her scrappy spirit was incredible.

I didn't speak Ukrainian very well at the time, though I had been taking lessons in Russian because the two languages were similar in the same way that Portuguese and Spanish are comparable. But we still clicked and when I asked her out, I couldn't believe it when she actually said yes. I'd never been the romantic type. I'd been schooled in how to shoot at moving targets, rescue pilots stranded behind enemy lines and spy on potential terrorists. Charming someone I was falling for was a whole other ball game, especially as I was clearly punching above my weight.

After six months of dating, I moved out of the Azov barracks and into Larysa's home. We got on great, shared many of the same interests and never argued. A small community formed around our relationship. Her friends accepted me as part of the group and there was never any sense that I was there as a tourist. Quite the opposite, in fact: I was known as the Englishman in Mariupol – *a somebody* – whereas in England I was nothing more than a number. I was also falling in love with the city and its people. By 2020 I'd applied for a one-year temporary residency (which was to be renewed annually) after transferring to the 36th Marine Brigade, First Battalion on a three-year contract in 2019, which would mean joining the battle against Russia in

Donbas. They were – like the Royal Marines in the UK – a wing of the navy rather than the army. We were sailors, not privates. Then, the following year, Larysa and I made our relationship official and got married. I felt like a pig in shit.

By 2021, I was earning $1,100 a month on the front line. Larysa was bringing in more with the demining organisation, but at times it felt like we were living off pop-star money. A pint of beer in Mariupol cost around £0.50, a steak £1.50, and the local produce was bloody cheap. There was no way I would have enjoyed the same lifestyle in the UK doing what I was doing, and it was enough to make it feel as if we were living it up. If we fancied a picnic on the beach, we'd call friends, light a bonfire and barbecue some lamb shashlik as the sun went down. There was a sense of freedom to go with it, too. The city council didn't bother with sneaky parking charges or speed cameras and you could fish for free, without a licence, because the authorities trusted its community.

Also, Mariupol had an identity. Yes, there were one or two historical throwbacks in its architecture and tram system. But the new city felt cosmopolitan and modern. It had a bustling population of nearly 440,000 people, with a large international contingent, thanks to the local university. I quite fancied retiring there when my military contract eventually ran out, and perhaps buying a house near the beach – once the Russians had stopped playing silly buggers, that is. Mariupol seemed as good a place as any to see out my golden years, and nothing was going to tear me away.

Then wouldn't you know it – *everything changed*.

2

Scrapping on the front lines with First Battalion from 2019 onwards was ugly, but nothing prepared me for my first Russian tank attack. *Whoomph!* When the rocket ripped through the ground with explosive violence, the whole trench seemed to shake for minutes afterwards. I sank into my position, praying for it to be a one-off, worrying that if another landed, our line would be ripped apart, killing everyone inside or that the threadbare infrastructure we'd taken so long to build would be destroyed – like the mud-walled bedrooms or the damp wood-lined caves that doubled up for kitchens and sewage pits. As the ground settled and the shouting began, the enemy's artillery proceeded to pound our position for another forty-five minutes. The noise and the force of the attack were relentless. From time to time I heard the ominous pop of mortar fire. On first catching the noise, I had approximately twenty seconds to find a place of cover before the blast turned everything to shit.

The type of fighting I was involved in wouldn't have looked out of place in a World War I drama. The company was operating from a boggy network of trenches and bunkers positioned between twenty and twenty-five kilometres outside Mariupol, in places such as Chermalyk, and no matter where we were stationed, our orders had a familiar ring to them: to watch and listen to the Russians. Ahead of our thirty-strong group, by no more than a kilometre or so, were hundreds of separatist fighters from the DPR, all of them tooled up by Putin's government. If everything went to hell and a convoy of enemy tanks rolled over the horizon with the intention of steaming into Mariupol and deeper Ukraine, we were the first line of defence. A lot of the time it felt as if I'd been stuck out on a limb.

If I could draw one positive from being bombarded by enemy artillery, it was the heat. During the breaks in fighting, or when yet another temporary ceasefire was being called, life on the front line could be incredibly uncomfortable. In winter, the temperatures dropped to as low as −28°C, and, in the morning, anyone crawling out of their *blindazh* – or sleeping quarters – usually experienced a flash-freeze. As the sun came up, it was common to see groups of soldiers doing star jumps or press-ups as a way of getting the blood pumping. The alternative was to stand still and die from hypothermia. In the cold, my fingers and toes ached and my eyes threatened to freeze over. At one point, during my first January on the lines, I looked down at my weapon and wondered if I'd been the victim of a practical joke. The metal had turned white. *Had some shitbag painted my gear?* Then I realised the colouring was the result of the cold.

I felt like absolute crap for 99 per cent of the time. In the freezing mornings, the puddles in the trench would harden with ice. The impact of my boot breaking through into the deep, gluey swamp below, sometimes up to my shins, was utterly demoralising. We were forever bailing out water in the areas outside our viewing posts and sleeping quarters, but they usually flooded again within hours because it pissed down with rain and snow for long periods of time. This type of trench maintenance was essential, though. We'd need to move sharpish if a special forces unit ever attacked or the DPR infantry came in. Getting pulled down by the mud and gloop would only slow our response, which might prove fatal.

Another downside of being so cold and wet in winter was that the body needed more calories to maintain its core temperature – someone reckoned it was an extra couple of thousand a day given the type of work we were doing. But the rations available to us were pretty thin on the ground, and that was before the invasion. Any fruit and veg brought to the lines tended to perish pretty quickly and most of the time we were forced to live off scraps. In our case, that mainly involved Grechka, a brand of parboiled buckwheat that was fairly easy to cook and swallow down with the right seasoning, especially if it was added to chicken or red meat. I soon got sick of the stuff, though I wasn't the only one. During a joint training exercise, some British soldiers pulled a face when Grechka was served up for the first time.

'What's this shit?' said one, gingerly poking at his pan with a spoon.

I laughed. 'Welcome to Ukraine, mate.'

Around three kilometres back from the front line was a shop, and whenever there was a lull in the hostilities, one of the lads was dispatched to pick up supplies such as pasta, cheese and spices. Sometimes, we would receive care packages from our families and one soldier was regularly sent home-made jam, which always went down a treat, especially at breakfast, though it rarely lasted for longer than a day. And when times were really tough, we lived off the land. There was a river nearby and the lads were often sent out to catch wrack, which was very similar to crayfish, and tasted lovely, like crab meat. But if a pheasant ever wandered by, which wasn't uncommon, we were ordered to shoot and gut the thing. A handful of chewy, roasted meat was the closest we came to five-star dining.

When the shooting eventually stopped, I would walk down the trench to check on the others, making sure that nobody had been killed or badly wounded. Death had become a regular event out there. During my first week or two of fighting in 2019, I'd walked towards an old green Vauxhall Frontera that was supposed to be taking a group of us away from the position. Suddenly, a barrage of 152 mm shells, fired from a Soviet-designed cannon, exploded around us. Some of the blasts were at our rear, others ripped up the ground ahead, and having learned that our position had taken a direct hit, we drove back to the carnage once the attack was over. Five of our lads had been killed and three others were badly hurt by shrapnel. Following on from my experiences in Northern Ireland, Bosnia and Syria, I considered myself to be fairly battle-seasoned, but nothing had prepared me for the onslaught in Ukraine. The fighting was never-ending and at times the heavy artillery rained down on us for hours at a time. *Bom! Bom! Bom! Bom!* Our only defence was to dive into the nearest hole for cover and pray.

My nerves were constantly frayed – not just from the artillery strikes that arrived without warning, but also from the threat of close combat and night-time raids. When stationed at Novoluhanske in 2019, I was part of a unit that sometimes dropped into separatist trenches during a series of high-risk reconnaissance missions. It was our way of checking the enemy's activities and the positions were always unmanned (which was why we were dropping in), but conducting a raid as ballsy as a trench reconnaissance had psychological implications. On the one hand, it was an exhilarating rush, like something out of an old war comic. On the other, it was terrifying, because knowing that an incursion of that kind was possible only increased the chances that we might be on the receiving end at some point. Our nights became very scary as a result.

The dark brought all sorts of thought-up terrors. A dog rummaging around was reimagined as an enemy recon unit waiting to deliver death. A pig snuffling through the trees was a special forces operator waiting to attack. When the fog and rain came in, it was impossible to see or hear any movement outside and that made the paranoia even worse. Because of my experience, I made the welfare of the other lads a priority, but I was also eager to maintain a high standard when it came to observing the enemy, which meant there was no downtime. I often went home from my six-month tours in the trenches feeling absolutely shattered – partly from the physical workload of being a front-line soldier, partly because my flight-or-flight response was frazzled.

I also had to watch my feet. During my first steps into the Grey Zone – a no man's land separating the two battle lines – my commander, Swampy, had shouted across to me as I crept forward, 'Watch out for the landmines!' Apparently, the place was dotted with them, and Khvat, another platoon commander, had lost both feet after stepping on one. From then on my eyes were out on stalks. But more than anything, these events proved just how brave and committed my Ukrainian counterparts were. I'd been employed to teach the lads some Western military techniques, to make them better soldiers, but it turned out they already had the most important attribute of all.

Heart.

*

In the Donbas War, the Ukrainian army was a rapidly evolving military force. The First Battalion was a 600-strong group and I was part of an Air Assault Company of ninety men that was split into three platoons of thirty. (Each platoon was then divided into sections of seven or eight men.) In many ways we operated like a reconnaissance unit and were parachutists and fast ropers and evidence of an improving infrastructure. After the outbreak of hostilities in 2014, Ukraine increased its armed forces to around 200,000 soldiers, with a further 60,000 members of the National Guard. It was being reported that this total was going to increase to half a million personnel. At the same time, the Ukrainians were participating in joint training exercises with other nations under the NATO cooperation programme, which allowed them to learn tactics from the likes of the USA, Canada, Sweden and the UK. A newly introduced strategy was to divert control away from one centralised command group – as had been their preferred method in a post-Soviet model – to a more decentralised entity, which allowed commanders on the ground to make decisions much more rapidly.

Under this new structure, we gave the Russians and their separatist counterparts a bloody nose from time to time. The fightbacks, when they happened, were impressive and the lads I'd trained and was serving alongside were solid soldiers. What they lacked in technical ability, they more than made up for with their motivation and a desire to improve, and we were holding firm against the enemy's attacks. Weirdly, a lot of the time we were told not to aggravate or provoke, and often our orders were to hold fire, even as the DPR's mortars and rocket-propelled grenades (RPGs) bombarded us. Under the Minsk agreement of 2015, we were not supposed to shoot. The higher-ups had decided that we should report any Russian violations of the treaty rather than initiate a dispute, though it was quite clear the other lot couldn't give a toss and happily opened fire whenever they felt like it. I struggled to understand the bureaucracy on our side. I even made a YouTube video about it.

'If something's not done, the Russians are going to take advantage of our passive approach and launch a mass invasion,' I said. 'We're being told not to fire back, so we're just getting hit by them, over and over.'

But nobody seemed to care. The story in the trenches remained the same.

I got on with the job because I bloody loved it and my enthusiasm and loyalty showed. The other lads quickly accepted me as being '50 per cent Ukrainian' – a Marine with a British passport and Ukrainian wife – and I soon picked up the nickname 'Old Dog' because of my age. To them, I wasn't a war tourist, a chancer who intended to run once the going got tough; instead, I was considered a fighter supporting their cause. *But it had become my cause too.* That's because I'd learned more and more about Ukraine's political struggles through Larysa. She had been through the mill, thanks to the Russian incursions of 2014, and having previously lived in Crimea, her home had been lost once Putin's forces stole the region.

There was a myth among foreigners living in Ukraine. It said that if a bloke like me married a local, their wife was bound to relocate to the UK. But from my experience, the truth was very different. Larysa was a proud citizen; she loved her county and wanted to fight for its independence. Running away at such a pivotal time was not in her story, even though her life would have become undeniably safer overnight, and there was no way I could have convinced her to drop everything and move to England. My company mates were just as proud. A lot of them came from Crimea and I soon learned they were a nostalgic bunch, like Larysa, but that's because they had witnessed the action up close. When the Russians snatched their land away, the group had been outnumbered in the stand-off. Faced with the choice of staying and joining the Russians or leaving Crimea, they had opted for the latter and departed without a shot being fired. Hating Putin's thug army became an obsession for all of them, and when the chance to defend Mariupol arrived, they went for it.

This attitude was most evident in my company commander, Captain Serhii Stratichuk, whose call sign was 'Bear', owing to the fact that he bore a passing resemblance to a full-grown grizzly. The bloke was twenty-nine years old and came in at around six foot two, though his width was his most imposing feature. Bear was a power-lifter. His frame was all muscle, but he was also incredibly agile and could race through the trenches like a whippet when he needed to. (It's funny what a round of incoming mortar fire can do to a person.) He was also heavily into Americana – the music, food and culture – and he talked so much about the souped-up motorbikes that race up and down the US highways that the lads nicknamed him 'Harley'. He was all for it.

Bear was a natural leader, with tons of charisma, and unlike certain people in positions of power, he wasn't a bully. Instead, he commanded respect through action. When he talked, we listened, and if he told us to move, everybody did so at top speed. But the dialogue worked both ways. When I approached Bear with a question or idea, he was open to dialogue. NATO often worked with us on joint training exercises and he was always keen to learn about the tactics and procedures in use across the Western armies. Bear often picked my brains about how things worked in the British armed forces and it wasn't long before he was translating those same conversations into effective battle strategies. When the company was sent on a joint training exercise with the Americans in 2021, our group came top in a series of mock section attacks, thanks to his leadership. Physically and mentally, the man was a beast.

I soon discovered that the hierarchy within the Ukrainian military was a lot more complicated than what I'd been brought up on. The armed forces were much bigger than Britain's, in terms of personnel, and there were many more ranks to learn. When serving with the Royal Anglian Regiment, I'd made it to the position of senior private. But when I joined the Ukrainian Marines I was given the role of *matros* (sailor), before later being made a *starshyi matros* (senior sailor), which was a rank equivalent to lance corporal. In a platoon, that made me point man and there was plenty of responsibility to go with it, especially as I had a fair amount of battle experience.

On training courses I was made a *Bronetransportyor* (BTR) commander, in charge of a Soviet-era armoured personnel carrier. My scores in a sharpshooter course later promoted me to senior rifleman. I soon learned that the Ukrainian forces were using a weird mix of weaponry comprising dated Russian hardware and modern NATO tech. Once I'd established myself in the group as someone who knew his way around a PKM, a Russian belt-fed machine gun that fired 250 rounds per minute, as well as the Swedish-made Next-generation, Light Anti-tank Weapon, or NLAW – a shoulder-mounted rocket launcher – I was looked upon as a senior bod. But when the bombs and bullets came down, my role and experience counted for nothing. I simply had to help win the firefight.

Towards the end of 2021, our company was dispatched to Pavlopil – a village about twenty-five kilometres north-east of Mariupol. At the time, talk of a potential Russian offensive was ramping up and there were rumours of gathering artillery along the borders. The Russian navy had also cut off the Sea of Azov under the pretence of a military exercise. Nobody seemed to think that Putin would do the unthinkable and actually invade, but as the Chinese strategist Sun Tzu famously wrote in *The Art of War* (and I'm paraphrasing here): shit happens when an army hesitates. By the look of things, there were a hell of a lot of Russian and pro-Russian separatist soldiers hanging about, scratching their bollocks. And if they eventually decided to invade, Mariupol would be for it.

As with our previous positions, the trench at Pavlopil had been established as a forward observation post, and it was down to us to watch the enemy. But with the various peace treaties now forgotten, we were able to distract them with returning fire if they lashed out with artillery, which they did regularly. We were located in an area of stripwood – a long, thin layer of trees dividing two open fields – though most of the branches had been brought down or burnt by artillery. I was soon on high alert. The enemy lurked in an adjacent treeline, about 500 metres or so to our left, but it was the opposite position that gave me the most nightmares because their forces had the high ground, around one kilometer to our right, with a woodland beyond. This situation was made even more precarious by the dug-out viewing slits in the trenches that allowed us to watch the separatists. They had become overgrown with vegetation, so anyone wanting to survey the terrain had to raise a scope over the parapet, or risk taking a bullet.

This spot was terrifyingly exposed and incoming fire was a real problem. The company we were taking over from had lost one or two men to shooters and their time in Pavlopil had taken its toll. Cheerily, someone had placed a warning sign at one end of the trench – *Beware Snipers*. And during the handover I realised that they all looked like shit and couldn't wait to get away, which was a worrying indication of the work to come. Rather than crumbling under the anxiety of copping a round, I told myself that fear was a good motivator: transforming negative emotion into alertness might be the thing that kept me alive.

I worked on rebuilding the stretches of trench that had fallen into disrepair, and there were plenty of them. If I were to count up the hours grafting on the front lines, I reckon the majority of it was spent shovelling away mud and rock. Sometimes it would take us three months to construct a new kitchen space from soil and wood, only for a shell to blow it to smithereens. So while I often prayed to the gods for my survival during an attack, I also wasted a hell of a lot of mental calories fretting about whether I would have to rebuild the sleeping quarters or gun positions. The effort required to survive was taxing enough, but working as a part-time builder on top of all that was often exhausting and demoralising.

The good news was that I liked to be busy. Sitting around and waiting to be told what to do didn't work for me, so I spent my time either digging or chatting with the British press – not just to warn the outside world of the invasion I thought was about to happen, but also to gather intelligence. By the end of 2021, the likes of Channel 4, *The Times*, the *Telegraph*, Sky and Al Jazeera were regularly in touch. All of them had questions: *What is happening in your position? What are the enemy doing ahead of you? How many Russians are there in the trenches?* They all wanted updates from the front lines and I soon became a valuable source of information on the enemy as the media tried to stay ahead of the unfolding story.

As far as I was concerned, my updates were an effective early-warning system for the Western media – and it worked. Before long, awareness of the Donbas War had increased, though the situation was rapidly becoming impossible to ignore. All sorts of Russian training exercises were now taking place in the borderlands, featuring rocket launchers, self-propelled howitzers and tanks – lots and lots of tanks. Meanwhile, tens of thousands of troops had poured into the area. I sensed that at some point Putin's sabre-rattling would turn to destructive action. When it did, there would be no hiding place for any of us.

3

The First Battalion was a functioning workplace, with rules and benefits, and everybody was granted a short period of leave during the course of a calendar year – even a year with a potential invasion on the way. The first holiday window usually opened in January and was always short on takers. Instead, most Marines preferred to rest much deeper into the tour, during the spring or summer months, when the beaches were at their best. Because so many in the trenches still figured that Putin was bluffing, my company mates opted for dates in May and June, and while I admired their optimism, my gut feeling was that a full-scale assault was inevitable. The latest reports suggested that around 120,000 enemy troops had massed on the border. The media carried images of armoured patrol cars and tanks, all marked with the letter 'Z' on their fronts.[1] Putin's claims that this represented nothing more than a training exercise weren't ringing true, especially as he was also making nonsense comments that Ukraine needed to be 'de-Nazified'.

Having assessed the odds, I volunteered for a two-week break at the beginning of January. My hope was for some restorative time with Larysa before everything kicked off,

---

1 The symbol was later reported to mean all sorts of things. Some experts speculated that it referred to the area in which the vehicles were positioned, with 'Z' standing for *Zapad*, or west Russia. The Russian defence ministry went on social media to claim that it stood for *Za pobedu*, which translated as 'For victory'. Other theories speculated it was simply a way for Russian forces to identify one another during the chaos of conflict.

and I travelled to Slovyansk, a Ukraine-controlled city in the north of the Donetsk region, where she was temporarily working, determined to make the most of it. Even then, the mood was weirdly sunny. Like my team-mates, Larysa was convinced that the threat of war was nothing more than a bluff.

'The Russians are always playing games,' she said, sounding pretty convincing.

'I don't know. There's a lot of them . . .'

'This will be no different, Shaun. You'll see.'

The idea was then floated that we should spend seven grand doing up the kitchen. Our apartment in Mariupol was perched on the city's left bank. Whenever I'd been there, I could hear the bombs at Pavlopil from our window.

Bloody hell, I thought. *Well, if Larysa reckons we should blow a load of money, maybe everything is going to be OK.*

As I rested up and contemplated a summer of home renovation and endless shopping trips for shelving and tins of paint, a crumb of comfort appeared in the news. There were reports suggesting that the French president, Emmanuel Macron, was in contact with Putin. His hope was to de-escalate the situation somehow. I wondered how successful such a diplomatic strategy would be given the Ukrainian president, Volodymyr Zelenskiy, was making noises that Ukraine might some day, hopefully, join NATO. He had made it part of his foreign policy, and it wasn't something that was likely to calm the Kremlin's bloodlust.

Despite the vaguely optimistic media dispatches surrounding Macron's peacekeeping attempts, a sobering reality sat at the back of my mind: everybody seemed to have forgotten we were dealing with Russia, the world's Death Star. Nobody really wanted to go up against them in a conflict, though I suspected that if push came to shove, the Ukrainian army would have enough muscle to kick back. We might not have had a massive navy, or much in the way of air support for that matter – not when compared to the enemy – but we did have the training and the motivation. There certainly wasn't going to be a repeat of the 2014 Crimean mugging. As I tried my best to relax, I couldn't stop thinking about having to return to my company if war was declared while I was away.

When my two weeks were nearly up, on 17 January, it was time to leave Slovyansk. On my last night, Larysa asked me what I fancied for dinner.

'Do you want a takeaway before you go?' she said. 'You're going to lose all that weight in the trenches.'

She was right. I was returning to a diet of Grechka, wrack and the occasional charred pheasant. My final civilised dinner for a while had to be one for the ages.

'I want everything,' I said. 'Pizza, burger, chips – *the lot.*'

I stuffed my face and the following morning made the always-emotional farewell with Larysa at the coach stop. I hated it. Saying goodbye was heart-wrenching at the best of times, but it seemed particularly brutal as I kissed her in the freezing cold.

'I hope this isn't the last time I see you,' I said, 'because I really—'

'Shut up, Shaun. It's not going to happen.'

I stepped onto the bus for Mariupol, not wanting to debate the matter. I just couldn't find the same level of optimism. 'I've got a really bad feeling about this.'

As I started the first leg in a journey that would eventually take me back to Pavlopil, questions and regrets bounced around my head.

Did I need to get on the coach that quickly?
Why didn't I linger for a few more moments?
Should I have run back and given her another kiss?

There would soon be plenty of time to contemplate them all.

Everything had turned to shit at the front line. The weather was deteriorating by the day and the temperatures had dropped to as low as −20°C. Despite our experience of toughing it out in such cold conditions, we were up against it, simply because the Ukrainian military wasn't equipped with modern fighting kit. Our uniforms, particularly the thermals, were old designs, the kind probably worn by European skiers in the 1980s. While they did an OK job of trapping the heat, they were hardly breathable. If anyone lit a fire or exerted a serious amount of physical effort, their skin became wet with perspiration. Once a soldier was soaked through and reintroduced to the cold, hypothermia and frostbite became real threats − enemies every bit as worrying as the snipers positioned across the Grey Zone. At times, my teeth chattered so much that my jaw throbbed.

I soon noticed that there was a new intensity to Russia's artillery attacks, and their military looked to have been upgraded to an alarming degree. In all the time I'd operated on the front line, no one had ever experienced a drone assault at night. That changed at the end of January, when my mate Yarik, an experienced Ukrainian soldier and a handy translator during my early days in Mariupol, was sent to the nearby treeline at dusk to chop wood for the platoon's fires. At that time of day, the fading light usually offered a fair amount of cover, as did the fog and snow. But on this occasion, there was no escape. The Russians launched the first of what would become a regular barrage of night-time drone strikes, dropping grenades and mortars into Yarik's position. In the blast, the poor bastard had his leg broken; another soldier alongside him suffered concussion. Really, it was a miracle they both survived.

There was no time to breathe and I was back in the thick of it almost immediately, with my section positioned around one kilometre ahead of the main company in an advanced listening post known as 'Mercury', where the work was unforgiving. Our job was to spot the source of any incoming artillery. We'd then call in the details to Bear, who would order a mortar strike based on our estimates. For weeks, we ran up and down the trench line, watching for enemy activity, avoiding sniper fire, all while defending ourselves from the wet and the cold. Just by keeping an ear out, it was possible to hear what the enemy were up to. Chainsaws buzzed in the woods to our right where they were working to outflank us, and every now and then a burst of machine-gun fire ripped above our heads. Most of the time, the DPR were firing blind from across the Grey Zone, but it was the snipers on the high ground that concerned me the most. I knew that looking over the parapet at the wrong time might cause me a whole world of trouble.

The mood amongst the lads was shifting too, partly because it had been announced that all leave was to be cancelled with immediate effect, but also because we were hearing rumours that the Russian war machine was again bolstering its numbers at the borders. By early February, intelligence reports showed how the amount of enemy personnel and hardware ahead of us had increased. The feeling that it was all about to kick off was only amplified when I received a text from an Al Jazeera journalist.

'Shaun, are you OK? How is morale?' they said.

'As good as it can be,' I replied. 'We are expecting an assault on Mariupol at some point. You?'

The response was chilling. 'We had to move to Dnipro as it was getting hard to report – my editor kept freaking out and has banned me from going out anywhere.'

I passed the message down the line, but nobody was too surprised. There was a grim inevitability about what was to come. Even the outside world was starting to stress, including my mum, who got in touch, asking me to come home.

'You don't need to do this,' she said.

'Look, if the Russians are coming across the border, then I'm staying to fight. There are a lot of guys here that have way more to lose than me, and I've been with them for nearly five years. I couldn't live with myself if I didn't stay.'

I was determined that if I died, nobody should feel bad in the aftermath. I didn't want Mum or anyone else blaming themselves because they hadn't been able to talk me out of fighting. This was my decision. I also had Mariupol in my heart. The last thing I wanted was for my home to fall under Russian control. The restaurants, parks and coffee shops would be lost for ever. As would those beautiful nights on the beach and my future life with Larysa, the pair of us happily retired, living in our home by the sea.

Mum understood, but it didn't make it any easier for her. 'OK. Well, then we'll be watching on the telly, thinking of you,' she said sadly. '*Please be careful.*'

Sometimes in the build-up to a big conflict, there can be a sense of excitement, especially among the younger soldiers. They want to see action, which is an understandable response, given it's what they've spent much of their adult life training for. In the same way that surgeons want to operate on sick patients, so Marines want to experience contact. I was a bit long in the tooth for all that. There were plenty of war miles under my belt and I carried a different attitude as a result. *We had a job to do.* Our resistance was the last stand, a blockade between Russia and Mariupol. What we hadn't been told was that if the city fell, the Russians were set to pour into Dnipro, Kherson and Odesa. Barring a miracle, the country would fall shortly after that. The pressure on the higher-ups must have been immense.

A steely determination linked the group. The senior lads had been fighting in the Donbas War for years. What was unfolding felt like the inevitable endgame of a horrible tussle in which everything was on the line, including Ukrainian pride. Yes, we were a little nervous, scared even. *And who knew what the Russian military were truly capable of?* Certainly, their recent attacks and incursions seemed to be devoid of morals and it was unlikely they paid too much attention to the rules of engagement as laid down by the Geneva Convention. That meant there was a chance we might experience a very unpleasant ending. Despite that, there was a sense of camaraderie and confidence within the company. We were trained for what was to come – and to a good standard, too. Though the West expected us to wilt in the face of sustained pressure, maybe within forty-eight hours of the first serious assault, I knew we were better than that. With drones buzzing around and heavy artillery ahead of us, I just had to keep everyone alive for as long as possible.

Ukraine was our home and we were defending its lands.

For days I kept busy, cooking for the lads and digging out new firing positions and trenches, always on the lookout for drones or listening for sniper fire. Occasionally we were forced to dive for cover from a small barrage of artillery or a machine-gun burst, though thankfully nobody was wounded or killed. Then, at 4 a.m. on Thursday, 24 February 2022, Bear ordered the company to stand to. My heart sank. *Was this it?* We'd practised this state-of-readiness procedure regularly, as I had done in the British armed forces, but these drills usually only took place at dawn and dusk. Given some of us had been woken this time, it didn't take a genius to work out that trouble was on its way. *The war had started.*

Our junior sergeant, Gluzsky, delivered the news. 'Russian forces have crossed the lines,' he said, coldly. 'Make ready.'

There were no platitudes, no rousing motivational rhetoric; there was nothing in the way of self-pity either, and no diplomatic word wishing fair fortune on the men. Junior Sergeant Gluzsky was an anvil, a military blunt instrument who showed 100 per cent commitment to the cause but very little consideration for the feelings of the soldiers scrapping around him, all of which made him the perfect candidate to deliver the news. *We only had time for the facts.* My section was immediately ordered to again take position at the head of the front line at Mercury.

Junior Sergeant Gluzsky then looked at me sternly. 'Old Dog, take the PKM,' he said.

Oh, God. Not that. I was forty-eight years old and the oldest in the group. In the boggy conditions, running around with an AK-74 was gruelling enough, especially as it was fitted with an under-slung grenade launcher. But the PKM was another beast entirely: a heavy-duty, belt-fed weapon that weighed around seven and a half kilos, and needed me to carry the hefty link of rounds that went with it. Part of me wanted to argue. I was the only soldier with experience in combat firing the much lighter, much more manoeuvrable

NLAW. *Surely it made more sense for me to take charge of that?* I watched moodily as someone stepped forward and draped a clunky necklace of bullets around my shoulders. The PKM was then shoved into my arms. As I cradled the weapon, I felt my boots sinking into the mud with the weight. It was like being sucked into quicksand.

The sky lit up not long afterwards. Everywhere was chaos. At times it was hard to tell what was ground fire and what was heavy artillery. Rocket-propelled grenades came at us from all angles, a lot of them from the treeline in the distance ahead. The air crackled with small-arms fire to our left. *Bup-bup-bup-bup-bup-bup!* At one point I watched a round from an SPG-9 anti-tank rocket launcher ping off the back wall of our trench before ricocheting away and exploding fifty metres behind us. There was nowhere to hide. I was deaf from the noise, blinded by the explosions and smoke, and the only sensation in my body was the aching hammering of my heart. *Was it bursting from my chest?* This was hell on earth.

And all the while I heard yelling on the radio.

Heavy fighting on the left flank!

Watch out for a full frontal attack!

One of our forward positions looks fucked!

If I knew anything about the military and war fighting, it was that we wouldn't be expected to hold our advanced position for too long. Not with the incoming fire hitting us at such a heavy rate. We needed to tactically retreat and regroup in order to strengthen our defences. Losing ground didn't bother or unsettle me. I understood that, sometimes, giving up territory was a useful tactic in a battle, especially if it helped to conserve resources. I crouched down in my trench and waited for the order to withdraw.

*

The first few hours of the invasion were all shock and awe. The Russians threw so much at us it was hard to get a handle on the battle picture, and I really had no idea whether they were flanking us, somewhere ahead of our position or already rolling away towards Mariupol. Our long trench was set up in three parts: shooters were positioned on the right and left flanks; in the middle was a centralised bunker with a crude sleeping area and a viewing and firing post. Through a lookout porthole in my central spot I watched someone firing the NLAW into the smoke ahead, towards a tank moving in the distance. Then suddenly an RPG exploded to the side of my trench. The blast rocked me to the floor. My ears buzzed, and when I looked up, I saw Junior Sergeant Gluzsky, who was also on Mercury. His hand was on my shoulder.

'Are you OK, Old Dog?'

He must have raced over to check on me. I nodded. *Yeah I'm fucking OK.* Then I heaved the PKM into the firing position again and opened up on the treeline, hoping to repel any Russian forces still in cover. The weapon barked like a feral dog.

Much of the confusion about what was happening had to do with how the Ukrainian military chain of command worked. While it was moving away from the old Soviet-style of leadership and into something a little more decentralised, with leaders on the ground calling the shots, the Ukrainians hadn't quite reached the standards of the British armed forces. Really, the only person who actually knew what was going on was the battalion commander, and his intel was then passed on to the company commander at the appropriate time. Everyone else was left in the dark. There were no quick battle orders, or QBOs, in which a group huddled together for a briefing, or even a sitrep (situation report). Instead, we were told, *Follow me! Do this! Go there!* As a result, the average fighter on the ground didn't have a clue what was going on.

This feeling extended even to me, an experienced war veteran with more than thirteen combat years combined in various conflicts and war zones. The type of assault we were experiencing was entirely new and incomprehensibly ferocious. It was as if I'd been transplanted into every war film I'd ever seen at once – *All Quiet on the Western Front*, *A Bridge Too Far*, *1917* – and occasionally it was hard to know what to do and where to go in all the noise and chaos. Physically I was blowing too. My back, knees and ankles felt close to cracking as I ran around in the mud, which was shin-deep in parts, all while being dragged down by the PKM and AK-74. Worse, it was pissing down with rain, and my eyes burned with smoke. At times knowing what was actually happening seemed impossible.

Throughout the day, my most pressing problem was weapon maintenance. The last thing I wanted was for my PKM to jam with mud or grime, and I was constantly wiping the link and muzzle clean, only for it to be splattered again. When I slipped and fell into the wall of the trench, I was covered in gloop and water. The PKM was covered too and I instinctively ducked down to wipe the metal with the outside of my sleeve. Then I heard a fizzing, whistling noise. A swarm of angry lead wasps ripped through the viewing slit in the parapet of the trench, into the space where my head had been a few seconds earlier. As they chewed into the wall at my back, I had zero doubts that an enemy gunman had spotted me and opened fire. Had I not ducked, my skull would have been blown off. Another SPG round then skimmed the back of the bunker and several rounds from a Dushka, a heavy Russian machine gun, exploded in the air behind me.

I took a breath. *How the fuck was I still alive?*

At the noise, Junior Sergeant Gluzsky rushed over again. He had seen the explosion from the trench's right flank and must have feared the worst.

'You OK, Shaun?' he shouted. 'Are you still breathing?'

'I think so.'

As he turned, I shouted out a warning. 'Positsii pizdets!' I yelled. '*Puli!*' Which translated to 'Position fucked! *Bullets!*'

But Junior Sergeant Gluzsky just looked confused. It had become clear that working with a second language during normal soldiering activities, while problematic and sometimes annoying, was something I could get away with. But during an invasion, my words had to be clear and precise. On this occasion it was a matter of life or death.

There was no time to explain my lucky break. I pulled Junior Sergeant Gluzsky down as more lead wasps zipped above us. 'We need a new position,' I shouted.

Everywhere I looked, the ground had been churned over by bullets, mortar fire and RPGs. By mid-morning, the enemy clearly had a bead on our positions and were laying down a constant barrage. Rather than cowering or finding a place to shelter, I stayed on the move, duckwalking through the gloopy mud, heaving the PKM with me as I went. Once I'd found a decent spot, I'd let fly with my weapon and then move away. The effort was so knackering that it was easy to forget the brutally cold and wet weather. My back and legs were soaked with sweat. I knew that if I stopped for any length of time I might catch hypothermia and freeze to death.

This might sound weird, but at no point did I feel frightened during that first full day of scrapping. I certainly didn't fear death, but that had a lot to do with the fact I'd seen people die in the past. I'd watched mates suffering with life-changing battle injuries and my old man had passed at an early age, so the reality of me going wasn't an issue. Sure, I got upset whenever a friend or family member died, but I rarely grieved and I was fairly pragmatic about situations in which my life was under threat. Also, when stuck in a trench, pinned down by enemy fire, there was actually very little time to feel scared. The radio buzzed with bad news throughout the day: there were casualties in the villages either side of us and talk of the Russians taking prisoners. None of it was cheery, so I decided to readjust my focus. I reimagined our hellhole position as another firing drill, of the kind I'd been used to as a young member of the British Army, where I'd slogged it out in Thetford Forest for days on end.

If this had been a drill, mind you, it would have been considered a proper beasting. We were massively overrun and after what felt like a full day of bombardment, the enemy were bearing down on us and showing very little mercy. Then the call I'd been hoping for came over the radio. *We were pulling back.* Bear had decided we were too exposed. My guess was that we'd withdraw to Mariupol in increments, village by village, slowing the Russians' progress as much as possible, while doing our best to stay alive so we could eventually add more firepower to what was bound to be a siege around the city. I couldn't wait to step back for a bit. Suffering the full wrath of the Russian army had been intense and I was knackered.

In the withdrawal I took the bare minimum: my rucksack stuffed with warm kit and living equipment, plus the AK-74 and the grenade launcher, with some extra rounds and grenades. I must have looked like a postman at Christmas with all the extra baggage. Junior Sergeant Gluzsky helped me with the PKM, thankfully, but in the chaos I realised my sleeping bag had been forgotten. I thought about going back for it but gave up on the idea, realising that if I fell behind the platoon at any point, our transport would have to move on without me. After running the trenches for God knows how long, my legs were on fire as I made the dash of nearly a kilometre to our fall-back position, taking a breather before sprinting 400 metres more to a group of BTRs that were waiting to ship us to another trench, in another battlespace, the metal, smoke and violence of Putin's force excavating the land behind me.

4

I clambered into the back of the BTR, my senses rattling, my body shaking with exhaustion, adrenaline and cold. *What the fuck was going on?* It was really hard to tell. Physically and emotionally, I'd been pulverised by the Russian war machine and had made it through more near-death experiences in one day than in my entire career combined. *Had I really only been fighting for less than twenty-four hours?* It was hard to tell. When I ran through it in my mind, I saw moments of darkness and moments of daylight. There had been at least one sunrise, but I hadn't slept , and now darkness was falling. In the intense fatigue, I couldn't tell whether my first contact experience of the invasion had lasted one day or two. My brain was a mess.

I looked around the cars and did a quick head count. Everyone was in place and, more importantly, in one piece. Across the platoon it was being reported that – *miraculously* – we had suffered zero dead and zero wounded, which seemed unbelievable. Having seen what Putin's forces had at their disposal first-hand, I'd feared the group would be decimated. Then I heard my name being called.

'Hey, Old Dog!'

It was Dima, a gunner for our BTRs and, at the age of twenty-one, one of the youngest soldiers in the group. He was waving out from his gun turret with an unlit cigarette in his hand.

'You OK?' he said, chucking the smoke at me with a smile.

I sparked up and laughed. 'Loving it,' I said, wryly.

I'd first met Dima in Mykolaiv in about 2020 and he'd originally joined up with our air assault company. At first, the pair of us hadn't really clicked – Dima was a bit cocky, but he was smart and he spoke several languages. Over the next couple of years I got to know him better and came to really enjoy his company. That was the funny thing about serving with people. The lads that initially seemed bloody annoying often ended up being the closest companions. I'm not sure what aspects of Dima's character I chimed with in particular, but I know he made me laugh a lot of the time.

I noticed a small wooden crucifix dangling from Dima's helmet. A few weeks ago he had confided in me about how he'd rediscovered his faith. The thought of heading into war will do that to a person, I suppose. We used to share the cooking duties, and over Grechka the two of us had several heavy chats about the meaning of faith, prayer and churches – all of which was a big deal in Ukraine, though it didn't really mean a lot to me. I couldn't get my head around there being one Jesus and one God, even though I loved the idea that when it was all over I was going to see my friends and family again, once we'd all made it to *The Big Reunion in the Sky*. For that reason, I understood why soldiers clung to faith in times of crisis. This certainly felt like a time when a little back-up might come in handy.

I pointed to the cross. 'You're going to need that today,' I shouted over the roar of more exploding SPGs and gunfire at our tail.

Dima laughed. 'You should try it today, Shaun. It will help you.'

'There's nothing I haven't learned in life, mate. I'm a little bit older than you and it's not going to change me now.'

'But, Shaun, the Bible can teach you so many things,' he said.

I pulled him close. 'I'm sure it can, but when I die, I'll be seeing you at the Gates of Valhalla. *Where the warriors go.*'

I was happy that Dima had something to hang on to for comfort. He was a good kid and I certainly didn't want to shut him down. Tapping into some extra source of strength was essential if we were to survive the Russian onslaught. But the way our day was going, Valhalla's gates were probably going to open up sooner rather than later.

I burned the first cigarette down in a matter of minutes. I reached for another as our next steps were planned out. As I'd guessed, the higher-ups had decided that we should move in three stages on a south-western bearing to Mariupol, which by all accounts was being smashed to bits by long-range artillery and air assaults. This sounded to all of us like a fighting withdrawal, though nobody was 100 per cent certain, and we knew to expect a scrap every bit as hectic as the assault we'd just survived. Our first stop would be a second-line position – a trench on a hill outside the town of Talakivka, which was twelve kilometres away. If all went well, we would then move on to the middle of Talakivka and finally to Sartana, an even smaller enclave on the edge of the city, all the while doing our best to slow the invasion. It was going to be a risky trip.

Our previous position was now being demolished by the enemy, and yet the battle picture ahead of us was just as intimidating. Intelligence was telling us that the type of assault we'd experienced in Pavlopil was going to be nothing compared to what Mariupol was currently enduring. The number of casualties was worryingly high and the fact that there were civilians on the ground seemed to be of no concern to the invaders. From what we were being told, the story was the same all around the country, in Kyiv, Odesa and Kharkiv. Russia's forces and their separatist allies were on a mission to crush Ukraine's resolve through sheer force and bloody murder. The worst-case scenario was too horrible to contemplate. I wondered whether Larysa was safe and if our home was still in one piece.

There's little chance of us getting that seven-grand kitchen now, I thought, darkly.

But I also thought of the things I'd fallen in love with – the coffee shops, the old tram system and the beautiful coastline. *Lamb bloody shashlik on a quiet beach.* I had no idea if any of it still existed. Part of me dreaded rolling back into our home town and not recognising any of it.

In the smoke and violence of battle there had been zero chance of getting a message back to Larysa, or anyone else for that matter. My mobile-phone signal had been next to nothing in Pavlopil, but as the BTRs moved away from our forward position, a series of pings echoed around the car as messages and voicemails from loved ones and mates came through all at once. There were texts from Larysa, Mum, my friends in the UK, and they all feared the worst. Communications also arrived from Channel 4 and Sky News. They had been cut off and were unable to get a clear sense of what was going on. Rather than answering every media request individually, I posted a message to my friends and family on Facebook:

I'm OK. Yesterday was hell.
I can't reply to everybody obviously.
All I can say it's the worst thing imaginable.
I'm really at a loss for words.

As we drove past bombed-out houses and burning cars, the roads were unsurprisingly empty. We arrived at the second-line position in twenty minutes and once the BTRs had pulled over, everyone grabbed a shovel. Just like in those firing drills I'd undergone in Thetford Forest, it was time to scoop out a series of shell scrapes – muddy, man-sized pits to sleep in and dive into when the firing started up again. The idea was to stay here for the night, but, knowing the Russians, they had probably already clocked our location and were making plans to attack. I fully expected a horror show every bit as traumatic as the one we'd experienced at Pavlopil, and once midnight arrived, I managed a few hours' kip, occasionally rolling over to watch the light show taking place ahead of us. Our old trenches were on fire. My mind raced at the enormity of what was taking place as bombs and tracer bullets strafed the skyline.

I'm right in it, in a war against the Russians . . . And I'm still alive? I shivered and thought about my lost sleeping bag. It was Larysa's and an expensive one too, much better than anything the Ukrainian military had ever given me. *She was going to chew my ear off when I told her the news.* I tried to give myself a break. This was a dangerous moment for me. With a little time to pause, take a breath and think, there was a chance my emotions might spin out of control. What I'd heard on the radio during the first assault had been disturbing: news of hostage-taking; details of mass casualties in several companies across the front lines around Mariupol; our positions being overrun. We were all locked into a fight for survival, in a battle that would decide the fate of eastern Ukraine and by extension the whole country. The following morning, we were heading straight back into the shit again, to the middle of Talakivka, which had once been a small town of around 4,000 people, though who knew what was left of it now. With nineteen kilometres to go to central Mariupol, all sorts of hell were sure to be aimed our way. I had to stay strong.

You can handle this, I told myself.

As a leader of men, it was important to keep my thoughts on an even keel. Freaking out would only cause my team to collapse. I needed every ounce of resolve to hold firm.

This is a drill, one you've done countless times before. Do it again . . .

The following morning, as we moved into Talakivka, taking cover in a small farmhouse with all its homely reminders of a civilised, peaceful life – family photographs on the windowsills, kids' toys, abandoned belongings – the bombardment started up all over again. Bear had been right. The Russians were showing no signs of slowing down. If anything, they were warming up, and despite the fact we had supporting artillery fire at our rear, we were now being pinned down by a more fearsome oppressor: Grad.

I had never experienced a barrage of BM-21 rockets before and it was a sensory overload. Launched from a mobile system, usually set on the back of a truck, Grad had the capacity to rip through a small urban area, but the rockets were so imprecise they were also regarded as being inhumane. Launching a Grad attack on a town or village was a surefire way of killing a lot of innocent people. Meanwhile, the name was chillingly apt because *grad* is a Russian term for 'hail', and during my first attack I experienced its full power close up.

At first I heard the scream of artillery fire overhead. It sounded like a fighter plane taking off and my hearing thrummed, even through a set of ear defenders. Then the shouting started.

'*Grad!*' screamed the bloke alongside me, as several tons of metal rained about us in a series of pounding explosions.

Duh-dum! Duh, duh-dum! Duh-dum-dum-dum!

I shouted over to Bear, who was crouching nearby. '*Fuck!*'

'You not heard Grad before, Old Dog?' he said.

I could have sworn the bastard was laughing, though it was hard to tell. My ears were still ringing.

'No, it's a new one for me.'

'Well, you better get used to it, my friend.'

As the farmhouse became still again, everyone checked in on the soldiers nearest to them. It had been a close call, but everyone was OK. Then I realised there had been a nagging familiarity in the exploding artillery's percussive rhythm. *Bloody hell!* It had sounded like the instantly recognisable drum solo from Phil Collins's hit single 'In the Air Tonight' – though there had been nothing fun about it and over the next twenty-four hours I learned to spot the warning signs of an incoming Grad attack, and when to remain calm and when to panic. If I was able to hear the tearing, metallic detonation of rockets in the air, I was OK – it meant they had already exploded away from us. But a loud crack followed by several seconds of silence was more scary. That meant the payload was detonating nearby.

With every blast, the shouts went up. *More Grad.* And my thoughts weirdly went to Phil Collins and his drum kit.

Duh-dum! Duh, duh-dum! Duh-dum-dum-dum!

Then I crossed my fingers that we would all make it to the end of the song.

For two and a half days, we stayed on the move through Talakivka in an attempt to avoid being hit, and our progress became a constant race for survival as the Russians destroyed the homes around us with wave after wave of attacks. Grad came in every hour or so, and we learned to stay away from any crossroads, because the enemy's aerial assets were using them as a fix with which to attack us. Anyone standing near one at the time of impact risked being blown to bits. We also realised that the only way to stay safe during these assaults was to dive for shelter in a dried-up well alongside one of the houses. Whenever the shout of 'Grad!' went up, the Marines patrolling the area or positioned in their shell scrapes would sprint for it, piling on top of one another from a height of three metres, huddling close until the bombardment had concluded and the whining in our ears had stopped. If my knees and ankles had felt sore before, they were creaking and groaning after a series of hard landings.

Despite all this, our spirits stayed remarkably high, and the positive vibes were most evident in Bear. The bloke showed no signs of wilting under pressure.

'This is like CrossFit, Old Dog,' he laughed, after yet another race for survival. '*Grad CrossFit.* You've got to keep up or get out of the way!'

I laughed. *But what else could I do?* The alternative was to go crazy with terror.

The First Battalion fought non-stop, striking the Russians from a distance. In between, we did our best to sleep and recover, though resting was almost impossible. At the most I grabbed a thirty-minute nap during the lulls in violence and my mind was in such a state that I often jolted awake as soon as I'd dozed off. In those merciful few seconds between sleeping and waking I'd always forget where I was. Then the scream and the crash of exploding bombs delivered a terrifying reminder and my nerves would frazzle all over again. Eating was just as tricky. We had limited supplies and there was barely a chance to grab a bite, let alone wolf down a ration pack. Certainly nobody had the opportunity to get a brew going. We were all running on fumes.

Beating a retreat in this way was a strange situation. But as far as I was concerned, we were making a tactical withdrawal to the city, where we would put up more concerted resistance. Mariupol was only 19 kilometres away from Talakivka; we could see plumes of thick, black smoke rising above the city skyline. Once we rendezvoused with the rest of the Ukrainian forces there, the hope was that we might hold the Russians off, so that any remaining civilians in the area could get away and we could defend the rest of Ukraine, though apart from those communications with our friends and family, none of us had any idea what was happening in the wider war.

Before the invasion kicked off, many military experts had reckoned that Putin would own the country within a matter of days, a week tops. So far, the battle had been raging for seventy-two hours and we were holding strong. Or at least we were in the company I was serving with.

But in the distance, my home town burned.

5

On 28 February, we pulled back to Sartana, on the north-eastern outskirts of Mariupol, and during our first patrol of the area I gained a heartbreaking perspective on the brutalities taking place. Bloody hell, it was awful. The little town was a smouldering ruin and at the centre of the destruction was a school, its windows blown in by a Grad attack. Drawings and paintings drifted about the place, and inside there were satchels, coats and art-class aprons hanging on hooks. The owners' names had been written in crayon below each one. I later learned that the pupils had managed to get away, but that didn't deflect from the barbarity of what was going on. The Russians had blown it all to pieces, not knowing or caring whether any civilians were sheltering inside. I'd long suspected that Putin's war machine had sod-all regard for the rules of engagement or innocent life. The realisation that even the tiniest of tactical gains were being made without any consideration for innocents sickened me.

'I didn't think it was going to be like *this*,' I said to Dima as we kicked through the rubble, despondently.

I filmed the ruins of the school building on my phone, recording a short message for social media:

I can't tell you where we are, because of op sec [operational security]. But this is a school the Russians have just bombed. It's about seven kilometres off the front line.
We're just taking a bit of a respite, we've just had a week

of intense fighting.[2] It's chaos, to be honest. This was a thriving little town. Until, obviously, the Red Army decided to show up . . .

The disregard for human life didn't end there. Houses were ablaze. A doctor's surgery, the local church and a parade of shops had been levelled. Anyone hiding inside at the time of the attacks would have been crushed too.

Before long, we were on the receiving end of a similar level of violence, and surviving it became increasingly difficult. We were clearly outgunned and outnumbered at that point, running from position to position and jumping into abandoned buildings and trenches for cover. There was more Grad and more bombs, and I even experienced our first aerial assault when a fighter jet raced overhead and unleashed a fireworks display of ammunition. To stay under cover as best we could, the company took shelter in a house. As an extra layer of security, Bear ordered us to park our BTRs in a nearby garage, so the thermals of the engines wouldn't show up on Russian surveillance systems. And then over the radio came the call that every soldier dreaded.

'We've got a couple of three hundreds over here,' the voice said.

I understood the code clearly. 'Three hundreds' were casualties; 'two hundreds' meant fatalities. From what we could tell, a Grad attack had taken down two of our lads – one had broken his leg; the other was suffering from shrapnel wounds. Having forgotten the warnings to stay away from the town's major intersections, they had been caught out at

---

2   I'd actually been fighting for five days at that point, but I was so tired that it was hard to tell.

a crossroads, by the school. From what we could tell they were in OK shape, but they would have to come off the front line for treatment. That meant we were down a couple of fighters. Every loss of personnel – no matter how small or temporary – increased the strain in what was already an incredibly overworked group.

As I patrolled the town with Dima at noon, the devastation inflicted by the Russians was yet again unavoidable. Mariupol, which had flickered all night with fires and explosions, was again shrouded in thick black smoke in the distance.

Thankfully, there were moments of relief to be found among the misery of war. As I kicked through the rubble of an old village store, picking up bags of sweets, chocolate bars and energy drinks, I heard a shout. Dima had been moving through the skeleton of the flattened school.

'Old Dog! *Shaun!* You have to see this,' he yelled.

When I caught up with him, Dima was sitting at a piano and checking the keys. It was the only item still standing in a classroom that had been otherwise crushed in an explosion.

I handed him some of the grub I'd found. 'Play a bit, do you, mate?' I said, gesturing to the keyboard.

Dima nodded. 'Yes, I learned as a child.'

He then put together a couple of chords. It sounded pretty in tune to me. And as his fingers ran across the top, I recognised a delicate, haunting piece of classical music I couldn't for the life of me name now. It sounded incredible and poignant at the same time, probably because of the person playing it. This was a twenty-one-year-old kid with his whole life ahead of him. An intelligent and good-hearted man who spoke four languages and could play the piano as well as anyone I'd ever heard. Yet here he was, sitting in the ruins of a school, creating something beautiful while a senseless war waged around him. Really, he should have been out in the world finding his way and building a life; making connections and creating something positive. The boy had ambitions.

As Bear and a few others joined us, I noticed that Dima was smiling. I sat down on the floor and made the most of what was a rare moment of civility, enjoying the music, trying to imagine myself as being somewhere else, *anywhere else*, and not in a bombed-out school. It was a timely reminder that even in times of total darkness, some people had an incredible knack for finding the light switch.

That evening, explosions in Mariupol rumbled away behind us like thunder and blasts of Grad hurtled through the sky towards our position, though their impact seemed a little easier to manage at night. In the gloom, it was possible to first spot the glowing rockets and then track their trajectory. If they veered left or right, it was a sign they were heading away harmlessly, but a barely-there flicker of light meant the strike was coming straight at us and we should sprint for cover. At times, the pyrotechnic show was strangely mesmerising, despite the horror of everything going on around us. The same went for the fighter planes heading for Mariupol. Their afterburners looked terrifying, a blaze of ultra-hot blue, red and orange, and from a distance the fast-moving shapes resembled a line of Christmas trees, though their baubles and fairy lights were powering a delivery system of hard-core destruction.

I wasn't the only one watching and gawping. At one point a soldier alongside me stood up for a better view. 'Oh, it's so pretty,' he said.

A voice in the dark snapped back, '*Pretty?* How the fuck can that be *pretty?*'

Before the bloke could respond, Bear had loomed out of the shadows. He sent a heavy slap to the back of the poor sod's head. 'Pretty!' he roared again. 'Is it fuck. *It's Russian.*'

If Bear had hated the enemy before, his stance was hardening by the hour. More and more fighter jets flew overhead, each one set on an attack run to Mariupol. Putin's air force had complete domination of the skies – I certainly didn't see any dogfights involving Ukrainian planes – and the city was being demolished as a result. Everything there looked to be ablaze and there was a growing sense that the fighting we were involved in, which had been taking place at a distance up until that point, would become a little more hands-on in the city, especially once Russia's ground troops were deployed to take the region and mop up any resistance.

This feeling only grew stronger the following morning, when I watched several BTRs from other units racing through Sartana. Upwards of twenty men hung from the back of each one and they all had yellow tape wrapped around their arms – a marking to differentiate them from the enemy. That meant the next stage of the conflict was about to begin. *A siege defence in Mariupol.*

'Fuck, it's getting up close and personal now,' I said to Dima. 'We'll be scrapping in the streets soon.'

We left Sartana at 04:00. By 1 March 2022, we were back in Mariupol, nearly a full week after the invasion had kicked off. So much had happened to our group in such a small space of time and none of it was good, though we had at least slowed the momentum of Putin's ground assault. Up until then, I'd only really seen the war from a weird, claustrophobic perspective – sheltering from Grad attacks and firing at any tanks we might have seen rumbling towards us in the distance. Once in Mariupol, however, it was possible to witness the war in widescreen and high definition – and it was horrific. The city was a wasteland. Vast areas of housing had been razed to the ground by artillery shells; concrete roads were cracked up like broken chocolate bars. There wasn't a soul on the streets because thousands of people had hidden in a network of makeshift shelters – basements and underground car parks. The pavements were a carpet of rubble and broken glass, and everywhere I looked smoke poured from windows and smouldering cars. Surveying the wreckage did my head in.

I felt sick. The loss of life in the city was on a scale I'd never experienced before, even in Bosnia. Thousands had already been murdered and many more had lost their homes and livelihoods. All while Russian military leaders were claiming that their intention wasn't to kill civilians. More lies, more gaslighting – it was the Russian propaganda playbook in a nutshell. I scanned the skyline, looking for familiar landmarks, checking the left bank for the spot where our home had once stood. *Was it in one piece?* I took some comfort from the fact I couldn't see any smoke, but at that point, I doubted it even mattered. The Mariupol I knew was long gone.

I was worried. There was little doubt in my mind that we were about to be locked into a brigade-level defence. The mobile artillery units that had bombarded us at Pavlopil, Talakivka and Sartana were soon to be coming down on us yet again. They would be backed by large numbers of troops who would flood into the city. Our job was to keep them at bay for as long as possible, but we were ill-equipped to survive for extended periods, because, while Ukraine's military had suspected this day might eventually come, nobody had thought to prepare the city or its protecting forces for a siege event, and we had very little in the way of MREs (Meals, Ready to Eat). On arriving, Bear estimated that we had one box to share between thirty men, which was probably only enough to last a week, and reports told us that the city had already been ransacked for food. Without discipline, we'd soon be fighting on empty stomachs. To make matters worse, the city was without power, water or gas supplies. In the freezing conditions at night, everyone was going to suffer.

Our first few hours in Mariupol were as chaotic as my time on the front lines. Section commanders from other platoons raced around, barking orders. Some of them were meant for us, some weren't, and it became hard to distinguish what were instructions of tactical importance and what was knee-jerk decision-making. As the company awaited clear directives, we took shelter in the awnings of the Volodymyr Boyko Stadium, home to FC Mariupol. Over 12,500 people bustled around this place on a match day. Now it was surrounded by troops hoping to avoid another drone or Grad attack. Waves of fighter jets flew overhead, delivering noisy explosions to the city, and I found myself thinking about Grandad's war stories. *Was this what life had been like during the Blitz?*

We were pulled from pillar to post during those aerial attacks. At one point we were pointed towards the Illich Steel and Iron Works on the north of Mariupol, an institution that had for so long been the focus of Larysa's environmentalist anger. And then we weren't. In a last-minute turnaround, the company was dispatched to a village green, where we dug out shell scrapes for an impending attack that never came. At one point we were even told to 'Make ready' again, as we had done at the very beginning of the invasion.

'Russian troops are on their way,' Bear said. 'And we should be prepared for a ground assault.'

Everyone focused. *They're attacking. They're attacking. They're attacking.* The company gathered at the BTRs, clambering inside for warmth, and some of the lads, like Dima, crossed themselves in prayer. *Good luck to you,* I thought, white-knuckling my AK-74, the adrenaline coursing through me. I reckon anyone meeting me at that moment would have wondered if I was the most hyped soldier in service – I was ready to go, full of energy and anxiety; wanting to fight but not wanting to die. And I wasn't alone. I saw the same grim expression of determination and worry in the others. The tension was so palpable that the body heat building in the BTR caused me to sweat. I cracked open the door for a little ventilation.

We must have sat there for six hours before the call came in to stand down and move on.

I still have no idea why our orders had changed, but the emotional effort was exhausting. I had been fired up, ready for battle, only to experience another false alarm. I was already fatigued from the Pavlopil withdrawal, not to mention several days of bombardment. Now I had to find the strength to readjust to a new mission, whatever that might be. I wouldn't have to wait long, though. We were sent back to Illich, a hulking mass of metal spires and chimneys that was being transformed into a fortress, having been ringed by Ukrainian forces. It was also serving as a shelter for thousands of displaced residents. As we moved into the area, heavily armoured vehicles passed us on either side of the road. All were loaded with heavy weaponry. I spotted convoys of civilian cars, packed with armed Mariupol residents wearing yellow armbands. Local volunteers with next to no military experience were also arriving at Illich to take up arms.

The scene was surreal, but it was easy to see why the steelworks was the most likely location for Mariupol's last stand.[3] The place was fortified thanks to its tall metal towers and several expanses of water that protected the compound on three sides. We were deployed under cover of darkness to the main supply route, which ran parallel to the steelworks. Adjacent to the road on a two-tiered bridge was a railway track that led into the city and would provide an escape route if we were overwhelmed by the enemy at any point. It was thought that when the Russian army arrived, some of the forces would head for that very road and those very tracks, and our brief, according to Bear, was to defend the area with our lives.

Oh great, I thought. *The whole Russian army coming down this stretch, tanks and all . . . What could possibly go wrong?* We weren't fighting alone, though. The area had been ringed by anti-armour and anti-tank weapons systems. The 501st Naval Infantry Battalion had positioned themselves alongside us

---

3   The other steelworks in the area was Azovstal and it also became a military stronghold during the siege. The building produced steel and iron for the Chernobyl nuclear power plant, and was known to have nearly forty concrete nuclear bunkers underneath the main foundries, as well as a maze of subterranean tunnels. That made it the perfect place to hide, and hundreds of civilians were running to its perimeters, even though the Russians had made no secret of wanting to destroy it. The people of Mariupol didn't care. In the catacombs, under the plant, they would still be relatively safe from attack. Much safer than they would be in a subway station or car park.

too, and behind them the 503rd. I also took some heart from the fact that the First Battalion had been trained for moments such as this and our group was considered an important component within the overall battle plan. On training missions, it had been our role to secure key positions, such as beachheads or steelworks, so that any other assets could come in behind. We were bloody fit lads. Or at least we were supposed to be. At the age of forty-eight, I couldn't help wondering how long I would last in yet another gruelling gunfight, with no end in sight, and for a few moments part of me wished I'd taken a job in the military kitchens rather than the Marines. Then I recalled my responsibilities. I was defending my city and my home, and I felt proud. There wasn't anywhere I'd rather be than in a battle, at the very front with the other lads.

If I'm going to go, it doesn't really matter where it happens, I told myself. *So it might as well be here.*

Then I hoped that if the date of my going *was* today, it would be quick and relatively painless.

6

For the first seven days of the siege, I felt like a spectator to a war being fought from a distance. Heavy artillery still shattered Mariupol's buildings and roads, torching the city and killing hundreds more civilians, but nearly all of it happened around me. The anticipated ground attack hadn't yet materialised and for the most part I spent my time digging out shell scrapes and readying our positions for when it did inevitably come. For my platoon, comparatively, the war had slowed for a week, but that was only because we'd spent so much time dodging death while fighting our way back from Pavlopil. However, despite the change in pace, our work at Illich was still bloody knackering. We were back in the business of trench-building – digging in and strengthening our defensive positions ready for the coming assault.

Handily, Bear was an innovative thinker. One afternoon, as we hacked into yet another wall of mud and rock, I heard an engine chugging towards us. Fearing the worst, I took cover from what I assumed was an approaching enemy tank, calling out to the others to ready themselves. But when I peered over the trench, I saw a JCB digger steaming towards our position. Behind the wheel, waving cheerily, was Bear.

As the vehicle's steel teeth chewed into the terrain, carving out a hole that would have taken me all day to dig by hand, he shouted out cheerily, 'Hey, Old Dog! What do you think of this?'

I laughed. 'You ever driven one of these before?' I said, as Bear scooped another hole from the ground.

'No, just took a few lessons when I was down there,' he said, pointing back into the city. 'It was just sitting around. So I decide, "Why the fuck not?" I hotwire it and now I give you boys a hand.'

In the space of an hour or so we were able to dig out a series of *yamas* – deep, man-sized depressions that would make for handy shelters when the Russians sent their next wave of fighter planes hurtling towards Mariupol. I reckoned Bear's quick thinking and light fingers would probably save a lot of lives.

Whenever we weren't digging, our focus turned to food and heating. Everybody was famished, so until the Russians struck us on the ground, it made sense to forage for rations. Our issue was that a number of air raids had taken out the city's biggest supermarkets in a presumably deliberate attempt to starve us into surrender, and we were living off scraps. The winter was biting hard too and as there was no power in the city, our only hope of staying warm during any rest periods was to light a fire in a stove heater, using broken-up bits of furniture as fuel.

This was a risky process, of course. The smoke often gave our position away and if we were lucky enough to be able to light a fire inside, we were troubled by the realities of getting too warm. Going back into the cold with a sweaty back could cause a soldier to flash-freeze. In the end, the dilemma of whether to light a fire came down to a simple question: *Do we light the fire and let everybody know where we are, or do we freeze to death?* Warmth won out every time, though we never lit our fires after sunset.

It was after emerging from one of those rest breaks that I became caught up in our first significant contact with the enemy. As I stood shivering in the cold alongside Dima,

I heard the crackle of gunfire to our right. A five-man, Russian reconnaissance unit had crawled from the nearby treeline and was sneaking under the railway bridge. My guess was that they were probably trying to lay explosives at the bridge and instil a sense of fear into the battalion by breaking through our lines. But they had been spotted. I grabbed my night-vision goggles (NVGs) to see what was going on and in the grainy green light of my optics I saw rounds and muzzle flashes. Two of our troops, led by Bear, were driving the enemy back into the trees, but I realised our sentry post on the other side of the bridge wasn't laying down any covering fire. When I called out to him, there was no response.

The gunfight was chaotic. *They were always chaotic.* And as I fired, it was impossible to tell whether any of my rounds were actually landing. In addition to my NVGs, the lads around me were also using an Archer thermal imaging system, which was a much more effective way to locate enemy targets in the woods. Their positions were then called into the comms so that Bear could move in, but because of the intense cold, the batteries in the Archer often drained of energy in next to no time. Before long, the kit had died on us.

'The thermal system is down!' I said into the radio, alerting the advance party. They were now fighting half blind.

In the sensory overload, all I could make out were branches breaking away along the treeline as a chainsaw of bullets carved through the wood. I squeezed off more rounds and saw a Russian soldier falling over a log. I wasn't sure if I'd hit him or if he had slipped and tumbled. (And I couldn't exactly run over to check on his vital signs.) The noise was just as disorientating. Dozens of AK-74s all sounding out their distinctive bark at once. *Bup-bup-bup! Bup-bup-bup!* When the enemy eventually withdrew into the darkness, an unnerving moment of calm and stillness settled in. I smelled cordite and heard shouting somewhere in the shadows.

When Bear returned, there was a body – Ivanov, our man in the sentry post. I hadn't known him that well, but we'd been in one or two hairy moments together over the past fortnight and I liked him. As his corpse was carried past my trench, a chilling realisation kicked in. *This was our first fatality.* We had done well to get so far without a death in the group, but our luck had clearly run out. Not that I took any time to grieve the loss. While Ivanov's passing was undoubtedly sad, I simply had to compartmentalise the horror and move on. The following day, as soon as it was light, I distracted myself by relocating our sentry post at the bridge to a more suitable position, feeling determined that the Russians wouldn't be breaking through again.

Later that night, Dima seemed to be processing the events very differently. 'Ivanov's gone,' he said sadly, shaking his head.

Because of his age and combat experience, I couldn't imagine that he'd seen much in the way of death.

'*Tovarish*, we've got all the time in the world to mourn him afterwards,' I said. 'Right now we've got bigger problems, so try not to dwell on it. It's happened. It might even happen to you or me. But to make sure it doesn't, we've got to stay sharp.'

It's funny how the small things can lift the mood in such a tragic situation. The following morning, on a routine shift in the shell scrapes, Dima excused himself to go for a piss. As he fumbled around in an alley behind us, I heard

72

giggling. *What the fuck's he doing?* The giggling then turned into a throaty laugh. *Dima was cheering!*

'Shaun . . . *Shaun!*' he shouted, excitedly. 'You'll never believe this . . . I found cigarettes!'

Fucking hell. I'd last smoked a ciggy on the retreat to Mariupol. They were in short supply within the company and if anybody was lucky enough to still have any, they were keeping it to themselves. Finding smokes in a war zone was like winning the lottery. I was gasping for one.

Dima jumped down into the shell scrape below me and tore open the packet. 'Here, help yourself,' he said, smiling from ear to ear.

We chain-smoked for an hour straight, chuckling like school kids, not bothered that we were sucking on a rancid Ukrainian brand called Monte Carlo, which we'd have avoided at all costs in peacetime. To us, the acrid, chemical aftertaste was like nectar.

By the second week of March, the Russians had turned up the heat and Mariupol was feeling the full force of the invasion. On the 9th, a bomb attack flattened a maternity hospital, killing three people and wounding seventeen. Seven days later, this horrific act was followed by a similar assault on the Donetsk Regional Theatre of Drama, where around 1,300 people were taking shelter. To identify who was hiding inside, the residents had painted the word *children* in Cyrillic on the concourse. Enemy air surveillance passing overhead would have seen the warning, and yet they still attacked. Officials later estimated that at least 600 civilians were killed as the theatre exploded and caved in on itself. The city streets were beginning to hum with the stink of death.

From my position at Illich, it was possible to watch the battle moving around us. While ground troops had yet to attack our spot directly, they were undoubtedly probing for weaknesses, and rocket assaults came in from enemy ships lurking in the Sea of Azov, hammering the left bank of the city. Mobile artillery moved in the distance, along our flanks. Clearly, the Russians were attempting to encircle the steelworks in some final climactic attack, as they were at Azovstal. But while this was going on, there was a growing sense that our fearsome enemy, the great Russia, might not be the all-conquering force we'd originally feared. Yes, they were brutal. The murders at the maternity hospital and theatre were evidence of that. But while their tanks assaulted our trenches from a distance and mortar fire occasionally pinned us down, none of it was having a significant effect. Instead, their shells rained on the embankment ahead of us for days without inflicting any serious damage.

'Well, they've got to be a shit army,' I said to Dima, one morning.

He looked at me, confused, and almost instantly another wave of blasts exploded harmlessly in the distance, proving my point.

'Their accuracy is way off. Maybe they're not as efficient as we thought.'

All the same, while I was OK with it, the explosions were having a terrible psychological impact on some of the other lads. At least one soldier in our company had freaked out in his shell scrape. I later heard the radio call that a medic was caring for another who had suffered from a full-on breakdown. My heart melted. *The poor bastards*. We were in a horrific situation, so I wasn't surprised to discover some of us were emotionally ill-equipped to survive. Overall, though, our group had proved to be fairly resilient during the opening onslaught. After each wave of attacks, we all gathered together, rebuilt any positions that had been damaged and cracked a few jokes. Then we pressed on for another day of trying not to die.

Our will was tested again and again as the death and destruction piled up around us. We lost Private Danilo, a bloke I'd bonded with while travelling to Kyiv a year or two earlier. I was going on a sharpshooter course, he was learning to be an RPG gunner, and when I announced it was my birthday that day, the pair of us celebrated my completion of another twelve months around the sun during the journey. Moments before his end, Danilo had been exploring the city on a scavenger hunt for food when a Russian tank spotted the car he'd been driving. I was later told that a direct hit turned him into pink mist and no trace of him was ever found. Miraculously, the guy alongside him suffered only a broken leg and shrapnel wounds. It was yet another reminder that life in a war zone could be a lottery.

Not long after Danilo's death, Bear jogged over to my shell scrape during a lull in the fighting. He looked pissed off.

'Old Dog, I think they've bombed your house,' he said, angrily. 'Go take a look.'

I moved to where I could see the enclave of Mariupol I had once called home, except it was now glowing orange. Smoke billowed into the night sky. The raging fire looked like something from a disaster movie, and it was obvious that no building would survive it.

I texted Larysa, knowing she was away from danger. 'Left bank's gone.'

She pinged me back straight away. 'I know, somebody's told me the house has been hit.'

I later discovered that an RPG had been fired through a window, blowing up the inside and taking with it nearly everything we had built as a family. I consoled myself with the fact that my wife was still in one piece. Then I thanked the stars we'd not wasted seven grand doing up that bloody kitchen.

Rumours of an imminent Russian ground attack were doing the rounds and with them talk of what would happen if we were captured. I heard all sorts of horror stories regarding the type of inhumane torture that might be inflicted upon us if we were unlucky enough to be imprisoned. I even knew of a number of people who were stockpiling civilian clothes in case we had to go on the run. Being taken as a non-combatant was bad enough, but survivable. Being mistaken as a member of Azov – a unit most Russian and separatist soldiers believed, wrongly, was a Nazi group – didn't bear thinking about. I'd rather have died in the battle than have my appendages cut off by an angry enemy soldier, high on Putin's propaganda.

The gossip was understandably demoralising for a lot of people. We were starving, down to the bare bones of our arses with malnutrition, and our military resistance looked to be waning. At the beginning of the siege, the city's anti-aircraft defences had put up a stiff fight. But by the middle of March their defiance had waned, either because their positions had been destroyed or they were all out of ammo. It was nothing but crickets on the artillery front, and Russia's warplanes were able to attack at will. The talk of torture and escape and evasion only added to the doomy atmosphere.

Dima even overheard two Ukrainian tank drivers as they discussed escaping the city. The blokes had been attached to our company, but they were talking about finding a tunnel and making a break for it, unannounced. For a young bloke, Dima could be quite vocal. He had apparently stood up to them, appalled at the idea that anyone should desert their posts.

'Without you, who will operate the tank?' he'd shouted.

I'd felt nervous when he told me about it. Our position was clearly becoming untenable; snipers were enclosing us and taking potshots, and a sense of panic was creeping in. Now these guys were openly discussing desertion, debating whether abandoning their post was the right thing to do under the circumstances.

I knew Dima was just as worried by our deteriorating morale. 'What do you think we should do, Shaun?' he said. 'Are you staying?'

'Well, command and control hasn't broken down,' I said. 'So it's not every man for himself just yet.'

I really didn't want to have to make a call like that myself, especially not one that could have been misconstrued as sounding overly negative or defeatist. Dima was a good mate. I hated the thought of letting him down or having to explain just how bleak our situation might turn out to be in the coming weeks. Though I'm sure he understood our option of last resort was to go on the run and that we might have to take it at some point. Still, I'd rather someone else was making that decision for us. I wanted the order to come from our higher-ups, not one of the lads.

'You've got to spend a long time living with yourself,' I said. 'So if you have to go, you need to be doing it for the right reasons, rather than running off and leaving your friends.'

Dima nodded. 'I won't be leaving, Shaun,' he said.

Eventually our tank drivers announced that they were staying in place. *Thank God.* Their departure would have left us massively exposed, but it was yet another sign that the Russians were making psychological gains. I wondered how much more we could endure.

7

There was a rare lull in the bombing one morning and in the stillness I peered over the lip of my shell scrape. There didn't seem to be much in the way of enemy movement on the horizon other than a weird blob in the distance. It was around 400 metres away and moving towards us along the train tracks at a speed of no more than two or three miles an hour.

What the fuck is that? I thought, reaching for my binoculars.

Having managed to get a visual, I realised that the shape was a bright yellow train engine. My stomach knotted. *Fuck.* For a while, the Russians had thrown everything at us. We knew that at some point they would probably make another attempt at blowing up the two-tiered bridge that crossed the waterways around Illich, given it was our most immediate escape route. From there, they would either send in the infantry and kill us all in a last-stand gunfight or pin us back as a way of starving the stragglers into surrender. The general assumption was that such an attack would kick off with a concerted air assault on the tracks running along the bridge's lower tier. What nobody had envisioned was that the enemy might explode an improvised, slow-moving train bomb on the same route.

I screamed at Junior Sergeant Gluzsky, who was crouching nearby. 'An engine's coming down the tracks. I think it's packed with explosives.'

He got on the radio to Bear. 'Shit, shoot it!' he yelled. I'd never heard him so close to panicking.

I crouched on the upper tier of the bridge with several others, all of us firing at the train as it rumbled towards us. It had closed the distance to 200 metres. Nothing seemed to dent it, and when I looked around I realised we were horribly exposed. If the train detonated directly underneath us, there was every chance we would go up with it, and the only safe place to shelter was either in the trenches or in a shell scrape. *But there was no time to get there.* As the engine moved closer, I saw a bright white light and . . . *BOOM!* I was thrown backwards in a huge explosion. My eyesight flickered and distorted like the image on an old telly. I couldn't see anything in my right eye and my ears buzzed from the noise. Talk about having your bell rung. As I staggered to my feet, I saw that forty metres of woodland on the embankment's right side had been shredded, leaving behind a smouldering crater, but the bridge was still holding together – barely. If needed, we could still use it as an escape route into the city, maybe back to the other steelworks at Azovstal.

There was a second or two of eerie silence as everyone checked themselves for injuries, and then the groaning started. When I looked down, I realised that bits of kit had been ripped from my body in the explosion – my tourniquet was gone, all my pouches too, and a chunk of shrapnel had embedded itself in my plate carrier. Next to me was a soldier, a civilian reinforcement called Kovalenko. He was on his knees, staring into space, his eyes locked into a thousand-yard stare, his jaw hanging open in a silent scream. The man's faculties were shot. And then the sky exploded with falling debris from the explosion. Tree branches, metal and concrete rained from above. I felt Junior Sergeant Gluzsky grabbing at me. His fatigues were covered in red blotches, but I couldn't tell whether it was blood, paint or something else thrown up in the attack.

'You OK, Old Dog?' he shouted. It was hard to hear him over the whining in my eardrums.

'I – I – can't see anything in my right eye.'

Bear was shouting on the radio. 'Send him down now,' he yelled. 'We'll get him to the hospital and clean him up.'

My peripheral vision was exploding with flashes and light. From what I could make out, two Russian tanks had followed in behind the train and were opening up at the position. Those soldiers not wounded by the detonation were fighting back, and as I slipped and fell down a muddy embankment and waited in a shell scrape, I heard the rattle of AK-74s. The stink of cordite and scorched wood burned my nostrils. Not for the first time, I feared the Russians were on the verge of overrunning us. I later learnt that their plans had been screwed by a stroke of good luck – in the explosion, the wreckage of the train had been sent across the tracks, making it impossible for any tanks to pass.

Everywhere I looked was nightmarish. Eventually, Bear ordered me to the medical officer and I was lifted into the back of the vehicle and sat next to another soldier on a stretcher. He was flat on his back, his uniform shredded, his body and face blackened with burns and blood. As a doctor treated the wounds, every muscle in his body twitched and spasmed with shock and pain. And then I recognised him: it was a Marine with the call sign 'Moldovan'. I tried to speak, to reassure him, but nothing came out and the medics were soon talking to me. *Sshhh.* I could make out calming words among the bangs and whooshing outside. *You'll be OK.* There were questions and my brain clanged. *What's your name?* A liquid was poured into my eyes. *You've got a contusion – it's treatable*. I sat back on the stretcher and wondered at what point my luck would finally run out.

By rights, I should have been dead.

Modern conflict is more like a horror film than a war movie and nowhere is this more evident than in the workings of an active battle hospital. We were driven to a subterranean bunker deep inside the plant and I saw soldiers and civilians, men and women, in various states of agony. Shrapnel wounds were the most common injury and victims had either been slashed to ribbons by chunks of razor-sharp metal or were limbless and bleeding out. Some people were so badly burned it was impossible to recognise any facial features through the charred flesh and gore. But the worst part was the sound. Mariupol had been cut off from the outside world and, as a result, the hospital had run out of vital medical supplies such as bandages, antiseptic and, most troubling of all, heavy-duty painkillers like morphine. Everybody was in a world of hurt, and with no sign of an immediate respite, there was an overwhelming sense of hopelessness. I don't think I'll ever unhear some of the screaming from that day.

I stayed under supervision for several hours, an IV drip hanging from my arm, one of the few resources still available. I even managed to drift off for a brief time. Then, as I prepared to head back to the front line, somebody called out my name. When I turned around I saw a medic walking towards me. With my cracked eyesight it was hard to make out the face at first. Then I realised. It was Mykola, a good mate from Mariupol. In happier times we'd often hang out at the beach with our wives.

'Shaun! What happened?' he said, giving me a hug.

I told him about our position on the bridge and the train attack. 'Have you contacted your missus?' I said.

Mykola shook his head sadly. 'No, I was conscripted to work as a medic, and I haven't been able to get a message to her, but she's away from the city at least. *You?*'

'Just the once. I got a call out to her recently and I get texts when the reception comes back. I know she's safe.'

'Thank God,' said Mykola. 'Look, if you talk to Larysa again, can you let her know that I'm fine, just in case she's still in contact with Alana?'

I promised him I would. We were close friends. As we sat chatting, my mind drifted back to those long days at the seaside. I'd have given anything to be back there.

Mykola looked around, as if checking for spies. 'Do you want cigarettes?' he whispered conspiratorially.

Fucking hell, did I? My last puff was a week previously, when the stash discovered by Dima had run out. I was desperate.

'Well, I can't give them to you here. I'll be swamped with people begging for one. We're in such short supply of everything.'

He took me to a side office and shoved a dozen ciggies into my pocket. Out of nowhere, he pulled out a brand-new pair of socks. The ones on my feet hadn't been changed for weeks. They must have stunk something rotten.

'We're close to breaking here,' said Mykola, handing them over. 'There's talk of maybe relocating the hospital because the front lines have pulled back and we're too close. We'll have to move everybody out, but I have no idea how we're going to do it.'

Mykola looked exhausted. He was clearly out of his depth as a war-zone medic. He'd previously worked in one of my favourite restaurants. I'd never expected to run into him here, but the war was making unlikely heroes of a lot of people. I didn't even know that civvies were being called up as field-hospital medics and my workload in the trenches hadn't exactly afforded me the luxury of checking in with my mates from the city. As Mykola left to finish his rounds, I wondered what would become of him if the Russians eventually broke through. Judging by their previous attacks on the maternity hospital and the theatre, very little thought was being given to the civilian death toll, and the latest reports reckoned that 25,000 people had already been killed in Mariupol. The city was now on its last legs.

I feared many more would lose their lives before the war was done.

Back on the front line just twelve hours after the train blast, I soon became resigned to the fact that our brave resistance was pretty much finished. Over the next few days, that feeling intensified and I realised that at some point we would have to sneak out of Mariupol in an against-the-odds evacuation. Seeing as the Russians weren't likely to open a humanitarian corridor for civilians to escape, most of us would probably cop it on the way. The only question was the timing of the move. Because of the communication hierarchy within the Ukrainian chain of command, very little information about what was happening was getting through to our position. We were left to wait and worry.

Then, at the end of March, I received more intelligence updates in one frantic conversation with Larysa than in two weeks of trench fighting. Phone signals were now almost non-existent at Illich. However, if the planets were aligned and the meteorological gods delivered a south-westerly wind, it was possible to hook onto a local network. Though even doing that was fraught with risk. The best area of connectivity lay just past the trenches, in a copse of trees that was a magnet for Grad attacks, but most of us were willing to take the risk if it meant chatting to our loved ones. Those moments of connection, no matter how brief, were enough to keep a soldier going.

One morning, the shout went up that the phone signal was back. I decided to take a chance and ran to the woods, where I got through to Larysa on the first attempt. Worried that the fragile signal might give out, I quickly delivered the highlights of our grim situation: *We're fucked, battered and bruised, but holding on; surrounded, but fighting back. The Russians are on top of us and have inflicted serious casualties, but they're yet to break through.*

Larysa did the same: *You're cut off; the Russians are making Mariupol a priority now. You'll be bombed to shit. And forget any chance of getting a humanitarian corridor on your way out – the ones that have opened up across the country are being attacked.*

The details hadn't exactly been a morale-booster, but just hearing her voice gave me the lift I'd so badly needed. I'd also been presented with a stark reality check regarding Mariupol's short-term future.

We were double-fucked.

The only reason the country hadn't yet fallen as a whole was that Ukrainian resistance, led by Zelenskiy, had turned out to be so bloody stubborn. Through an understanding of the country's terrain and infrastructure, plus a fearless desire to defend its sovereignty, the army had held on to a number of key territories. The battles were bloody and ugly, but Ukraine was still standing strong, and the longer Mariupol remained out of Putin's hands, the better. Once the city fell, however, Russia would have her land bridge with occupied Ukraine, allowing them to push deeper into the country, all while controlling the supplies that went out of the Azov Sea and Black Sea ports. Putting a squeeze on Ukraine's vast exports added muscle to Russia's future international dealings, especially as they attempted to wriggle out of the various sanctions being levied against them by those nations in need of grain.

Meanwhile, more enemy snipers had encircled the area and it was becoming increasingly difficult to hide. A call was made that the lads lucky enough to be off duty for a few hours should sleep underneath the city in a nearby sewage works. Though it was slightly warmer down there in the tunnels (if −10°C can ever be considered hospitable), the place stank, as you would expect. It was also a health hazard because we usually gathered beneath the filtration systems, doing our best to stay comfortable on the damp concrete floor, without pillows or blankets, as a channel of filthy water ran alongside us. We weren't animals, though. Anyone needing the toilet would take themselves away from the group for some privacy. Every now and then, the dull boom of detonating rockets and missiles reverberated through the tunnels.

The Russians were applying more force, and shortly after my call with Larysa, another tank attempted to break through our perimeter wall at the rear of the plant. Some of my platoon were ordered to defend it; others were asked to hold at the railway bridge. I drew one of the short straws and was dispatched to attack, while Dima remained in our shell scrape, and as I sprinted to the gunfight, I spotted more and more indicators that we were close to breaking point. Dead bodies littered the streets. Presumably, they had all been killed by sniper fire, though the most chilling detail was one corpse at the centre of it all. It was a man slumped across a hospital stretcher. My guess was the Russians had attacked a team of medics as they carried a casualty to Mykola's hospital and the dead and dying were then used as bait. Anyone assisting them in the aftermath would have been gunned down too.

I had to push on. I ran to a wall with a small unit of fighters, comprising Bear, an armed medic and a reservist in his late fifties who in normal times would have been militarily retired. Crouching down, we waited for the tank to crawl across our line of fire. As we hid, two soldiers from the heavy weapons unit approached us.

'Can we borrow the NLAW?' said one, gesturing to the rocket launcher.

His tone was so casual it was as if he'd asked to borrow a mobile-phone charger or cigarette lighter.

Bear didn't want to give it up. 'We're going to use it.'

The soldier then pointed to a blown-apart office block around thirty metres away. He explained their plan was to move into the wreckage, climb to a higher floor and take out the tank from above. The building was a shell. It looked close to toppling over. I couldn't believe the balls of it.

'Mate, in that case, knock yourself out,' I said, gesturing for our lads to hand over the NLAW.

I then watched in disbelief as the two soldiers edged forward, occasionally taking cover in a doorway or ripped-open office front. Eventually, they slipped inside their chosen kill position.

There was a noise and I froze. From just behind the nearby wall, I heard the chatter of Russian soldiers. They were only a few metres away. *Shit! The bastards were on us.* Presumably, they were waiting for the tank to destroy one of our nearby positions. After that they'd have little bother in storming the steelworks before killing everyone inside.

Wanting to avoid detection, I gestured to the others to stay quiet. I then crept away from the wall and ran into a nearby building. Stepping carefully around a carpet of broken glass to avoid making any noise, I took up an elevated position on a flight of stairs, grabbing a line of sight at a smashed-in window. Below me, Bear and the others had slipped away from the wall and were heading back to the embankment. Our survival, and that of everyone in the company, was now in the hands of the heavy weapons unit.

But where were they?

I scanned the bombed-out block ahead and spotted a shadow on the second floor. It was the bloke with the NLAW. He had moved into a prime position. The launcher was at his shoulder and aimed at the tank rolling through the street below.

WHOOSH!

The flash of light came first, then a loud bang as the rocket tore through the tank's armour, destroying everything inside with a ball of fire. The ground shook. Thick black smoke billowed across the street and several nearby Russian soldiers, recovering quickly from the attack's explosive force, opened up at the shooter's position. Bullets ripped into brickwork, bringing down chunks of stone and plaster, and the air was clouded with so much airborne debris that it was hard to assess the battle scene ahead. But through the dust clouds I saw our heavy weapons unit sprinting for cover as a volley of enemy RPGs and mortar rockets blew up at their rear. They were soon over a wall and out of sight. I smiled grimly. In what was an increasingly bleak situation, that one act of bravery had given me a glimmer of hope.

But it wouldn't last for long.

Within minutes our radios had delivered news of yet another setback. While we'd been neutralising the tank, a Russian fighter plane had launched an attack on our embankment positions, destroying two of the company's BTRs – the vehicles we'd used so effectively during our withdrawal to Mariupol. Our hope, in the event of an evacuation, had been to sprint from the city in those same vehicles, and I knew that losing them seriously reduced our capacity to carry the group away. At the very least, it would be a bloody uncomfortable ride. The mood among the lads in the trenches was bleak. And as I crawled back to our shell scrapes, I noticed that everyone was downhearted.

'What's going on?' I asked.

'We're out of NLAWs,' said one Marine. 'And there's another tank coming round to our position.'

He pointed to a wall ahead and the gaping hole that had been exploded open during a previous attack. 'The Russians are going to come through there at any minute. We've heard them shouting.'

Everything was so close. The fighting was claustrophobic. Then I spotted Bear in the distance. He was making his way over to us. When I tried to deliver a sitrep, he listened thoughtfully for a moment, then raised a hand to stop me. 'Shaun . . . I'm so sorry. Dima's dead.'

Everything froze for a second or two. What Bear had said – *it didn't make sense.*

'*What?*'

Bear repeated himself and I rolled onto my front, digging my fists into the mud for stability. The ground beneath my body seemed to be slipping away.

'No. *How?*'

'He was in the BTR when the rockets hit. He didn't stand a chance. At least it would have been quick – I doubt Dima knew anything about it.'

My mind ran through everything we'd done together, all of it, all at once. I thought back to that time when we'd kicked through the shops in Sartana, Dima picking out a piece of classical music on an old piano in a bombed-out school. He'd briefly brought some beauty to a day of overwhelming horror. *Twenty-one years old.* I couldn't get my head around it. *Dima was about the same age as my kid.* He'd been popular in the platoon too, and it wasn't just me who had clicked with him. He'd always shared his food – and his ciggies. *Bloody hell: the news was going to crush his girlfriend.* I'd met her in Mykolaiv a year or so back and they'd seemed so happy together. *Who would break the news to her?*

Everything felt unsteady. I couldn't believe Dima had been snatched away. Up until that point, I'd survived several dark moments when an emotional breakdown would have been a completely understandable reaction. But I'd somehow clung on, partly because I'd become inured to so much of it, but also because he'd been alongside me. This was the toughest moment of all, no doubt. Dima was my best friend on the front line. We'd made each other laugh when everything had turned to shit; we had propped each other up during the heaviest moments. I hated the thought of facing the war without him. Then, remembering the crucifix hanging from his helmet, I wondered if Dima had finally found his God.

Bear sensed my spirit was crumbling. 'Shaun,' he said, calmly. 'Listen . . .'

But I didn't want to listen. I was a million miles away, staring at the wall where I knew the Russians were lurking.

The bastards were probably prepping another barrage of senseless murder. *Who would they cut down next?*

Bear raised his voice to reach me. '*Shaun*. We deal with this after, yes? We need to keep pushing. Be strong. We need to keep pushing.'

I nodded, knowing that Dima's death was the last straw for me.

'When are we going to get out?' I said. 'Where are we going to go?'

Bear shrugged. 'I don't know, my friend. Anywhere is better than here. I just want to see my wife again.'

8

Dima had been close. *So bloody close.*

Only three or four days after his death, the call went out to evacuate. President Zelenskiy was urging anyone still fighting in Mariupol to flee the city and rejoin the battle with another unit, if possible. Those that couldn't escape should surrender.

Bear was eager to leave. 'We're folding, Old Dog,' he said. 'We've got no hope.'

I felt relief. 'You sure?'

'Yeah, we are on our last legs. Now we've got the call, it is time.'

Nobody was less surprised than me. I did a head count: I think around 60 per cent of our total fighting force had been either killed or injured. Some of them, like Dima, were mates; others were good soldiers, *brave men*, and we needed to move out if their efforts weren't to be in vain. Our position was untenable. More Russian tanks were smashing through the heavily fortified walls around Illich; the enemy's shock troopers were pouring into the city too, and at times it felt as if we were living in the closing scenes of the Steven Spielberg war film *Saving Private Ryan*. Worse, fighter jets were now focused upon our compound, and they attacked it over and over again, presumably because there was nothing else in Mariupol to destroy. We did our best to move around from defensive position to defensive position, but as soon as we settled into one spot a drone would quickly ping us. We were also dangerously malnourished and dehydrated. At the start of the siege, the group had made a daily ration bag last for as long as a week. By the end, I was thinking about those days with a weird sense of nostalgia. At least I had *something* back then – especially that twenty-five-kilo wheel of Parmesan cheese Bear had found in the rubble. The lads lived off the find for ten straight days, even though it gave most of us constipation. Now the pulsing, hollow hunger pains in my stomach had become as bad as the stress in my guts, and living off nothing but scraps of mouldy fruit and veg was crushing our morale, especially as our situation wasn't going to improve.

A lot of the inexperienced soldiers in the group had become increasingly bitter. Some were bitching that their government had abandoned the forces in Mariupol, but as far as I was concerned, starvation was one of the unspoken consequences of war. Quickly accepting our lot was the only option – positivity in the face of adversity and all that – and I was always trying to find something to joke about. Really, it was the only way to stop yourself, and the others, from going stark raving mad. Even when our guts had become blocked with Italian cheese, there was often plenty of laughter whenever one of the lads tried to take a shit in the woods. The grunting and groaning was hilarious and we had to make the most of it.

Considering these realities, I felt OK about retreating – either alone or as part of a group. I had done my bit, no question, and as far as I was concerned, survival represented the smartest tactical choice. While I was still fighting fit, with two arms, two legs and a clear head, it felt right that I should do everything to move past the enemy lines around the city. Hopefully, I could join up with another battalion in a more tactically advantageous position and start with the scrapping all over again. Bear reckoned there was one such group near to the city of Zaporizhzhia, in the Zaporizhzhia Oblast, which was a couple of hundred kilometres away. Covering that distance was a bloody ambitious target, but if my luck held out and I could find food along the way, my aim was to join them. Surrendering was out of the question. As a former British soldier, I didn't fancy doing time in a Russian prisoner-of-war camp. There was every chance I'd be executed or tortured.

Before we could do anything, though, we had to escape the city in what was left of our road fleet, plus some commandeered military lorries, and that would be no easy task. Mariupol was surrounded by woodland and every treeline was sure to be occupied by enemy gunmen, because that was where soldiers were usually trained to hide out. There was also my age and condition to consider. My body had been ravaged during the siege and I wasn't sure how much more physical punishment I could take. My SERE training had taught me just how brutal an escape-and-evasion mission could be, and because I was already rinsed from the siege fighting, I knew I'd have to tread carefully. Finally, we had the enemy to consider. Russian armoured vehicles, drones and aerial assets had been set up to spot and presumably kill anyone fleeing the city. I wasn't optimistic that we'd survive an attack from above.

That doomy reality hadn't fazed Bear one bit. As we circled the wagons and tried to survive the latest Russian assaults on our position, he drew up a seating plan for the retreat convoy, so that the remaining members of the company could escape as a group. A commander was assigned to each vehicle and the idea was to fill the seats and then cram as many others onto the back as possible. Once we were out of road, or the Russians had spotted us from the air, we would run into the woods for cover. If luck was on our side, we'd disembark in an area not taken by the enemy, which would allow us to progress on foot. The journey wasn't likely to be comfortable, and it was definitely going to be a lottery as to whether we'd survive or not, but I comforted myself with the fact that a lot of lives would be saved if everything went well. For me, our evacuation couldn't come quick enough. I wanted to get the fuck out of Dodge.

The waiting was torturous, so I attempted to call Larysa. I didn't want her to worry about me. Miraculously, I got through, and I told her of my plans to dump the phone at the first sign of being captured, so that the enemy couldn't get their hands on the personal information it contained. I didn't want her to stress over any extended periods of radio silence.

'If you don't hear from me, I'm not necessarily dead,' I said. 'I'm going to get out. But the fight is coming to an end and at some point we might be captured.'

There was a pause on the other end of the line. For a second I assumed that Larysa was crying. Then the shouting started.

'Live. Fight. Survive!' she yelled. 'Don't fucking die!'

'*What?*'

'I said: Live. Fight. Survive. *Don't fucking die!*'

This was the Larysa I'd fallen in love with: the woman who enjoyed sticking it to the polluters and the Mariupol business leaders putting profits before people. No way was I going to disagree. Larysa could be a force of nature when the mood took her.

'OK . . . OK! I get it.'

'You've brought the world's attention to Mariupol. Everyone can see that Ukraine is fighting hard. Keep going . . .'

It was exactly what I'd needed to hear. Part of me had doubted that we'd make it out of Mariupol alive. Now she was ordering me to keep the battle going. *Live. Fight. Survive!* Her words ran through my head like a mantra, over and over.

I would need them to keep me going in the battle.

Our plan was to flee the city on the early morning of 12 April and we gathered together at 3 a.m., creeping towards the pick-up spot in the dark. I was exhausted. I'd barely eaten anything for three days and there was very little water to share among the group, but at least we were on our way out of Mariupol. As we moved on foot through the rubble of a flattened city, I couldn't help but feel a sense of relief. The town I'd previously called home was gone. It was almost unrecognisable, apart from the steelworks towers. The Russians had destroyed everything else. I wanted to be as far away as possible.

We walked for twenty minutes. From time to time a sniper would spot us and open up. A couple of mortars exploded nearby, though fortunately nobody was hit. But when we arrived at the rendezvous point, the mission became a clusterfuck. Our transportation hadn't yet arrived and reports were coming through that a Russian armoured vehicle was patrolling our chosen route away from the city.

Bear then made the call. 'We're going to delay the mission for twenty-four hours,' he said. 'We go again tomorrow.'

I crawled back to an area of woodland near to our old shell scrapes, not knowing whether the Russians had already moved in behind us, feeling totally confused as to what was going on. For the next twenty-four hours I counted down the minutes, waiting for the 3 a.m. call to come so I could get the fuck away from our position. I daresay everybody else was pretty much in the same boat: we were starving, exhausted and frightened. During the day, our company was bombed to hell and a drone attack killed one territorial army soldier in his trench, but eventually we were able to attempt our escape once again. Depressingly, as we crept away, the Russians detected our movements and opened fire. All hell broke loose.

We ran through the streets to our vehicle rendezvous point, the shooting and bombing continuing around us, passing another dead body along the way. After everything I'd been through – Ivanov's death, Dima, my time in a makeshift military hospital – I was able to tune out most of the grisliest sights. But not everyone was built the same way. Some of the blokes around me, especially the ones who were carrying injuries and couldn't move as quickly as the others, became visibly rattled. One or two were on crutches; others had their arms in a sling. A lot of soldiers were suffering from shrapnel injuries. They'd endured a torrid time and their morale had been crushed. Seeing a corpse abandoned on the ground only compounded their misery. Despite my brush with mortality during the train attack, I was able to handle the horror. I couldn't help but count my blessings that I hadn't broken down.

I'm a lucky fucker, I thought, not entirely sure whether my good fortune was down to random circumstance or the fact that my past combat experience had helped. I knew how to function during moments of hard-core violence. I hadn't flapped or made a mistake.

I pushed the thought to one side. We weren't yet away from Mariupol and the worst thing would be to cop a round during the early phases of an escape and evasion. Ahead of us, the Russians were lighting up a treeline on the city limits with artillery fire and white phosphorus. The chemical was usually applied to bullets so they could glow in the dark as tracer rounds. When detonated in large quantities, however, white phosphorus worked as an even bigger marker for heavy rockets to pile in – though, chillingly, it also burned through everything it touched and made for a crude chemical weapon. As the phosphorus rained down from the sky, there was a deafening, psychedelic explosion. The attack must have struck a nearby ammo dump and I heard RPGs winging around and rounds popping off. The skyline ahead of me twinkled like Christmas tinsel.

Oh, fuck. A phosphorus attack at the city perimeters was a sure sign that the Russians knew which way we were heading. The odds of our making it out in one piece had been cut drastically, though at least the vehicles were waiting for us this time. We had a convoy of two open-topped lorries, a couple of cars and at least one armoured patrol car, all of which had been reinforced with welded steel plates, *Mad Max*-style. I counted forty soldiers from my company, plus some civilians. Many had been scrapping on the other side of the steelworks for weeks and they were now clambering into the back of our trucks. I recognised one or two fighters and called out to say hello. Some were OK; others were covered from head to foot in dry blood. When our mission brief had been laid out, nobody had mentioned that we'd be transporting so many injured, but here they were – dozens of them. Our seating plans were ripped up as we worked on squeezing everybody aboard as best we could. Anything that wasn't a human body was left behind, including some of our fighting kit. One woman had even brought her dog. She was distraught when we told her to say her farewells.

'Why can't I?' she screamed.

Another soldier had to pull the whimpering animal out of her arms and place it on the ground. 'There's no room. You can't take it!'

The mood was end-of-days stuff. When I clocked the driver in the lead lorry he was sucking the end of his cigarette down to the butt. Once done, he instantly sparked up another. The bloke was bricking it, though at least he had nicotine for comfort.

I heard the rumble and grind of tanks to our rear. Rockets were being fired over our heads, towards the road and woodland. The bastards were attempting to cut off our route, but we had no choice but to press ahead. At around 4 a.m. the small convoy moved off into the dark and who knows where. I squeezed into the back of a truck alongside several groaning, injured team-mates and barely-holding-it-together freedom fighters, my weapon trained on the shadows outside. Every bump in the road brought a chorus of moans. Those standing had little room to manoeuvre and if they adjusted their feet and trod on a casualty, there was a scream. I was terrified. Even though we were unlikely to be spotted with the naked eye, if a passing jet picked up our thermals we would be compromised. Our chances of survival hung by a thread.

But the tanks missed us, the rocket attacks tailed off. For more than twenty minutes we seemed to be OK and my mind calmed a little. I told myself that everything was going to be fine – maybe, hopefully. *And at least you're not stuck in a trench outside Illich, waiting to be blown up.* We passed friendly checkpoints outside the city. One or two Ukrainian soldiers waved to us from their posts. And then, all at once, the convoy slammed on the brakes and everyone was ordered to get out. I sighed.

This can't be good, I thought. *Shit. Shit. Shit.*

My gut feeling was spot on. A fighter jet scorched overhead and bore down on a cluster of small industrial buildings to the side of the road, blowing them apart. The sky was lit up. We had been ambushed. Rocket fire trembled the ground around us. When the air stopped vibrating, I heard the familiar rattle of small-arms fire in the distance, though in the confusion it was hard to tell if it was aimed at us or if some other gunfight had kicked off along the road. I jumped away from the lorry and ran.

We were screwed. I really had no idea of what to do next. My mobile-phone signal was patchy at best, so even if I'd wanted to refer to an online map, which was an absolute fail in terms of an escape-and-evasion mission, the chances of me picking up an accurate reading were next to nothing. The only instructions Bear had offered us in the event of our convoy being bumped was to run for the nearest treeline, so I did just that, making a mad one-hundred-metre dash for the woods. In my condition, it felt more like ten kilometres. As I did so, I saw people struggling. The injured were barely able to keep up and when a medic called out, I ran over to help. She was supporting a bloke in civvy clothing, someone I recognised as a battalion officer. He had been hobbling along on crutches. Grabbing an arm each, we dragged him into cover.

The firing stopped and there was a brief moment of stillness. Everyone was out of breath. I heard the pounding of blood in my ears. When I peered out to the smoking ground behind us, I realised that daylight was breaking above the horizon, which made us even easier to spot. Looking back into the woods, I listened for the rustle or crack of under-growth and waited for some sign of movement, but all I caught was silence. The main body of the platoon was scattered. We had been pulled apart.

'What do we do now?' whispered the medic, fearfully.

I shrugged. 'I don't know. Let me take a look.'

A quick scan of the area told me that the group had sprinted off in different directions. In the distance I heard the sound of moving vehicles and more gunfire. It was hard to know whether the engines belonged to them or us. Maybe it was both. The only thing I was certain of was that we were vulnerable. The Russians knew exactly where we were and if we didn't move quickly, there was a good chance we'd be blown up or captured.

The medic pointed to a small gatehouse across the road. It looked like the entrance to an industrial estate.

'I don't know,' I said. 'It's a pretty easy target for them to lay fire down on.'

There was no changing her mind. Her English wasn't great, but there was also the fact that she was a master sergeant, which meant I was outranked. I had to defer. Reluctantly, I heaved up the casualty and stepped out into the open ground, moving cautiously towards the gatehouse. As we did so, I heard a shout behind and, swivelling, looking for the source, I spotted two more Marines in civvy clothing as they stepped out of the woods from different directions. They shuffled towards the building like extras from a zombie film.

I kicked in the door. There on the floor was another wounded Marine. He was lying on a stretcher and his torso had been so badly shredded by shrapnel that he was unable to stand. Somebody must have carried him to the building and then left him. The medic tended to him straight away as I took a second to regroup and assess. Six of us had made it inside. A few more had spotted our move and were now following, but I knew staying put was the worst thing for me to do. Out of the group I was the only one in full military fatigues and the only person still armed. I had my body armour, weapons and ammo, and although I'd been a combat medic in the British Army, I was vastly under-qualified compared to the medic who was now tending to some of the wounded. The bloke with the shrapnel wound was moaning. He was in a bad way.

I searched the space for food, my mind racing, and by luck came up with a mouldy old cabbage, which I shared around the group. It tasted disgusting and the smell was horrendous, but it was better than nothing. Then I weighed up my options. I knew that if I was captured by Russian or DPR forces, I would be tortured, or maybe even executed on the spot, because I was (a) a soldier, and (b) a Brit. Talking my way out of trouble was an impossibility, though the others could at least pass themselves off as Ukrainian civilians, which meant they would probably be transported into occupied Donetsk. They were going to be treated a damn sight better than me. After making a quick 360-degree patrol of the exterior, I realised we were alone and that nobody else was coming. *What should I do?* I remembered my orders to regroup with my platoon. *It was my duty.* Bear had instructed me to get to another battalion in Zaporizhzhia. *I had to make a break for it.* There was also the fact that if my weapon was spotted, it would make all of us a target. *By staying I was putting everyone at risk.* I crouched next to the medic.

'Look, I have to go,' I said.

She shrugged. I don't think she understood me at first.

'If the Russians or DPR find me here,' I said, 'they'll assume that we're all military and that's everyone fucked. You lot are mainly in civilian clothing, so you'll be taken into occupied Donetsk. I've been ordered to get to another unit so I can carry on fighting.'

One or two of the others who spoke better English nodded. *They got it.*

It was probably the hardest decision I've ever had to make in my military career. I hated leaving, though I'd been presented with very little choice. Staying would make me a liability to the group rather than an asset. At the same time, I had to do what I could to rejoin the fight. I pushed the door open, scanned the treeline for enemy gunmen and stepped into the early-morning gloom.

9

How was I going to reach Zaporizhzhia?

I assessed my location. Before the war, Larysa and I had often driven along this route and I knew of at least one petrol garage nearby. If I recalled correctly, there was a food store too, so hopefully I'd find something to eat. Beyond that there was a village a little farther down the road. I scouted around the gatehouse, moving cautiously towards the treeline, noticing the telltale signs of a gunfight. Spent shell cases were scattered across the mud and grass, meaning the enemy were probably somewhere nearby. Making a note to stay alert, I hid in cover as best I could. In the distance I heard more small-arms fire and the ominous rumble of heavy artillery. The last gasps of resistance in Mariupol were being snuffed out. *Surely it must have fallen by now.* I imagined Russian tanks steaming through the steelworks and then the city streets, laying claim to whatever and whoever was still standing, which probably wasn't a lot.

My stomach grumbled. Those mouldy cabbage leaves had barely touched the sides and if I was going to walk a couple of hundred kilometres, I'd have to eat something sharpish. But as I approached the garage, I noticed the smashed windows. Its doors were swinging open on their hinges. The attached mini-supermarket had already been broken into, and when I stepped through the wreckage and searched the toppled shelving, everything had been stripped. It was as if a hurricane had ripped through the place.

I crouched down low and bear-crawled towards a window. The garage sat on top of a small hill and from its vantage point I was able to study the village ahead. It had been built on two levels, and like nearly everywhere else, the Russians had attacked a lot of it. I saw blackened cars and crumbling homes. Furniture had been dumped into the street and discarded clothing and rubbish flapped about in the wind. An entire community looked ransacked, presumably by a mob of heavily armed enemy fighters. At some point, a scene of pandemonium must have kicked off, and I tried to imagine the horror of watching as an invading force wreaked havoc on my home. Then I pictured our burning house on the left bank. *How much more damage would the Russians cause before all of this was done?* They seemed relentless.

I left the garage and moved forward cautiously. It was around eight o'clock. The sun was higher now and a beautiful morning was in the offing. There was a cold bite in the air. My ears burned in the freeze and my breath plumed like vape smoke, but because of the frost and ice on the ground everything twinkled. It reminded me of a wintry country walk in England and I became weirdly elated, even though that life was a million miles away. *All I needed now was a dog and a takeaway coffee.* For the first time in months, my nerves weren't being jangled by the crash and clatter of incoming artillery and gunfire. Yeah, I was on the run. An enemy soldier would happily clack me off as prey. But a strange sense of freedom had kicked in, as if I'd become the master of my own destiny, probably for the first time since my short holiday with Larysa. I suddenly felt optimistic about my situation.

I'll survive, I thought. *If I can find water and a little food, there's no reason why I can't get to Zaporizhzhia. I can do this.*

When I arrived in the village and viewed the scene close up, everything felt ghostly. The lower level was definitely abandoned and part of me wondered if I'd already slipped past the first line of Russian units around Mariupol. Certainly the noise of artillery was all behind me and I hadn't noticed any drones flying overhead. If that was the case and I *had* broken behind the enemy, the hardest part of my job was done, though I held off from celebrating. For one thing, I didn't have anything to celebrate *with*. And secondly, the last thing I wanted was to become cocky or careless.

Edging towards the first house in a small street, I slipped inside, rummaging through the kitchen drawers and cupboards, looking for edible scraps, but everything had been taken. I checked my phone in the hope of picking up a signal, but I was all out of luck there too. Carefully pulling back a curtain, I surveyed the terrain ahead, thinking back to my SERE course in Washington State. Bloody hell, the lessons had taken place years ago and were now a distant memory, but the thought of my performance back then gave me a sense of confidence that I might stay ahead of the Russians, despite the fact I was starving and bloody knackered.

I waited in the house for a few minutes more, checking the windows so that I could study the rhythm of life outside. On the second tier of the village I noticed one or two people wandering around. They were dressed in civilian clothing and were probably locals who had refused to leave when the Russians rolled through. I also spotted an abandoned enemy vehicle with a 'Z' painted on the bonnet. The bodywork was splattered with bullet holes, but that didn't mean the original occupants, or their mates, weren't still somewhere nearby. There was also the risk that one of the civvies might be a Russian sympathiser and would mention my arrival if I was spotted. I had to be careful. Pushing forward again, I sneaked into the next house in the street, then the next. Over the course of two hours I moved from home to home, kitchen to kitchen, hoping to find something that would keep me going for a couple of days or so, but every cupboard was bare. Even the rats must have been starving.

And then I saw them at the end of the street. Three big storage containers, the kind brought in on transport ships and freight trains. When I shoved the first door in with a loud metallic groan, my mood lifted. There was no sign of food or water, but at some point the space must have been used as a storage depot because it was full of non-military clothing – jackets and jumpers, socks and woolly hats. As I rifled through the piles, checking sizes, I knew I'd been thrown a bone. Losing my military fatigues gave me the chance to go undercover, though my weapons would give me away. I picked up a duffle bag to carry my bulky AK-74, but it was too small.

Think, Shaun. Think.

Because of my physical state, making my way to Zaporizhzhia while weighed down with forty-five kilos of body armour, ammo, gun, grenades and heavy-duty boots was going to be a slog. I was already soaked through with sweat and rapidly dehydrating, and, as I stripped and changed, I made a call that went against everything I'd been taught during SERE training. I was ditching my weapons. Travelling light was my best course of action, and the only equipment I intended to keep on me was my watch, torch and knife, plus my phone and charger.[4]

---

4   When we first arrived at the Illich steelworks, there had been a plug socket in the accommodation next to the embankment. When the power was cut after a week on the position, I used a battery bank. I turned my phone off as a rule and only used it when I wanted to call Larysa.

Once I reach the other unit, someone's bound to give me a weapon, I thought.

My next task was to plan the route. I'd done well to evade capture so far, but I needed to work out exactly how to get to Zaporizhzhia. Although I knew from memory where I was in relation to Mariupol, my exact bearings were a mystery. Following the main transportation routes was off the table because the Russians were bound to be watching them. But if I could get to the highest point in the village and spot a familiar landmark or two, then I might be able to find some clue as to which direction to take. If I walked into an area of mobile reception I could even check Google Maps for a clearer perspective. It wasn't an ideal tactic, and, as with the idea of ditching my heavyweight kit, it was regarded as a bad idea during an evasion mission, but I was in a desperate situation.

The moment for a desperate measure had arrived.

I checked my watch again. *Eleven o'clock.* To get my bearings, I'd have to take a risk in daylight – the chances of me spotting any landmarks after dark weren't high – and now was as good a time as any. Checking for moving figures outside, I stepped into the street and walked towards a wooded area that separated the village's two tiers. Above it was a steep incline of around six metres and it looked to be the most advantageous viewing point. I jogged towards the treeline, before advancing slowly up into the dead ground. My head was on a swivel: I looked left and right for signs of soldiers, glancing up to check for drones, all while scanning the ground for mines. I might have been the master of my destiny, but every step was loaded with jeopardy.

More than anything, I wanted to find a water source and

I didn't care what it was. *Fast and flowing, I'll make the most of it.* If the worst came to the worst, I'd use my sock as a makeshift strainer, which wasn't the most effective of tools, but it would do. The good news was that my mind was still alert and busy despite the physical struggle. SERE training had taught me that fatigue, lethargy and indifference would only result in mistakes. Of course, there was also a chance that I might miraculously run into my platoon or another group of Ukrainians, in which case nearly all my problems would be solved, but until that moment arrived, I had to survive. I zigzagged in and out of the trees until I'd reached the top of the hill, eyeing the ground ahead of me nervously.

CRACK!

A shot rang out and I instinctively dropped to the ground, burying my face in the mud, wriggling my body down into the wet grass as the noise reverberated around me. *Fuck. Fuck. Fuck. I'd been spotted.* I was done for. My body trembled with adrenaline as I tried to work out what might happen next. The first question was the identity of the shooter. If I was lucky, it was a trigger-happy local and he or she had let a bullet fly, having mistaken me for an invader. If that was the case, talking my way out of trouble was a possibility. However, if I'd been spotted by enemy soldiers, I was facing a very different scenario. Being captured by Putin's gunmen would be a shitty turn of events, especially if they were members of the DPR, or even worse, Chechens, who were known to be fighting for Putin and were considered to be lawless pirates. My understanding was that both were ragtag groups of thugs and killers who operated with very little discipline. There was every chance they might shoot me for fun, or take their time torturing me while streaming my suffering online.

I glanced up. *Well, shit.* Below me on the hill, set in front of a small stone building, I counted eight shell scrapes. A soldier was nestled in each one, their weapons raised. They were probably around thirty metres away and the set-up resembled a forward observation point or mortar post. I knew instantly that I'd caught a bad break because judging by their mismatched kit they were almost certainly DPR, and my guess was that they had been attached to the shot-up vehicle in town. I looked around. There was nowhere for me to run to and no point of cover – if I made a move for it, the enemy would stand and gun me down.

Bollocks. The game was up. I tried to gather my thoughts because the next few minutes would be vital and I had to get through them unscathed. If I was badly beaten in the arrest process and any bones were broken, or if I lost a limb or an eye, an extended period of captivity afterwards would become a living hell. I'd been told that during hostage situations the biggest battles were waged in the captive's head, especially when it came to interrogation – and they had to be won. With a weakened body, a prisoner was more likely to crack. The DPR would want to know who I was and where I was heading. They would also drill me for any intel on my company, their identities and our activity in Mariupol. My job was to keep my team-mates safe. I had to stay strong.

Then I remembered: my phone. *Shit!* It was a digital dossier on both my military and home life, with plenty of exploitable data, such as my previous GPS coordinates, bank details, social-media pages and phone numbers. These were all vulnerabilities during an interrogation because they represented leverage, which was why soldiers on the ground usually established a series of rules regarding their mobiles, one of them being *No photos*. I knew that any investigator examining a captured phone would immediately check the data inside. From there it was usually possible to identify a prisoner's team-mates and any people of importance, such as a senior officer or commander. Behind me at the foot of the hill was a small pond. Realising I was partially shielded by the terrain, I lobbed my phone towards it, breathing a sigh of relief as it entered the water with a gentle plop and sank.

A voice called out in Russian and ordered me to stand. I raised my hands.

'Don't shoot!' I shouted back in Russian. 'No weapon.'

Then I rolled the dice. 'I'm English.'

My hope was to startle them in some way and, luckily, it seemed to work. The soldiers looked at one another. They seemed to be conferring. Then one of them ordered me to move forward. Cautiously, I stepped down the hill, knowing the game was up, all the while wondering if someone was going to freak out and pop a round in me.

'I'm English. *I'm English*,' I repeated as I reached their position.

'English?' shouted one of the men as they surrounded me.

I nodded. The poor bloke looked terrified; they all did. His eyes were on stalks. Of the group, nobody appeared to be a day older than twenty and one or two had wispy crops of facial hair on their upper lips. Imagine if Jay from *The Inbetweeners* had tried to grow his first moustache – that was the look.

I'm old enough to be a dad in this rabble, I thought.

Physically, they looked like a bag of shit. Judging from their gaunt expressions and bloodshot eyes, they had all been through the wringer. I checked them up and down. Their kit was piecemeal and ragged. They wore mismatched helmets and scratched-together bits of camouflage clothing, and just that one detail made me extra cautious. This was clearly an inexperienced group and they were probably prone to poor judgement. One wrong move might see me shot or badly wounded.

Weirdly, I didn't feel intimidated at any point. Concerned? *Yes.* Pissed off? *No doubt.* But there was no fear as several hands reached down to punch and grab at me. I was dragged into a nearby trench and shoved face down in the mud. Someone took my warm coat and outer layers, ransacking the pockets as they did so. Another soldier snatched away my watch. My wallet was emptied. My hat and cargo belt followed soon after. It was more like a mugging than an arrest.

Eventually, a more senior figure stepped into the scrum with an AK-74. The order was made that my hands should be tied. Finally, there was an adult in the room.

'Who are you?' he said, calmly.

'I'm Shaun. I'm English and a Ukrainian Marine. I speak a little Russian.'

There was no point in holding back on those facts. They already had my military ID – it had been in my wallet.

The information didn't faze him one bit. 'OK. We're going to take you away,' he said, pointing to a beat-up Lada parked nearby. 'You're going to get in that car.'

I felt sick, not through dread but embarrassment. I was supposed to be SERE-trained. I'd only been running for five minutes and I'd been captured by a bunch of spotty, streaky-piss kids. They weren't soldiers. They were part-timers with kit picked up from a Toys 'R' Us shop. To add insult to injury, I was being hauled off in a car that looked to have been reclaimed from 1976. If I ever saw my friends and family again, I wasn't sure how I was going to live down the jokes.

10

I was shoved onto the Lada's back seat. One of the Inbetweeners put his foot on the accelerator and attempted to drive away from the shell scrapes and onto a nearby road, but the car had sunk into the mud and was stuck. The wheels churned. If a gun hadn't been pointed at my belly, I'd have offered to push.

'Keep your head down,' one of the boy geniuses shouted as I looked around me. 'Don't move.'

I wondered if the poor kid's mum knew what he was up to.

After a series of wheel spins the Lada pulled away and ten minutes later we arrived in another small village. Somebody hooded me with a carrier bag and my hands were retied with masking tape. Whenever I wriggled my wrists, the material knotted and tightened painfully. Then I was pulled from the car and shoved against a wall roughly.

Here we go, I thought. *This is where the fun begins.*

I didn't have to wait long for the first slap. My hood was lifted and I saw a soldier with long blond hair. He was eyeballing me, his face contorted in rage, and there was zero time to pacify him. I was belted across the jaw with a punch that would have made Tyson Fury proud and, tipping over like a skittle, I tasted warm metal as my mouth filled with blood. Everything was blurring and fuzzy. I realised the soldier had been standing with two teenage girls and they were now laughing at me and pointing. I seethed. He looked like the clichéd bodybuilder I'd seen in just about every gym ever: the grotesquely muscular steroid head in a too-tight T-shirt. The type that stood by a weight rack and took selfies of his biceps.

What a prick. Then I noticed that a 'Z' patch had been stuck on one of his sleeves and my anger intensified. As far as I was concerned, the letter was a symbol of evil and defined everything the enemy had been doing over the past few months – the shelling, the murders, the wilful destruction. Dima and the other lads at the steelworks had nicknamed it the *zwastika*, and seeing it made me feel sick and increasingly unsettled. It was known that the Russian military tended to promote brutish thickos to positions of power, like the one standing over me now. The higher-ups wanted a cruel authority imposed on the weaker individuals in their ranks and these thugs were used as blunt instruments, in place to terrify their team-mates and victims into compliance.

Another soldier, who looked more like a section commander, had joined him. 'Where is your phone?' he yelled, prodding mé in the back with his boot.

I spat blood and mumbled.

There was more shouting. 'Who are you? Where are you from?'

The atmosphere seemed to have changed. For a fleeting moment I'd held the upper hand. My captors, presented with a British soldier in Ukraine, hadn't known what to do. But these guys were different. The mood was immediately more hostile and questions came at me like body blows. I shook my head and attempted to babble out what I hoped would be a plausible cover story. *I'd married a Ukrainian and was defending the country on principle.* I'd developed the alibi when the war had kicked off, in the event of a situation like the one I found myself in, and the tale had the benefit of being mainly true. I'd hoped it might lend me some credibility. More importantly, the information wouldn't compromise my unit in any way.

The commander leaned over me. 'And where is your phone? Don't make me ask again.'

I shook my head. 'I don't have one.'

'So why are you carrying a phone charger?'

I had no answer for that one. In the chaos of capture I'd not had a chance to ditch the lead and it was now an incriminating piece of evidence. My mind catastrophised and reached for the worst-case scenario.

One of those teenage soldiers at the village is going to discover my phone in the pond, isn't he? Then the Russians will pick through my data, calling the numbers for Mum, Larysa, my mates . . .

I cursed my bad luck. Because I hadn't been able to access a decent signal or even wi-fi at Mariupol, it had been impossible to deactivate my social-media accounts. Even if my phone remained undiscovered, a quick trawl online would lead a half-decent investigator to my Facebook page. With that information they could paint a fairly comprehensive picture of who I was and what I did.

The commander turned to another goon standing nearby. 'Go back to the village and look for his phone.'

I prayed for a rainy month or two. If the pond remained full, I'd be OK.

The following moments are a blur, a series of snapshot memories that sometimes come back to me in fragments. I was standing in a long residential street. Houses ran along either side of the road and my guess was that the original inhabitants had been forcibly evicted. The place was now being used as a temporary garrison and its new occupants were in the front gardens and taking a look at their latest trophy. As I was marched down the length of the street, everyone gawped.

'We've captured another one, and he's a Brit,' said the commander proudly.

One or two people were shouting angrily. I braced for another blow to the head or body, but it never came.

'No, we have to take him away for questioning,' said the commander as several people gathered around. From what I could tell, I was quite the attraction.

We arrived at another building, where I was hooded again. Somebody punched the muzzle of his rifle into my chest. The blow was so hard it knocked me to the floor. I heard a voice call me a *nayomnik*, or mercenary, and unable to see through the hood, I imagined one of my tormentors running at me with a knife or cosh.

I'm in for it now, I thought. *This is going to turn nasty.*

The end of the weapon was jabbed into my chest again. Whoever was doing it had become enraged.

'You're a faggot,' he hissed. 'A faggot mercenary.'

I tried to pivot away but there was no escape.

'You are fighting the wrong war, *nayomnik*.'

My hood was taken away and, having clocked the attacker, I had to stare to make sure I wasn't imagining things. He was a short, stocky bloke, probably in his mid forties. But with his goatee beard and floppy haircut, he was a dead ringer for David Brent, Ricky Gervais's character in *The Office*. I groaned. First *The Inbetweeners*, now Wernham Hogg's bellend-in-chief. The humiliation would have been excruciating if it weren't for the pain in my sternum. Under any other circumstances, I'd have given the bloke a hiding for jabbing me with his rifle. As it was, I had to hold my temper because losing it and kicking out would only end in an extra beating, especially as the Russian looked to be ramped up on adrenaline. I bit my tongue and rolled away.

Someone grabbed my shoulders and ordered me to stand. I was on the move again. The thought that I might be heading for a public execution briefly crossed my mind as I was frogmarched out into the street and another hood was yanked over my head. It was a cheap plastic bag, the type you might get from a budget off-licence in the UK, and every time I inhaled, it clung to my face. Before long I was a hot and sweaty mess. When the hood was taken off I was in another building and being led towards a wooden door with a latch.

This doesn't look good, I thought, remembering every horror film I'd watched as a kid.

The door was opened and I was shoved forward. A flight of stairs led down into the dark. When I looked back, David Brent was eyeballing me angrily.

'Go down, *nayomnik*,' he shouted, gesturing to the black space below me with his gun. 'Down!'

Gingerly, I stepped forward, pressing my hands against the wall for support. *Bloody hell, the place stank.* There was strong fug of bin juice and human excrement, and I tried not to gag. The basement honked like a music-festival toilet. Having reached the bottom of the stairs, I realised I was ankle-deep in rubbish and God knows what else, and though it was hard to see anything, the sound of movement told me I wasn't alone. As my eyes adjusted, I noticed several figures looking back at me in the gloom. They were all emaciated, skeletal-thin and stooped, as if they'd been living amongst the waste for years. My breath fogged. It was colder down there than it was outside. Seeing as most of my warm kit had been stripped away in the mugging, I didn't fancy my chances of surviving for long in these conditions.

Someone waved me over to a group of men who were huddling under a threadbare sheet. He pointed to the mouldy fabric and I understood implicitly. *You're going to freeze to death if you don't get under here.*

I waded forward and crouched down, pulling the covering around my shoulders. Then I looked across and started to speak, but one of the guys put a finger to his lips. *I had to be quiet.* Then he pointed to the stairs. *They were afraid the guards would hear and beat the shit out of us as punishment.* They all looked broken and terrified. I nodded my thanks and joined in with the shivering. I'd ended up in a very bad place.

Only five minutes had passed when the door opened again. A soldier was shouting in Russian.

'*Nayomnik! Nayomnik!*'

Someone nudged me in the ribs. *That's you.*

Whoever was yelling had become agitated. '*Nayomnik!* Come on . . .'

I pulled myself up the stairs, thankful to be leaving such a hellish spot, then my hands were bound and somebody led me outside the house. I blinked against the bright sunlight and tried to get a handle on what was happening to me. And then I realised. A silver RAV4 had pulled up nearby and two men stepped out, dressed in matching Russian fatigues that were totally unlike anything the DPR had been wearing. Both were tall and muscular, and they moved with purpose. One was blond, in his early twenties and built like a profes- sional rugby winger. He was quite a good-looking bloke, with styled hair, and didn't look ravaged by combat. The other was dark, middle-aged and much smaller. His swagger screamed *killer*, as if he'd been born to inflict pain. Both were tooled up with all sorts of high-tech weaponry and body armour. They carried chem lights and multi-tools; they wore helmets with fittings for night-vision goggles, ear defenders and microphones. Their Lowa boots were clean and polished. More chilling was the fact that neither of them wore any noticeable patches or insignia.

Shit, I thought. *Spetsnaz. Special forces.*

I was pushed against a wall. One of the operators was up in my face, hammering me with questions in fairly fluent English.

'What is your name?'

'Shaun,' I mumbled.

'Are you Azov?'

'No,' I said. And it was true. Technically, I was a Ukrainian Marine. I didn't have to divulge any of the groups I'd trained in the past. There was also a good chance I'd be shot on the spot if I mentioned my previous employers, given Putin was still pushing the made-up narrative that Azov was riddled with Nazism and far-right ideology.

'Do you have any tattoos?'

I felt a surge of panic. *I had ink.* My chest tightened. Tattoos were a big deal in the Ukrainian military, as they were in most armies, and I had a Native American on my right shoulder and a Japanese tattoo on the left side of my chest, as did Larysa. The words *Happy Days* were also sketched out on my right forearm in ammo-box-style stencilling. My guess was that Russia's special forces wouldn't need much of an excuse to top me, especially if they thought one of the designs was somehow connected to Azov.

The story of how I'd got my *Happy Days* tattoo was an innocent one too. I'd been in Moldova with a few other soldiers. We were on our way to Ukraine, having survived in Syria, and there was a sense that we were fighting the good fight and living at our peak. The World Cup was on, we were drinking a bit and there was a tattoo bar near the hostel we'd been using. When Tony – my best friend of thirty years – suggested we should get inked up to commemorate the latest chapter in our lives, everyone had laughed and agreed it was a great idea. The ink also acted as a sobering reminder that we were still living when so many people we knew had died while fighting alongside the Kurds. Afterwards, whenever we were wearing short sleeves and shooting or saluting, the words *Happy Days* were always in view. That rite of passage now felt like the worst decision of my life, but I reassured myself that I'd only encounter trouble if the DPR had picked up any of the other lads with the same tattoo, which seemed unlikely.

Without warning, my shirt was ripped open with a knife. One of the operators saw the design on my shoulder. He studied it carefully.

'Hmm. We like the American Indians,' he said. 'They are no problem.'

He pulled down my shirt and looked at my biceps. Then he yanked at my trousers to check my legs. Miraculously, he didn't bother to look at my forearms. I was off the hook – for a little while at least.

More and more questions were yelled out, but the words came at me too quickly. I couldn't respond. I was stuttering, in a state of shock, my jaw still throbbing from the earlier beating. Then, in my peripheral vision, I caught the shimmer of a blade. It was moving in front of me at speed and in a scything motion. Before I could react, it had torn into my thigh and carved along the side of my leg. The steel was nearly down to the bone. Finally it twisted.

I stared down at the wound in horror and screamed. A large chunk of flesh had been sheared away like kebab meat and was dangling grimly. Blood pumped and pooled on the floor and any hopes of getting through the first phase of capture unharmed were now done with. There was a good chance I might be killed here and now. Larysa's mantra looped around my head. *Live. Fight. Survive!* It was the only thing distancing me from the pain.

Someone was laughing at me. 'Whoops – *sorry.*'

Then the questions came in again. It felt like someone was taking a hammer to my brain.

'Who are you?'

'Listen, my name's Shaun. Wait—'

'Who are you fighting for?'

'I'm a Ukrainian Marine . . .'

'Are you MI6 or SAS?'

'Mate, I'm nearly fifty years old. Please . . .'

It was hard to focus. The pain in my leg was now spreading outwards; every nerve ending in my body felt pinched and my vision had blurred. Nausea washed over me. Then somebody grabbed my shoulders and I heard the ripping and tearing of masking tape again. When I looked down, one of the operators had wrapped my thigh in an old blue T-shirt and was clumsily sticking it across the wound. Within seconds it had soaked through with blood.

The dressing was a poor attempt at preventing a mess. I was hooded, then dragged and bundled into the back of the RAV4. As I collapsed on the back seat I smelled the intoxicating waft of new leather. The car was box-fresh and there I was, leaking red all over the seats. When the shivers started, I knew the shock of what was happening had kicked in.

One of the soldiers whispered in my ear. 'Don't move or we will shoot you . . .'

Like that was going to happen. I could barely hold myself upright, and when the car moved away I slid into the stomach of someone sitting alongside me. They shoved me back across the seat violently. I tried to settle my mind. Despite the physical and emotional trauma, I needed to gather as much information about the journey as possible, as I'd been trained to do. *Who knew when the intelligence might come in handy?* Through the gap at the bottom of my hood I looked for maps or notes in the footwell of the car, something to give me a clue as to our destination. It was empty, so instead I focused on the direction of travel. As we moved away from the village, I noticed the rumble in the wheels had become smoother and more consistent, which meant we were driving along a main road. There was only one route in and out of Mariupol in this area, and I doubted very much they were taking me back there. Instead, we were heading towards the city of Donetsk, which was under Russian occupation.

After thirty minutes, the car pulled over and I was hauled from the vehicle like an oversized bag of shopping. I saw my feet moving across a gravel path. Walking was agony and every step left a gory, size-nine splodge. As I was forced through more doors and more corridors, my feeling was that I'd been taken to a former Ukrainian police station. The Russian special forces were probably using it as an operational area. Then I was left in what looked like a bathroom. By looking down, I saw the perimeter of a square space with white-tiled floors and walls that dripped with stagnant water. The place was dank; it stank of death, but there was no sink, toilet or shower. My chest tightened with fear. In the floor was a circular drain hole, positioned so that any trace of blood or teeth, even toes or fingers, could be washed away with a hose. *I was in a wet room.* People suffered and died in places like this.

I'm fucked, I thought.

A bloke in a tracksuit stepped in front of me and lifted up the hood. He was holding a laptop and seemed to be cross-checking my face against whatever social-media platform he had logged onto. The briefest of glances around the room revealed a reception desk with a flip-up hatch, the kind you might see in a hospital ward or dentist's waiting room. Then my hood was yanked down again and I was forced into a chair. Someone strapped my wrists and ankles with tape to the wooden legs and the seatback. Through the gap in the bag over my head, I clocked the boots of people walking around me. There were at least four others in the room. A Ukrainian flag was being draped around my shoulders. The fear that I was about to be executed had intensified.

This is going to be filmed and my death will be used as propaganda.

I felt my hands being pulled and when I looked around, one of the special forces operators was attaching a set of plastic paddles to my fingers. There was a moment's pause, some footfalls and a click. And—

Dit-dit-dit-dit-dit!

Without any warning, a blast of electricity ripped into my body. The pain was even more intense than the wound in my leg and I was forced upright in a hyperactive spasm, my bones locking rigid. Every muscle expanded, clenched and threatened to burst. The blast can only have lasted fifteen seconds or so, but it felt like minutes, and when the power was turned off I deflated back into my chair, twitching and drooling, my neck unable to support the weight of my skull, my chin lolling across my chest. Saliva and snot dripped into my lap.

The shouting started again soon after.

'Who are you?'

'Who are you fighting for?'

'Are you MI6 or SAS?'

I heard a word or two being repeated over and over, and over. At first it was hard to make out exactly what was being yelled. Then I recognised a name amid all the ranting. *Condoleezza Rice.* The former US Secretary of State.

'The black witch of the USA!' yelled one of the interrogators. '*You've* kept Russia back. *America* has kept Russia back . . .'

Attempting to explain my nationality was impossible. I could barely talk. My whole body rattled with the numbing, metallic echo of live electricity.

One of the operators lifted my hood. He was clicking through my social-media pages. I saw photos from happier times – with friends and family, on holidays. Then he stopped and pointed to a picture from my days as a sniper trainer. I was on operations and holding a rifle.

'I see you have a Light Fifty?'

The guy knew his stuff. The weapon was a Barrett .50 rifle, which was popular with a lot of military marksmen.

'I'm not a sniper.'

'Your pictures tell other stories . . .'

'I'm not a sniper. I get pictures with weapons all the time. I'm Marines.'

'You're a sniper and a Nazi . . .'

'I'm not a Nazi! You have my ID, I'm not a sniper!'

'And why are you here, sniper Shaun Pinner?' he continued. 'Because of your wife?' He looked down at a piece of paper. 'Larysa? We found her business card. She works for an NGO, I see . . .'

Shit. I was so tired that I'd forgotten about my wallet – the one snatched off me by the DPR. Several scraps of paper had been shoved inside, including Larysa's work card, and the mention of her crushed my spirit, but only a little. I knew she was safe, a million miles away from this hell because, before leaving Mariupol, I had received two Post-It Notes from another British soldier called Aiden Aslin, who had been based in a bunker deep in the steelworks and had access to wi-fi. Two words were written on the first: *We're fucked.* The second contained Larysa's location after Aiden had learned that my wife and his girlfriend were travelling together.

The soldiers then talked amongst themselves in Russian, not knowing that I understood a fair bit of what they were saying, and it became clear my story had brought a little respect, as I'd hoped. The fact I was defending Ukraine for love, a country that wasn't my own through birth, was thought of as being commendable. In my captors' minds, I'd been willing to die for my beliefs and that placed me slightly higher on the pecking order than a contract soldier. But only just.

I heard another voice behind me. 'You should not be here in this war.'

Looking up, I suddenly realised that the paddles clipped to my digits were probably attached to a field telephone. It was known that the Russians plugged them into the mains as a repurposed torture device. My suspicions were confirmed moments later.

'Oh, Shaun . . . You want to phone home to your wife?'

I tried to shake my head, but my neck muscles couldn't respond.

'No.'

'Do you want to call Condoleezza fucking Rice?'

'Please—'

Dit-dit-dit-dit-dit! The staccato snap, crackle and pop of barely tethered electricity ripped through the air, leaping from the telephone box and lightning-striking the paddles. My body was gripped with power, lurching and tightening. Veins seemed to be exploding all over my back and neck. And all the while, I heard the yelling of my torturer, a bloke who might or might not have been an off-the-leash psychopath.

'Condoleezza Rice!' he screamed.

Two, maybe three more blasts of electricity followed until, eventually, I blacked out from the pain. I'm not sure exactly how long I was tortured for. It's hard to guess, and if someone had told me the agony had lasted for days, I'd have believed it. But I wasn't broken. When I came to, a 9 mm pistol was shoved into the back of my head and I felt unafraid.

'I've made my peace,' I whispered. 'If you're going to do it, *do it* . . .'

I heard the clicking of an empty chamber and felt the crack of steel on bone as a pistol whipped across the back of my head. When I looked up, my captors were laughing. Human suffering was a joke to them.

I know what you're thinking: *Did he piss himself?* The answer is no, though I must have come close. Still, I took pride in the fact I was able to hold my bladder together through the torture, but I knew that more psychological misery was inevitable. The Russians had found my identity. They had my social-media profile and with it a contacts book of loved ones – people who could be emotionally tortured from afar, for fun. Sure enough, a smartphone was shoved into my face shortly afterwards. On the screen was a video of me in a chair with a Ukrainian flag draped around my shoulders. I was bucking and lurching with live electricity. An image of my passport appeared. The word 'DECEASED' had been stamped over the top.

'You're dead on the internet,' whispered a voice.

I had no doubt the abuse I'd experienced would be in the inbox of every friend and family member within minutes.

PART TWO
The Weight

Blacking out: *good*. Being awake: *not so much*.

Over a few hours I endured several more episodes of horrific, unimaginable pain as I was kicked across the room like a football. Particular attention was paid to the stab wound in my leg. The Russians seemed happiest when stamping a boot into the gory, pulpy mess, over and over, until the pace changed and I was unexpectedly fried with a cattle prod. Like a hubristic Bond villain, one of the special forces operators then explained to me how Putin was hoping to steamroller Poland – that's once he had finished his business in Ukraine. The idea was even floated that I might be sold to a Chechen-led militia group who were scrapping alongside the Russian and DPR forces. Apparently, the going rate for a Western fighter was around two million quid. But as the Chechens were hoping to free a general being held in the West, and in double-quick time, my captors were holding out for a more profitable deal. *Market forces and all that.*

Then the early phases of capture became increasingly surreal. A plastic bag was thrown over my head and I was forced back into a car, but for some reason the mood had changed and there was immediately a genuine concern for my well-being. As I slipped about on the back seat in a puddle of my own blood, my vision blurring, the blond soldier leant over to check my breathing. A few hours earlier his face had been contorted in hatred as he'd put a few extra dents into my ribcage. Now he was offering up a bottle of water.

'Are you going to live?' he said.

As if you fucking care, mate. I didn't have the strength to answer.

Then I heard another man's voice in the car. 'Don't die,' he said, sounding increasingly agitated. '*Don't let him die.*'

It was impossible to know whether I was hallucinating or being screwed with.

At some point we changed vehicles, having driven for a couple of hours. My hood was lifted and a gang of officious-looking men gawped at me through the window and laughed, and I couldn't shake the feeling I was being mocked by several members of the Russian secret police, or one of their spy agencies, like the FSB or GRU. In their fresh, neatly pressed uniforms, they looked important. They certainly seemed to command a level of respect from the special forces thugs holding me, which meant they must have been pretty high up the food chain. The humiliating circus didn't last for long and I was soon being driven to yet another facility. *Was it the second of the day? The third? It was hard to keep track.* And having been led through a series of doors, I was greeted by a DPR guard. As he moved around me, I could make out some of his physique through the gap at the bottom of the plastic bag on my head. The bloke must have been the size of a Portaloo. He had hands like shovels and he stank of booze. But what caught my attention was his combat uniform – it was a design I hadn't seen before, a blend of forest green, khaki and black.

'Welcome to Russia!' he boomed as I was placed onto a medical trolley.

All sorts of activity went on around me; I glimpsed more details from the bottom of my hood. Orders were delivered. Commands were being obeyed. There seemed to be a hierarchy to the place, and aside from one or two DPR soldiers standing nearby, everyone was wearing the same pressed combat uniforms as Captain Shovel Hands and top-quality, military-issue boots. That meant I wasn't being handed over to the Chechens just yet. Those fighters were known to be ragged and unprofessional. They rarely fought in body armour and often wore trainers rather than battle-ready footwear. *These people?* I had little doubt that some of the men gathering around me were FSB or GRU (Main Intelligence Directorate) agents. As I sat there, awaiting even more pain, I caught a brief glimpse of a stocky man wearing a thin, military-green balaclava. He looked and acted like a professional killer.

Mr Balaclava soon established himself as point man and he briefly lifted off my hood to check my face against an ID photo in my wallet. Then he jabbed me with questions – about who I was and why I'd been fighting with the Ukrainian Marines. Repeating everything I'd mentioned previously, I added one or two details that were readily available on social media. Mr Balaclava then explained that I was being held in the city of Donetsk. He said that my leg would be stitched up and I would be given a painkilling injection.

'Shaun, I have a question,' he said, almost absent-mindedly.

'Go on . . .'

'Why did you stab yourself in the leg?'

I was confused. 'I didn't stab myself,' I said. 'Why would I stab myself? One of your soldiers did it. Then they brought me here.'

There was a pause. I wondered if notes were being taken. 'Please tell me what happened from your perspective,' said Mr Balaclava.

'Your guy knifed me. He was cutting at my clothes, looking for tattoos. Then he stuck me in the leg. It came out of nowhere.'

After some thought, he said, 'Hmm. I will look into this.'

The penny dropped: this was all part of the game, and thanks to my SERE training, I'd recognised one of the initial stages of capture and interrogation. Mr Balaclava's plan was to establish himself as the Good Guy, whereas the special forces operators on the front lines had been the Bad Guys. It had been their job to pulverise me into submission through extreme violence, setting a physical precedent for what I could expect if I didn't comply with any future requests. My guess was that Mr Balaclava was hoping to present himself as a potential lifeline away from pain. At some point, the promise of help, or even freedom, would arrive. But only if I told him everything.

A painkilling injection was stuck into my neck and my leg was patched up. From time to time, I blacked out on the spot. Eventually, I was woken up, pushed into a nearby cell by two DPR guards and ordered onto a pull-down bed affixed to the wall. The space was probably no bigger than two metres in width and three metres in length, though it was warm at least. I was dressed in only a damp T-shirt and what was left of my ripped and bloody trousers, plus a pair of plimsolls, and my teeth were soon chattering with adrenaline. I grabbed a thin blanket that had been left for me and wrapped it around my shoulders for warmth. *How was I going to get out of this?*

SERE training had taught me that the best chance of escape usually arrived during any moments of transit, but given that opportunity had passed for now, and I was stuck, I assessed my situation instead. There were no windows in the cell, only the typical trappings of solitary confinement: one bucket for a loo and a single ceiling light that glowed way too brightly. But weirdly the threadbare fittings looked new and the place smelt of fresh paint. When I checked the bed frame, its metal edges were still shiny. The fabric on the pillow was clean too. *The Russians have only just thrown this place together,* I thought. Compared to my sleeping quarters under the sewage plant in Mariupol, it felt like an OK Airbnb. Then I noticed a surveillance camera fixed to the wall. It had been trained on my bed. That meant Big Brother was watching me – and listening too.

My head buzzed. All those beatings and electric shocks had given me a banger of a migraine, and, as my senses adjusted, I heard the noises of wartime incarceration just outside. There was shouting in the corridor. Shutters and grates were being slammed shut. *And was that music?* The throb and grind of death metal was only faintly audible at first, but then somebody cranked it up to full volume, presumably to drown out any artillery blasts that might have been exploding nearby, or the agonised screaming that I imagined was being forced out of someone, somewhere, on the inside.

It's that type of place, I told myself.

Suddenly the thrashing guitars faded and a more familiar but no less unsettling tune kicked in. *The bastards were playing 'Eye of the Tiger'.* I sighed. *Now they were trying to annoy me.* Death metal was one thing; the soundtrack from *Rocky III* was a step up on the pain scale. *And what was that smell?* I realised somebody had placed a tray at the foot of the bed and on it was a bowl of piping-hot chicken stew and a loaf of bread. I sniffed the contents before wolfing down the lot in no time at all. *A bed, some hot food and a bucket for a khazi?* For a brief moment I wondered if I'd done the impossible and landed on my feet. Then a quick retrace of the day told me not to be so stupid.

I was screwed.

The following morning, I ate and drank and slept some more, only waking to use the bucket, before taking the first slap of the day. Two guards came into the cell and ordered me to the back wall, but because nobody had explained the rules of solitary confinement, I hadn't known I was supposed to wear the plastic hood I'd been given. As I stepped to the edge of my cell, somebody clumped me around the skull and my vision speckled with stars.

'You need to write,' shouted a guard, shoving a pen and some paper into my hand.

'Write?'

'Yes, write. Write everything from the time you come to Ukraine until now. We will come for it tomorrow.'

I weighed up what was happening. The first forty-eight hours of capture were crucial, for both sides in the battle, because prisoner information was usually most valuable during that timeframe. For example, the movements of various battalions or the locations of any hidden compounds could very easily change within a day or two. Battalions shifted course; compounds broke up and moved on. The interrogator's role was to extract that intelligence as quickly as possible. Mine was to resist as best I could, though the position was double-edged. In one way, I was in a good spot because my knowledge of the overall battle picture in Mariupol was fairly out of date and therefore any intelligence I shared was unlikely to endanger anyone. The reverse was that nobody would believe my claims of ignorance and my torturers were going to inflict serious levels of pain to extract the information I didn't have. If their methods became too extreme, I might die. I also guessed that if I could stay alive for a little longer, there was a very slim chance I'd be thrown into a cell somewhere and forgotten about, left to rot until either the war had ended or some form of prisoner exchange or release was agreed. And then there was always the possibility that somebody might execute me out of boredom or rage.

I looked down at the paper and wondered what the hell I was going to write. Eventually, I scribbled down the basics of who I was and what I was doing in Ukraine. I mentioned my time serving in the Marines and the fighting at Pavlopil, Talakivka and Sartana, taking care to gloss over any details regarding the people I was fighting with, before adding one or two basic snippets on my time at the Illich steelworks. All of it was utterly irrelevant. Our positions had been overrun and destroyed, and the Ukrainian Marines were scattered to the winds. I feared a lot of them might be dead already or banged up in establishments similar to this one. As I wrote, I played the smart card and made sure to slow the process down, and throughout the day, my captors motivated me with cups of coffee and hot food. The DPR were clearly at the bottom of the military pecking order and weren't the brightest buttons in the box. At some point, a spoon was left in my cell. I shoved it under the mattress, in case it became useful later on.

There were stressors to consider, my phone being one. I worried that a bizarre twist of fate might have led to its discovery and that my previous movements were being analysed on the GPS, as well as any messages or emails I might have shared with team-mates during the build-up to war. I really didn't want my data to expose another Marine in another prison, someone who might be masquerading as a civilian. I also knew that to mention my time spent training the Azov National Guard would probably end with a bullet to the head. As far as my captors were concerned, they were Nazis. Finally, I reiterated my *why*. I was fighting with the First Battalion because I'd fallen in love with a woman in Mariupol and wanted to defend our home. There was no point in saying otherwise. The Russians had Larysa's business card and, from scanning through social media, they knew exactly what we were all about. Put together, I hoped my story would be enough to satiate my interrogators and keep my team-mates safe.

My interrogation began the next afternoon and almost immediately I understood that a session of hurt was approaching. I was hooded and put in an armlock as two guards pushed me up a flight of stairs, kicking and punching me as we walked. Their treatment was so rough that the stitches in my thigh flexed and pulled. Eventually, I was pushed into an office space and shoved towards a chair. My ankles and wrists were taped to the legs. Then a plastic clip was fixed to my ear. I recognised the shape and feel at once: it was a paddle, the type that could be attached to a power source. *Oh fuck, no. Not this again.* I could only think that something in my backstory had angered the Russians, or that another piece of incriminating information had been discovered.

Don't let them have found my phone, I thought. *Please don't let them have found my phone.*

I shifted around in my seat, but my limbs were bound tight.

'You don't need to do this,' I said. 'What have I done?'

There was a moment or two of silence. Then a voice spoke calmly. 'Thank you for your biography, Shaun . . .'

It was Mr Balaclava.

'. . . but you lied to me.'

I shivered. When I was electrocuted a day or two earlier, ignorance had been bliss. I had no idea what was coming and, in a way, it had spared me some anxiety – but only a little. Now I was acutely aware of the torture to come and it was hard not to freak out. It felt important to do everything I could to stop the switch from being flicked.

'What's the problem?' I shouted. 'Why have you got me here? What do you want from me? *What did I lie about?*'

I sounded desperate because I was.

'Shut up,' said Mr Balaclava. 'I'm the one who talks.'

Footsteps moved around me. It sounded as if several people were gathering in the room. I imagined them watching and laughing as I squirmed.

'You lied to me, because you missed out one very important thing.'

'And what's that?' I said, my voice cracking.

'That you were with Azov.'

I tried pleading. I wanted to explain. The words tumbled over one another as I began to blurt out my story, but Mr Balaclava had crouched down by my ear. He was making a series of soothing, shushing noises.

Then he spoke coldly. 'Aiden's told us everything we wanted to know – *everything about you.*'

There was no way out for me now.

My chest tightened. I felt short of breath. *Aiden Aslin.* A fellow Brit in Mariupol. Another Ukrainian Marine. The guy who had passed on those notes in Illich telling me our situation was 'fucked', and that Larysa and his girlfriend were in a place of safety. The pair of us had scrapped side by side in Syria and, for a while, in Paplovil. During the siege of Mariupol, Aiden had been somewhere underneath the steelworks, but he must have been picked up by the Russians during the battalion's withdrawal.

For a second, I was pleased. *Great, he's alive.*

Then relieved. *Well, I wasn't the only one to have been scooped up by the enemy.*

And finally concerned. Aiden knew my story. A surge of power suddenly corkscrewed into my body. My ears burned, my head felt ready to explode and every tooth buzzed and rattled. When the spasms eventually slowed and my muscles contracted and relaxed, I sank into the chair and farted loudly. There was nothing I could do to stop it. My body had been blitzed.

'You didn't tell us you were in Azov, Shaun,' said Mr Balaclava.

In that moment, I realised Aiden must have thrown me under the bus by mentioning my time training the National Guard. At first I felt angry. *Why couldn't he have kept his fucking gob shut?* Though the rage soon faded away. I couldn't exactly blame Aiden for spilling my story. Militarily, he was inexperienced; he hadn't served with the British Army at any point and I doubt he'd been trained to the same level as some of the soldiers I'd worked with previously. A halfway competent Russian torturer would have subjected him to all sorts of abuse near the front lines. They might have played one or two dirty tricks, like showing him my torture video on a phone while claiming I'd been killed. As my legs and wrists bucked with aftershocks, a part of me wished that I had been. I cursed Aiden. *Why couldn't he have been a bit more experienced?* Anyone could have worked out that the enemy weren't to be trusted and any stories regarding my death were probably greatly exaggerated. My neck went limp and floppy again. Snail trails of snot and saliva dangled from my chin.

'Is he OK?' asked a voice.

'Yes, he is fine,' said Mr Balaclava.

Then he whispered in my ear. 'Shaun . . . *Shaun* . . .'

'Yeah?'

'Do you speak Russian?'

I nodded. 'A little bit.'

I then proved it with a fluent sentence: 'My wife is from Mariupol and most people in Mariupol speak Russian.'

Another voice shouted out from across the room. 'If he speaks Russian again, electrocute him,' he snapped, presumably to whoever was controlling the buttons.

Who the fuck was that? My mind sprinted. Someone even higher up in the secret police must have arrived to witness my pain and was standing behind me. I felt disorientated, but there was no time to settle down. Mr Balaclava was asking me about Azov again.

'Why didn't you tell us?'

'Because you would have shot me on the front lines,' I said. 'I didn't hide it. It's open on my social media. You can read it. I just had to pick the time to tell you. So I can tell you now.'

'And why do you think we would have shot you?'

'Because I've been living here for nearly five years. I know that you look for right-wing tattoos. I know you hate Azov. But I didn't choose Azov. Think what you want about them, but I'm no Nazi.'

Mr Balaclava began conferring with someone else and he seemed deferential. There was no doubt about it now: an even more senior individual was with us in the room. As the two men whispered conspiratorially, I reassured myself with one or two basic facts. By now, the Russians would have rifled through the Azov and Marine bases in Mariupol. Every related document was probably under examination; any surviving military members in the city, like Aiden, were being interrogated. There was no benefit in my hiding too much personal history because they knew everything already. Also, had I originally denied my links to Azov, someone would have ordered my execution. *I had done the right thing.*

'So tell me, *Nazi*—' said Mr Balaclava.

'I am not a Nazi,' I interrupted. 'Yeah, I was posted to Azov, I was an instructor there. It's not what you think it is. I left Azov to join the Ukrainian Marines . . . I'm not a Nazi. I'm not right wing.'

'Then what are you?'

'A soldier. *A contract soldier.* That's very different to being a mercenary or a soldier of fortune, before you start thinking that . . .'

Mr Balaclava was in my ear again. 'Go on. Explain.'

'Well, I'm a foreign soldier with a proper position in the Ukrainian military. It's a bit like how a Gurkha is a soldier from Nepal, but they fight for the British Army.'

I suddenly realised there was an additional benefit to opening up about my previous career choices. It was temporarily deflecting attention away from my time spent scrapping in Mariupol and our middle-of-the-night retreat. Mr Balaclava hadn't yet asked me about the other lads in 36 Brigade and what they might have been doing. If I could keep him fixated on my background, and whether or not I was a Nazi, it would buy more time for any team-mates still on the run.

I heard more talking in Russian as several hands reached down to grab me. The tape was torn from my ankles and wrists. Two guards put me in an armlock again and I was marched back to the cell. Along the way they made comments and joked around.

'What happened in there?' said one.

The other bloke snorted and made a loud raspberry noise – a reference to my failing muscle control during the electric shock.

'No way!' said the other, falling about laughing.

I could not have cared less. I'd estimated that more than forty-eight hours had passed since my capture. That meant anyone still on the run from Mariupol had most likely broken past enemy lines by now – Bear, Junior Sergeant Gluzsky, maybe even the medic and her walking wounded. If that was the case, then being humiliated was a price worth paying.

I'd done my bit.

All privileges were revoked. The room-service meals stopped, the coffee deliveries were cancelled and my life at the Black Site was immediately locked into a repetitive and painful rhythm. The music that afternoon was never-ending, and in addition to the churn of death metal and

Survivor's 'Eye of the Tiger', I endured gangster rap and, weirdly, a loop of 'Fuck tha Police' by LA rappers NWA. As well as masking the prison's inner workings, this soundtrack was designed to crush the spirits of anyone caged underground, but during breaks in the playlist I heard several clues that at least one other person had been banged up nearby. There was shouting and yelling, instructions and insults. It felt strangely comforting knowing that I wasn't alone in this hell.

The DPR guards were my biggest psychological tormentors and that night they drank heavily and issued threats. They banged on my door with their truncheons and sang abuse as they staggered along the corridor.

'We're coming for you, faggot. *We're coming for you . . .*'

The intimidation tactics were terrifying. When the violence began several hours later, it was brutal. I was hooded and dragged away from the CCTV cameras. Someone big, probably Captain Shovel Hands, pinned me down and punched me in the gut. I was cracked in the kneecaps, hips and thighs, and I soon realised that the guards were striking at the few areas covered by my barely-there trousers and T-shirt. At no point did anyone smack me about the face, which meant the beating hadn't been authorised and was being done 'off the books'. As I wriggled around in an attempt to avoid the worst of the body blows, it was impossible to keep my bandaged wound away from the filthy floor. The last thing I needed was a grisly infection.

Over the next twenty-four hours, I endured several kickings and most of the time the attacks felt random, though every now and then I was presented with a demand for information. At one point somebody showed me a map of Mariupol.

'Tell me where you were on this,' said one of the guards. 'We are still meeting resistance here.'

Well, that's a load of bollocks, I thought. All our positions had been abandoned during the retreat, but rather than telling the truth, I handed over some vague, out-of-date details on posts I knew had either been abandoned or blown up by Russian artillery. I guessed that eventually the interrogators would push me really hard on the matter, but until that time arrived my job was to delay, and then delay some more. I'd learned from my SERE training that torture broke most people at some point – or they died. I hoped that holding out in a tactical fashion would save me from both outcomes, even though I knew full well I'd have to experience a lot of pain before reaching the other side.

And that pain was relentless. I soon learned that there were more rules to follow in the Black Site, though none of them were explained to me fully and any accidental violations resulted in another beating to the legs, arms and body. Part of that process included being bludgeoned with a tool several guards had cheerily referred to as the 'Black Mamba' – a heavy, wooden truncheon that was big enough to break an arm or leg if swung with sufficient power. After every beating, somebody dropped the Black Mamba onto my spine from a height. The pain was excruciating and I struggled to breathe for several minutes afterwards.

Trial and error was my only way of working out the various protocols and it was a horrible process. I quickly came to learn that I wasn't allowed to do push-ups, sit-ups or any form of exercise in my cramped space. Every time a guard entered the room I had to face the back wall. A buzzer woke me in the morning and ordered me to sleep at night. I lived in fear of making a mistake. Then, on the fourth day of captivity, as I sat on my bed, staring into space, the guards ordered me to stand up. I was then pushed against a wall.

'You are to stay like that for twelve hours,' said one, 'until the buzzer goes at ten o'clock tonight.'

I made to ask a question but thought better of it. Standing for that long was going to be job enough. Remaining upright following a kiss from the Black Mamba would probably prove impossible. I stood still, watching the camera as it watched me, doing my best to avoid cramp or falling asleep on the spot. Inevitably, as the hours passed, my mind started to stew. I pictured Larysa and wondered what she might be up to. I thought of my team-mates – the ones that had died and those that were hopefully still alive. I wondered if Aiden was somewhere nearby. Though we hadn't exactly been close, the fact that he might be in the cell next to me or somewhere down the corridor helped me feel less alone.

Avoiding an emotional downward spiral was tricky: I had no window, nowhere to walk and no one else to talk to. But I knew the Russians were hoping to break my spirit, so I had to get a positive grasp on the situation. I realised that the only productive step I could make at that point was to turn defiance into a game. Because if the unimaginable happened and I was released at some point in the future, it was important to leave captivity with my head held high. I didn't want to crumble or land anyone else in trouble.

Do a good job, I told myself. *Don't shit on your friends, whatever happens.*

Every now and then, I heard a jangle of keys outside the door and my adrenaline spiked. *Were they coming for me?*

The sound would then disappear down the corridor. *Thank God for that,* I'd think.

For a full day, I was like a cat on a hot tin roof, until, eventually, the buzzer sounded. I collapsed onto my bed in relief and for a few hours I slept soundly. Whenever I woke, my mind was full of horrendous possibilities. *What new torment would be coming my way in the morning?*

My food allowance had been massively reduced and I discovered the Russians were dishing out starvation as a punishment.

'You lie, so only bread and water for you,' I was told.

The rations now consisted of one stale loaf, which arrived at 10 a.m. and was thrown through a hatch in the door, plus a five-litre plastic bottle of piss-coloured liquid that seemed to ripple with bacteria and parasitic worms. It stank of bleach and tasted vile. If I was away from my cell being questioned or beaten during the morning delivery, well, *tough*: I would have to wait for the next day's round of food. When I'd first been captured, I was hardly in the best of shape, but I was deteriorating by the day and becoming skinny and ill; smashed up and starved. My guts felt as if they were being pumped with polystyrene and on the rare occasion I was able to pass something, it would hit the bottom of the bucket like a brick. The long-term lack of nutrition was becoming more worrying than the beatings.

The unpredictability was the worst part of being banged up, though, and the anarchic atmosphere in the Black Site was intensified by the violent characters working within it. To regain some sense of control, I attempted to build a picture of what was going on outside my cell door. The fact that I had no window made it impossible to judge the time of day, so instead I focused on the pattern of life taking place around the facility. The buzzer ordering me to sleep went off at 22:00. I knew that because the guard had said so when instructing me to stand still for hours on end. I also knew that it sounded again at 06:00. In between those times I was left alone – nobody had beaten or questioned me while I'd been sleeping. I also knew that between approximately 08:00 and 08:30 there was a changeover in personnel. Any new scrap of intelligence felt empowering.

During my SERE training, I'd been taught about the psychological power of gaining small victories like these and how they could keep a soldier alive in a prisoner-of-war situation. The concept was simple: when captured, an individual often feels helpless, hopeless and utterly demoralised. However, by recording one or two small victories against the enemy, it was possible to regain a sense of control in unpredictable and depressing circumstances. These gains were often marginal, and usually went unnoticed by those in charge, but they meant everything to a prisoner facing emotional collapse. For example, if at some point in the future I managed to get a cup of coffee, then that was to be taken as a small victory. Blagging a cigarette or gathering some information about home, or the wider war, would be an even bigger small victory. But the greatest win of all was to keep a secret from the interrogators or to plant some small seed of misinformation.

I'd also been taught how to reframe painful or negative events I was experiencing into something that felt like a positive. Later that day, two guards barrelled into my cell, their fists ready to fly, but after only one or two 'love taps', they walked away. *Well, that wasn't so bad,* I thought. *Result.* Shortly afterwards, when a medic knocked on my door and asked if I needed any painkillers I took that as a win too — albeit a confusing one. *Why were they offering pain meds?* Then

I realised that with a keen imagination, even a beating could be twisted into a positive event.

Don't get me wrong: these fleeting moments of achievement weren't massive dopamine hits – like scoring the winning goal in a cup final or landing a dream job. Instead, they gave me a flicker of relief; they told me that not all hope was lost. In many ways, these scores represented tiny emotional stepping stones that would eventually – *hopefully* – lead me away from a bloody dark place. I only had to cling on to the latest one for stability and as soon as I spotted the next, I'd make a bold leap for it. Step by step, small victory by small victory, I hoped to stay alive long enough to taste freedom again.

The next day, I overheard a snippet of news that gave me an even greater sense of hope. I listened as two DPR guards discussed the rumour that certain 'Russians of value' incarcerated in the West were being exchanged for Ukrainian soldiers caught on the front lines. My optimism rocketed: I was British, and I believed – rightly or wrongly – that my nationality gave me more of a prestigious cachet, especially when discussing swaps or negotiations. *Surely I'd be traded?* I tried not to get over-excited, but just the *idea* that I might be swapped at some point felt like an emotional boost and I clung to it in the dark moments. Later that night, as I worried whether Larysa had enough money or if my mum was doing OK, I remembered there was a chance I might get released. That was usually enough to bring me back into a position of emotional safety, like a life raft in a churning sea.

13

The following day I strategised. It felt more important than ever to turn the idea that I was a person of value into a stone-wall, 100 per cent *certainty*, though the challenge, clearly, was to figure out how. In the end, I was nudged towards an extreme plan by yet another prison mind-fuck. Shortly before the buzzer sounded at 22:00, several DPR guards roughed me up, sending me to the floor with a punch to the guts. The Black Mamba was then dropped across my shoulders. Finally, I took a volley of boots in the ribs. A scowling guard loomed over my body.

'Nazi, you are going to be executed tomorrow,' he said, throwing down a sheet of paper.

When I lifted my hood to look, I saw a prepared statement. It had been written in Russian and some of the words were difficult to translate.

'I don't understand. What does this say?'

The guard then took another swing at me with his boot. 'You are to read that on camera,' he said, drawing a finger across his Adam's apple in a slicing motion. 'Then we are going to slit your throat and send the video to your friends and family.'

Oh God, no. I thought back to the hideous execution films that had been made by ISIS. In one, they had murdered a Jordanian pilot and posted the film online. Then I imagined meeting a similar end. I pictured my mum, son and Larysa seeing the footage. I'd rather have taken my own life than have my friends and family go through that ordeal. Fearing an emotional tailspin, I reminded myself of those overheard conversations. My hunch was that the DPR guards were probably full of shit. Mr Balaclava was clearly pulling the strings in the Black Site, though there was a slim chance my execution had been ordered by a warden wanting to free up some POW real estate. In the end, I rated my chances of surviving at around 70 per cent, which was pretty good, but not so good that I could relax.

Over the next few minutes, my thinking flipped from hope to fear, optimism to pessimism, until I was struck by a detail from one of the war books I'd read a few years previously. In it, the author had claimed that, when held as a POW, it was imperative that the captive should become visible to the outside world in some way, either through a propaganda video or some photos, or by making themselves memorable to the other people in the camp. The thinking went that if somebody else learned of their existence – and if they were later freed before them – they might talk about it in an interview or debrief. More than anything, though, I wanted to be moved out of isolation. I had no one to talk to, *or even look at*, and living inside my own head was getting tougher by the hour. If I could make myself into something of an issue for the guards or become regarded as a loose cannon, I might be moved in with another prisoner or shunted to another facility altogether.

Fighting back against the guards was out of the question. No way would it be a fair scrap, and striking out would only give Captain Shovel Hands and his mates free licence to work me over in even more unpleasant ways. They had truncheons and I really didn't want to see out my days in the Black Site with a broken leg or shattered ribs. Then I remembered: *the spoon*! It was still stuffed under my bunk.

Turning away from the camera, I dug into the bed and pulled it out, bending the handle this way and that until it sheared and snapped in half, leaving two jagged steel edges. In a prison scrap, a home-made shiv could badly injure or even blind an enemy. It would be just as useful when turned on myself. *Suddenly, I knew how to become memorable.* I would stage a pretend suicide attempt by slicing open my wrists.

I stewed on the idea for hours. The thought of jamming the metal handle into my arm made me feel sick. My mind twisted with questions.

Is this really what I want to do?

Wouldn't it be better to stay uninjured?

They might just find me, beat the shit out of me and leave me bleeding to death in the cell. Then what?

I fretted all night and my anxiety was heightened even more by the night-shift guards. Some of them had been on the piss and were singing and slurring. I later heard Captain Shovel Hands beating up one of his colleagues in a nearby room, which I'd established was an office or break-out area. There was the crashing of furniture and shouting, and eventually a man yelled out, 'No! Please, no!' A few moments later, when the telltale symphony of violence had stopped, I recognised the whimpering sound of a badly beaten man. The brute, tired of pummelling his own staff, then turned his attentions to me. *Dink! Dink! Dink!* The prick was tapping his truncheon against my cell door. He called me an 'Azov paedo' and promised to open up my throat the next day.

Not if I get there first, mate, I thought darkly.

When the buzzer went the following morning, I made my decision, convincing myself that this was a death-or-glory mission and I had very little to lose. If I was left to bleed out in the aftermath, then at least I'd have reclaimed control at the very end of my life and spared my loved ones the experience of seeing me being slashed across the throat. But if the guards panicked, rushed me to a medic and took me out of isolation (so I could be watched over more effectively), my theory that I was truly a person of value would be confirmed. The doing would be painful, but either way the results would be worth it.

There was also a very good chance my wounds wouldn't actually prove life-threatening. As a schoolkid I'd once had a grisly accident in geography class while mucking around with an old golfing umbrella. The end had been bent out of shape and as I'd tried to straighten it, my hand slipped and a sharp edge sliced open my wrist. The cut was deep. I could see a criss-crossing network of ligaments and muscles inside the bloody flesh wound as red sprayed and squirted all over my desk and exercise books. But having been patched up by a hospital nurse, I was told that it was actually quite hard to die from such an injury. Yeah, I could have nicked an artery, but the chances of that were slim. By carving the split spoon across my wrist, I hoped to achieve a similar result.

Turning away from the CCTV camera again, I bit the bullet, and stabbed the metal into my flesh, taking care to miss the bigger veins while still being determined enough to make a gory mess. Then I did it again and again.

My jaw clenched with pain and I felt my teeth grinding. *I'm going to be OK,* I told myself with every gouge. *I've got to get out of here.*

I punctured the skin five or six times, the spoon's jagged metal edge sawing into flesh and sinew. Blood ran down my arm and dripped to the floor. When I saw the heavy splodges at my feet, nausea washed over me. I felt light-headed. Then I squeezed at the holes in an attempt to make more of a mess, spilling red all over my bed sheets. For dramatic effect, I finally flicked a serving of blood at the wall with my fingers, like a psychotic Jackson Pollock.

The effort must have taken thirty excruciating minutes and with the last slice I dropped to the floor. Shortly afterwards, I heard a key in the door and the groaning of metal. A guard was standing over me, taking in the horror show, but rather than checking if I was OK, he walked away.

Shit. Maybe I'm not so valuable after all, I thought, consoling myself that if I died, it would have happened on my terms rather than the Russians.

Minutes later, everything kicked off. The door swung open again, only this time the same guard had a tourniquet. He applied it to my arm forcefully.

'You're stupid. You're stupid!' he shouted. '*Stupid, stupid, stupid!*'

Over the yelling, I caught the sound of a panic alarm in the distance – either we were under attack or I'd caused a real scene and my theory was being proved correct. When two medics arrived, I knew I was in the clear. Judging by the way they were sweating and panting, the men must have sprinted to the cells. *The Russians wanted me alive.* One of them immediately squirted a frothy white foam onto my wrist. At first glance, it seemed to be similar in texture to shaving cream – I later learned it was designed to clot heavily bleeding wounds. The second bloke grabbed my uninjured arm and handcuffed it to the metal bar above my bed.

'No more being stupid,' he shouted, checking over my wrist.

'Is he going to be OK?' said the other medic.

'Yes. He hasn't got arterial bleeding. He's fine.'

Assured that I was going to survive, the medics scooped up the two gore-covered bits of spoon that had been sitting in a puddle of blood, before laying me out on the bed. The door clanged shut behind them as they left.

I closed my eyes and evaluated the situation. My hand felt like it was hanging off and I'd lost a bit of blood, but my tactic had worked. I now had a clearer idea of where I stood. The Russians had been furious. Whether that was because of some plan to exchange me down the line or because I had some other important value, I wasn't yet sure, but they clearly needed me alive. Any fears that I was being executed that day had vanished. Hopefully I was to be moved out of isolation and into a spot where I would be visible to other prisoners. I drifted into a half-sleep.

What followed was more evidence that my health was something of a concern. The door opened again. The medics were back. But this time one was carrying a bucket of water. I sat up to get a clearer view of what was going on, but as I did so the contents were tipped over my head.

I was soaked through and shocked awake. 'What are you doing?' I shouted.

'Wake up! Wake up! *Wake up!*' yelled the medic. 'You're looking delirious, I'm waking you up.'

The other medic thrust a glass of water into my free hand. 'You're dehydrated. Drink it all.'

The handcuffs chaining me to the wall were unlocked and a hood was placed over my head. 'You're to come to the office,' said a voice, and I was led away to the same medical room where I'd first been processed four or five days ago.

Hello darkness, my old friend, I thought.

When I was seated, the hood was lifted and my wounds were cleaned and stitched. Then another gruff medic grabbed my hand and stared at the ring finger. I was still wearing a copy of the band I'd exchanged with Larysa during our wedding vows. So far, the Russian interrogators and DPR guards had paid very little attention to it.

'Give me your ring,' said the medic.

'But it's a copy. It has no value.'

My mind flashed back to the day of our wedding. We had married in September 2020 and while the party wasn't as big as I'd hoped, mainly because Covid was a massive problem and none of my English family could travel over, it had still been an amazing and emotional event. At the time, I'd been working on operations at the front lines, and so a lot of the heavy lifting had been left to Larysa: she had organised the photographers, our hand-crafted rings and the bridesmaids' dresses. When we got married on Mariupol's left bank, her son gave us away at the altar and the place was packed with friends. A lot of them were people I'd trained and lived with in the trenches. People I loved and trusted with my life. *People I considered to be family.*

The bloke gripped my hand tighter. 'Give it to me.'

I felt heartbroken. My body was physically ravaged and my brain wasn't far behind. Reluctantly, I slid the ring from my finger and handed it over. The medic dropped it into his pocket and smiled. There was nothing I could do to resist and when I was eventually returned to my cell, I sat on the end of my bed and tried not to fall apart. Of all the things that had happened to me over the past few months, this felt like the lowest point.

He's nicked my wedding ring, I thought. *He's nicked my bloody wedding ring.*

I'd been dumped in a really dark place. *Could it get any worse?*

Stupid question: of course it could. A mate of mine had

told me a memorable story a few years previously about his break-up with a long-term partner. He had fallen into a financially bad place and it wasn't long before his rent had become unaffordable. Evicted from his home with nowhere to go, he shoved what he could into a bin bag and walked down to the embankment of the local river, wanting to consider his next steps.

What am I doing? he thought.

Then, out of nowhere, a random bloke made a grab for his possessions. A few punches were thrown and as they wrestled over the bin bag, the plastic shredded and my mate's underpants and socks were strewn all over the path. A few years later, once he'd got his life back together, it was something he would laugh about. When anything went wrong in life, one of us would jokingly remind the other: *At least nobody's nicked your bin bag.* Just recalling those words gave me a little lift.

And then I remembered my tattoos. Both Larysa and I had a Japanese symbol inked onto the left side of our chest. The design covered our hearts. I pulled down my T-shirt and looked at the scrawl across my flesh. My wedding ring might have been stolen, but nobody could take that shared ink away from me – not unless they burned it off or sliced it away with a knife. In that moment I decided that Larysa was right there with me in the battle. Her mantra looped around in my head. Live. Fight. Survive. Live. Fight. Survive. *Live. Fight. Survive.*

There was a noise. The cell door opened and a bucket was pushed inside. It had been filled with bleach. A mop was thrown at me soon after.

'You're going to clean the cell,' said a guard, slamming the door noisily. 'All of it.'

For the next four hours I scrubbed and washed the floors, walls and sheets, wiping away the messy evidence of my violent protest until, finally, the change of scenery I'd been hoping for arrived. The door swung open again, a dark blue, US college-style hoodie with the number '89' emblazoned on the front was dropped at my feet and a voice ordered me outside.

'For what?'

'You're going to meet the Prosecutor,' it said.

14

Same shit. Different wrapper. My captors were creatures of habit. On went the hood, the cuffs clicked shut around my wrists and I was marched down a series of corridors and up a flight of steps. I treated every footfall as an intelligence-gathering exercise. While I understood that an escape was unlikely, over the years I'd heard one or two tales featuring prisoners of war who had managed to escape from a high-security compound, usually after a bomb had exploded nearby, destroying the walls and security cordons. In the chaos that followed, the incarcerated were able to exit through the wreckage. Having fantasised about a similar slice of good fortune, I made sure to memorise my route away from the Black Site cells, just in case.

In the moments before being hooded, I'd taken a moment to size up the DPR guards. Captain Shovel Hands had stood nearby and, apart from Mr Balaclava and his mates, he was clearly the senior figure in the facility. The other staff seemed afraid of him, which was unsurprising given his size. But there were other interesting details to note. Half of the guards looked like senior soldiers put out to pasture – they were overweight and probably not up to scrapping on the front lines. The other half were presumably soldiers on their way up. They were much younger and looked fitter and stronger, as if they lifted weights two or three times a day. As a whole, everything about the group seemed amateurish, from the manner in which they conducted their business to the way in which orders were issued. The chain of command was loose, unstructured and at times drunk, which was the scariest realisation of all. The lack of discipline made them unpredictable; the unpredictability made them dangerous.

Having arrived at the DPR Prosecutor's office, I was led into a holding area that resembled a kangaroo court and forced to sit at a picnic-style table. My head was then pushed forward so that it rested on the top. Staring down, I counted ten pairs of feet. *These guys must all be Ukrainian POWs,* I thought, desperately looking to see if I recognised any familiar markings or styles of clothing from the Marines. I heard one guard talking about fingerprint records and guessed that we were in a processing room of some kind. Other than that, there was an eerie silence. When one of the prisoners coughed noisily, he was heaved out of his seat and beaten. I heard him being roughed up and thrown into the wall.

An official grabbed me by the shoulder. 'Has this one been through the fingerprints procedure yet?' he shouted.

'No, do him next,' said another voice.

My hood was removed and I was led forward. An official checked me over and I was taken into a drab-looking office. I saw pale-blue walls and heavy wooden doors. The furniture was cheap and rickety and on the shelves were framed photographs of Vladimir Putin and various other Russian generals and officials I didn't recognise. The Prosecutor, a baby-faced man dressed in dark green combat fatigues, was sitting behind a desk. I noticed a fancy-looking watch on his wrist – either it was fake or the DPR were paying their staff way above the going rate.

Alongside him were several other people, and I was introduced to a few of them. The elderly lady with dyed blonde hair was my translator. She smiled at me sweetly. A bulky woman named Yulia Tserkovnikova I later learned was a lawyer, though she seemed more interested in taking self-ies and texting. And the heavyset bloke wearing a mixture of DPR and Russian combat fatigues, trainers and thick-rimmed glasses was a total mystery. Presumably he was the muscle. My estimate was that he was in his mid forties – though, judging by his face, he'd had a tough paper round as a kid. His skin was saggy and grey, and when I looked down, I noticed that he was sporting a pair of camouflage trainers.

What a weird bunch of people, I thought, studying the incon-gruous collection of lawyers, prosecutors and soldiers. *They don't seem professional at all.* As if to prove my point, the Prosecutor stood up and offered to make me a cuppa. Then he asked if I fancied a cigarette.

These bellends want something, I thought.

At first, the mood was curious. Apparently, I was the first Brit to have been processed through this particular office, and that had made me something of a novelty among the staff. It was then explained that the DPR would be conduct-ing an investigation into my military activities and the usual questions followed – about who I was, what I'd been doing and why I'd been doing it. As the Prosecutor spoke, the old lady translated into English, even though I understood him pretty well.

'There will be another interrogation this afternoon by some investigators. But for now we are charging you with treason and for going against the fabric of the Donetsk People's Republic. As a matter of course, you will be put on a three-day statutory investigation, to see if we can then send you to trial.'

That was hardly a shock. Being set up as a fall guy in some kind of Mickey Mouse trial was a familiar wartime tactic – it had happened in a lot of conflict zones.

Finally, the mystery man in the room spoke up. 'What about Aiden Aslin?' he said.

So, Aiden was coming in here too at some point. This was getting interesting.

The translator shook her head. 'He is *funny*,' she said.

I didn't know what to make of that. Raising my hand cautiously, I said, 'Who's this guy?'

'That's your defence lawyer,' said the Prosecutor.

I tried not to laugh. The man was clearly an enemy soldier. He might even have taken potshots at one of my positions during the last four years. Now I was relying on his skills to defend my case during a war trial. *A war trial in Putin's Russian-occupied Ukraine.*

My defence lawyer smiled and waved cheerily. 'Hello, I am your defence lawyer,' he said slowly, in poor English. Right then I knew my case was dead in the water.

The Prosecutor went on to explain how I was being processed through a military court and, if found guilty, the punishment would be a lot more severe than in a civil or criminal proceeding.

'Do you understand the seriousness of your charges?'

I nodded, realising that whatever I said wasn't going to make a blind bit of difference and any naive hopes of building a strong defence had been dashed. For starters, my one-man legal eagle probably wanted me dead. Secondly, even if I did manage to put across a solid case, I was fairly certain the guards in the Black Site would see to it that I ended up changing my statements. The Black Mamba was a pretty effective persuader when coercing a prisoner. The Prosecutor then explained that I was additionally being accused of working as a mercenary, which could result in the death penalty under the DPR's code of practice.

Someone asked me for my social-media passwords. The translator passed on the request gently, as if butter wouldn't have melted in her mouth.

'Well, I can't think of them offhand.'

She looked at the Prosecutor and whispered, in Russian, '*Bullshit.*'

'It's not bullshit.'

The translator's face darkened. 'You speak Russian?'

I nodded and her eyes drilled into me. Straight away, I knew the translator couldn't be trusted. Up until that point she had cut a fairly harmless figure. Now that she realised I understood most of what was being said, her mood sharpened. As did mine. *I'd got her all wrong.* She was probably another member of the Russian secret services and was acting undercover. Their hope, presumably, was for her benign appearance to lower my guard, and if that happened, well, I might talk more freely or give up some valuable information. I wasn't falling for that, though.

Noticing the change in mood, the Prosecutor quickly slid a series of maps across his desk. One was a satellite image of Mariupol. The Russians wanted me to detail any locations I'd fought in during the siege, plus any places around the Illich steelworks that had previously been used by the Marines. I shrugged and pointed to one or two old tank positions, knowing they had fallen to Russian forces long before we'd fled the city. The Prosecutor sighed. I sensed he was close to moving on. Trying to shift his focus away from my recent military past, I enquired about a potentially depressing short-term future.

'How do the DPR execute people?' I said. 'Firing squad? Hanging? Lethal injection? How are you going to kill me?'

Everyone in the room became strangely awkward. The

translator coughed nervously. My defence lawyer riffled through his papers. Finally, the Prosecutor, who resembled a rabbit framed in the headlights of an oncoming BTR, offered a non-committal answer.

'As you know, we've never caught Westerners before,' he said. 'We certainly haven't executed one, so we don't know how this is going to work exactly. The mechanisms are not there to deal with you.'

I could have sworn the bloke was making a half-arsed attempt at an apology. *Funny,* I thought. *I've never been in any trouble with the Old Bill. I don't even have a caution to my name. Now here I am, being trialled as a mercenary and facing either a life-time of back-breaking work in a Russian labour camp or the death penalty.* The idea might have been comical if the verdict and potential punishment hadn't been so horrific.

The Prosecutor continued. 'Then there's the small matter of the referendum.'

'*Referendum?* What referendum?'

'Well, in Donetsk, the people are currently deciding whether to be ruled by Russian law or the current DPR laws. If they opt for Russian law, which looks like being the case, the death sentence will probably be abolished. There is no death penalty in Russia.'

That, at the very least, was a small crumb of comfort, though the irony was excruciating. To survive prosecution and fight another day, all I needed was for the Russians to win a presumably fixed election in an illegally annexed cor-ner of Ukraine – a part of the world I was hoping would be liberated one day.

When the questioning was wrapped up, another uni-formed man walked over. He had been standing quietly at the back of the room, almost unnoticed. He smiled sheepishly.

'You're the first English guy I've ever met,' he said.

'Oh, right . . .'

'Have you ever seen a rouble?' he asked, pulling out a crumpled note.

I nodded, feigning interest. Then he went a step further. 'Do you mind if I get a selfie with you?' he said.

I couldn't get my head around what was going on. *Were these people taking the piss, or were they as thick as mince?* But having been taught that plenty of value could be drawn from a tenuous connection with a captor, I played along. Maybe at some point down the line this bloke, whoever he was, would turn out to be a useful source of information, food or even cigarettes.

'Sure,' I said, posing alongside the soldier – him with his thumbs up, me with my thumbs down – hoping the photograph would soon be shared on social media. I made certain my bandaged wrist was in full view. My hope was to alert as many people as possible to my current status: I was alive and still clinging on, but in a world of fucking hurt.

I was frogmarched to another room, where the mood changed as I was shoved roughly into a chair. Looking around, I saw several people wearing neat combat fatigues, all of them senior military figures. Mr Balaclava was there too. Out of everybody, he was still the only one hiding his face.

He has to be FSB or something similar, I thought. *Why else would he wear a mask?* He was also the only competent interrogator among the group. He was authoritative, to the point and bloody intimidating – the standout in a ragtag bunch. Whenever anyone else spoke, they came across as shambolic or contradictory and every lie sounded comically transparent. One of them told me that Ukraine had fallen and so there was no reason for me to withhold information. Another claimed that Ukraine was still resisting and any intel I gave them would help my case in the long run. One minute I was being threatened with execution; the next I was being asked if I needed painkillers for my injuries. I was able to dodge every line of inquiry.

But that all changed whenever Mr Balaclava spoke and the atmosphere became a little more unsettled. A lot of that had to do with his physical presence. The bloke was probably six foot one and stocky, with the build of a slightly-past-his-best MMA fighter. I could see muscles under his too-tight T-shirt and the early signs of an advancing dad-bod paunch. Meanwhile, I'd noticed that he was the only person not dressed in military clothing. He wore a green, aviation-style bomber jacket with orange lining, jeans and a pair of smart, shiny boots. Poking out from one of his sleeves was a clunky silver watch.

But his eyes were the most revealing detail. They were bloodshot. His gaze darted about the room constantly, as if he was trying to figure out how to win a war, interrogate a prisoner and put together an IKEA wardrobe all at once. Sometimes, he seemed to be somewhere else entirely, and the biggest tell that he might be under heavy pressure was the rate at which he smoked. Whenever Mr Balaclava finished one cigarette, another was sparked up shortly afterwards. *The bloke was stressed out but doing his best to keep a lid on it.* And as always, everyone in the room was bowing and scraping to him.

'Shaun, why did you do that?' he said, pointing to the bandage on my wrist.

I shrugged. 'Your guys came in and beat the shit out of me last night. They told me they were going to execute me today.'

'Which ones?'

He was doing his best to come across as matey. It wasn't going to wash. 'I don't know. I couldn't see all of them as I had a hood on most of the time.'

'Well, I'm going to talk to them about th—'

I cut him off. 'So, I thought, "If I'm going to die, then I want to go out with a bang." I just decided there and then that I wanted to kill myself. I wasn't going to let you lot do it.'

Mr Balaclava crouched down beside me. I flinched, wondering if a punch was coming. When he spoke, the hairs on the back of my neck bristled.

'Listen. It is better to let another soldier kill you than it is to kill yourself,' he whispered. 'There is some honour in it at least.'

More talk, more mind games, I thought, unsure whether to feel relief (because I understood the games being played) or annoyance (at being taken for a mug).

'Look, it's a misunderstanding. I'm sorry,' I said eventually. 'If you can promise I'm not going to be knifed today—'

'You're not going to be knifed. They're just fucking around with you.'

I marked the conversation down as a psychological win. But the motive behind Mr Balaclava's false sympathy became clear almost immediately. More people had entered the room. One had a video camera and it was being positioned on a tripod. The lens was pointing right at me. A small, dumpy man sat down next to it. He had cropped, thinning dark hair and was dressed all in black, the look topped off with a cheap leather jacket. I immediately clocked him as the wannabe alpha-male type. The bloke was smirking. He seemed pretty full of himself, though I'm not sure why. From a distance, he resembled a pound-shop version of the Milk Tray Man.

'This is Andrey Rudenko,' said Mr Balaclava, 'a prominent journalist in Russia, and he will be interviewing you for television.'

Rudenko burst out laughing. 'Yes, a "journalist",' he said, using his fingers for air quotes.

This was the reason why only my body had been targeted during the previous beatings: my face was about to become a tool of propaganda. I'd seen the movies; hostage rescue books were considered standard reading material among my mates in the military, and I'd suspected that the Russians would look to feature me in a propaganda film at some point. I would be questioned and the footage would be edited to make it appear as if I'd had some change of heart about Ukraine's political position. Or maybe somebody, somewhere would attempt to cut the footage in such a way that I looked anti-Ukraine or pro-Putin. It made sense to assume that Rudenko was a paid-up employee of the Kremlin. I had to speak carefully.

Prompted by Mr Balaclava, Rudenko started by framing me as a Nazi. 'The Azov battalion has been accused by the United Nations of committing war crimes and atrocities,' he said. 'And I've seen, time and again, people detained by the Azov battalion. They have swastikas painted all over their body. They have been accused of Nazi affiliations by the BBC, by Vice News, by many different news media around the world. Obviously, you know more about them since you have been in closer contact, if you will. I'm not saying in direct... But still . . . What can you tell us about their Nazi affiliations, about their atrocities against peaceful civilians?'

That wasn't going to fly. 'I don't know too much about these accusations and atrocities against civilians,' I said. 'So

I can't really comment on that. I would if I knew, to be honest. Some of the guys I met in Azov are generally guys that can't get work in their villages.'

I then explained how there might have been the occasional rogue individual, as there was in any military group, but I hadn't seen anyone throwing Nazi salutes or goose-stepping through Mariupol.

'I've lived in Ukraine for over four years,' I carried on. 'If this is about de-Nazifying Ukraine, I've never seen a Nazi flag, never witnessed any Nazi behaviour, no street parades. I've been to Kyiv. I've been to Bakhmut. I've been to Kramatorsk. I've been all around Ukraine and I've never seen it.'

In a never-ending stream of lies and gaslighting, Rudenko then insisted I was part of a group of mercenaries that were attempting to topple the DPR. To pacify him, I offered up the basics about my life, something that couldn't be manipulated in an editing suite.

'I am Shaun Pinner. I am a citizen of the United Kingdom. I was captured in Mariupol. I am part of 36 Brigade First Battalion Ukrainian Marines. I was fighting in Mariupol for five or six weeks and now I am in the Donetsk People's Republic.'

Whenever I spoke, I brought my heavily bandaged wrist to the table, hoping that somebody watching might notice I'd been injured. Sometimes Mr Balaclava spotted the move and ordered me to put my arm down; other times he didn't.

'Tell me how you were captured,' said Rudenko.

'We were in the factory area of Mariupol. It was decided we'd move from the factory, but we did not know exactly where. At about four in the morning we left the factory. There wasn't much time to think.'

Rudenko then pointed to a map on his phone. 'You didn't have a single chance to reach this settlement Zachativka, since Russian and DPR troops were everywhere.'

I nodded my head and pretended to know what he was talking about. 'I had no idea,' I said. 'You know more than me. I don't particularly know anything.'

I was setting out my stall on a Russian propaganda video. Pleading ignorance regarding any military positions outside of Mariupol was the next phase in my cover story. I intended to take it into any future interrogation sessions, though I wasn't sure if it would do me much good.

Rudenko brought his interview to a close. The equipment was packed away. Mr Balaclava had left the room. But just beyond the cameraman's shoulder was a window. Through it I caught a brief glimpse of the world beyond captivity, and the banality was disorientating. The sun was setting low over the buildings of Donetsk. There were people strolling around on the streets as if nothing of significance was happening in the wider world. *And was that the sound of chirping?* I couldn't remember the last time I'd heard birdsong. Gunfire and explosions had drowned out everything while I'd been on the front lines.

It's so bloody normal here, I thought. *There's meant to be a war going on, but it looks so beautiful.*

For the first time in ages, I experienced a sense of peace. Just one brief glimpse of sunlight had been so rejuvenating that any concerns about facing the death penalty temporarily melted away. When I was hooded and cuffed shortly afterwards, I tried to hang on to the feeling for as long as possible. It was another shot of hope.

15

Back at the Black Site, I got my first sense that things might be moving in a slightly different direction. The car journey had been the same as usual – I took one or two digs in the kidneys – but as I was walked through the corridors, we took a new route. I was led past my cell and down a flight of stairs, where the temperature dropped drastically. It must have been around zero degrees and my breath fogged under the plastic bag. My sense was that I was in a basement of some kind. *Maybe I was going to be topped after all?* I heard the clanking of keys and the metallic groan of a heavy door being opened. A pair of hands shoved me forward. When the door slammed shut behind me, I removed my hood. It was the happiest I'd felt in months.

I was in another grim cell, in another grim part of the Black Site. The room was a similar shape to my previous home, with a camera on the wall, a bright light in the ceiling and a bucket for a toilet. I also noticed there wasn't a bed and everything felt damper and much colder. But standing in front of me, smiling nervously, were two skinny, stooped men. They were both wrapped in a paper-thin blanket and shivering. I smiled, wryly. *Finally, someone to talk to.*

The taller of the two stepped forward. 'Are you crazy?' he said in broken English.

'What? *No.* I'm not crazy.'

He offered to shake my hand. 'Guard says you crazy. I'm Dimitri.'

His grip was bony and frail. His joints were visible through his skin. Dimitri was so malnourished he looked like a carrier bag stuffed with coat hangers.

'Shaun,' I said, making sure not to squeeze too tightly. 'You speak English pretty well.'

'A little,' said Dimitri. Then he pointed to the other bloke. 'That's Oleg. He speaks no English. He is stupid.'

He gestured that we should all sit on the floor. 'So you are not crazy, then?' continued Dimitri. 'We have been told you tried to kill yourself.' He pointed to my bandaged wrist and made a manic slashing gesture, Norman Bates-style.

I shook my head and told him the story: my idea, my plan and my mocked-up suicide attempt.

'Good, we will get along, if you are not crazy,' said Dimitri, before explaining the situation to Oleg, who seemed to visibly relax.

Suddenly, he raised his hand. Dimitri wanted us to be quiet. I heard the familiar jangle of keys. When the door opened and we reached for our hoods, a guard walked in with a heavily stained mattress.

'Sleep on it,' he said, before gesturing to a series of vents in the wall. Each one was funnelling in icy cold blasts of air. 'You can block those up too if you want. We will not beat you if you do.'

When the guard left, Dimitri looked at me incredulously. 'I've been here forty days. They've never treated us this well.'

I smiled. There was no doubt about it now. We had value. Or at least *I* did.

We huddled together all evening, talking quietly. It was the first civilised conversation I'd had in weeks, maybe since before Dima's death, and I was desperate for information, anything that might give me a clearer picture of where I was. Dimitri told me he'd been captured around forty days previously and that when he arrived much of the Black Site hadn't been set up. It had been his job to paint the walls, clean up a carpet of broken tiles and fix the beds in the isolation wing where I'd been staying. His punishment for refusing had been the first in a series of heavy beatings.

'If the CIA had a headquarters in Donetsk, this would be it,' he said, confirming my feeling that Mr Balaclava was a member of the FSB.

Dimitri then told me that when he was arrested, he'd been trying to sneak *into* Russia in order to escape the bombs that were raining down on his position. Although he was a soldier, he'd been dressed as a civilian at the time. He'd also destroyed his military ID, but when his captors did a quick scan through his mobile, there was evidence of him being a Ukrainian fighter. I thought back to my phone, hoping it was still sunk.

'The prison wardens here are MGB,' said Dimitri. 'Which is the DPR equivalent of the FSB – the secret police.'

Then he whispered, 'It is not a nice place.'

I laughed, unsure of whether Dimitri was being ironic. *No shit.*

'What about him?' I said, pointing to Oleg, who had already staked out his territory on the mattress.

'Oh, he is going to be fine. He's a taxi driver, a civilian. He was arrested for posting anti-Putin views online. He went out to see the Prosecutor the other week and when he came back he looked so sad. He kept crossing himself. He said he was looking at a three-to-four-year sentence for supporting Ukraine. But the Russians now need workers in the Donbas region, so they will relocate him there, I think. Me, I'm never getting out.'

'*Why not?* Come on, mate, you need to hold on to hope.'

'Look, Shaun. I am Ukrainian, a soldier, but I am no use to Russia because those facts can't be proved as I have no official ID. It is not likely I will be swapped for some officer. But you might be a different story.'

Dimitri was in a bad way. His cadaverous frame was skeletal and hunched. He grimaced with stomach pains and at times he seemed unable to move properly. Given he had been holed up in the Black Site for forty days, I realised he was a dark premonition of my future health. In a couple of weeks I would be just as fucked as him. Dimitri then asked me what was happening in the war. I told him everything I knew up until the moment I'd been captured. Beyond that, I was as much in the dark as him. Other than the thugs that were holding me captive, I'd not spoken to another soul and the state of Ukraine was a total mystery. For all I knew, Zelenskiy's government might have fallen already.

'What about Azovstal?' said Dimitri, hopefully.

'Well, I heard of battles going on while I was still fighting, so it might still be standing. Even though we've been captured, Azovstal may be OK. But, look: you'll have to accept the fact that the Russians have passed through a lot of places very quickly.'

Given our perilous position in captivity, my lack of knowledge felt like a gift rather than a curse. The translator in the Prosecutor's office had shown that anyone could be a mole and should be viewed as such. It wasn't uncommon for military POW camps to plant spies among the prison community, within the cells. Any intelligence they picked up could be used as either tactical information in the war effort or leverage to coerce a prisoner into handing over more valuable intel. For now, I was keeping my cards away from Dimitri. The finer details regarding who and what

I knew would stay secret, even if much of it seemed out of date.

I also viewed secrecy as a safety measure, one that might help Dimitri in the long run.[5] If he knew very little about my life, Dimitri would have a legitimate level of plausible deniability to fall back on when questioned about me. Hopefully, that made him less likely to experience any torture. As much as I could, I repeated everything I'd told Mr Balaclava, making a point not to deviate from the script. When Dimitri suggested that I might be an Azov fighter, I corrected him firmly.

'Not Azov,' I said. 'No, no, *no*. A Ukrainian Marine: 36 Brigade First Battalion.'

He then blurted out that the guards were referring to him as 'Drone Operator' because of his expertise in that area. Dimitri hadn't exactly helped himself, either. During an interview with Mr Balaclava, he'd explained how he'd killed Russian soldiers in the line of duty – lots of them. He'd taken another beating for that too.

From what I could tell, the rules in the basement cells were fairly similar to the ones I'd experienced during isolation. When the guards showed up, I had to stand at the back of the room and face the wall with my hood on. The

---

5 I later learned that this was the right move. Once I'd got out of the Black Site, another Ukrainian prisoner told me that Dimitri had been badly beaten during an interrogation in which the Russians had pressed him for intelligence on me. I can only assume that Dimitri didn't mention the real reason for his beatings because he didn't want me to feel guilty. I know he used to get smacked about very badly, though. One time he fell asleep during the day with a woolly hat pulled down over his eyes. The guards hated that sort of thing. Dimitri took a real battering afterwards and he raged at us for not waking him up. We honestly hadn't known he'd been sleeping.

buzzers went off at 22:00 and 06:00 and the buckets were slopped out first thing. If we were lucky, a loaf of bread and some piss-coloured water would arrive during the day. There were also rules for when we were taken out of the cell. We had to stoop down low, with our heads as close to our knees as possible, and our arms outstretched. We then had to step backwards into the corridor so we could be cuffed. But the absolute worst thing to do was to attempt any form of physical exercise.

'They don't want you to get strong,' said Dimitri.

I got off the mattress and moved up and down on my tiptoes, feeling the stretch in my aching calf muscles and hamstrings. 'What if I did this?' I said, trying to make him laugh.

Dimitri yanked me down. 'No! Don't do it, *please*. They will see on the camera. Shit is going to come if you do.'

The bloke was terrified. I decided to put my prison aerobics plan to one side. No workout was worth a broken rib.

It was so very hard to keep track of the date. The only events to hold on to for clarity were the two buzzers that sounded during the day and the clawing, hollow ache in my guts. I was either starving hungry or painfully constipated; my intestines were bunged up with stale bread and my tummy had tightened from the parasite-riddled water we were being left to drink. At one point, I became convinced that some gruesome living thing was going to crawl from my body somewhere, like the extraterrestrial predator from the horror film *Alien*. On those rare occasions when somebody was actually able to pass something into the bucket with a groan, the noise was more like a heavy book being dropped onto a tiled floor than a broken man going for a shit.

A brief release from the boredom came a couple of days later when I was hooded, cuffed and driven into Donetsk to see the Prosecutor and learn more about the charges being levelled against me. My main objective was to catch a glimpse of sunlight again, but as I was led from my cell, I got the sense that I wasn't travelling alone. There seemed to be another pair of feet shuffling alongside me. *Was it a new prisoner?* I stepped forward. By now the new route to the car park had been committed to memory, but unexpectedly I was dragged into a side room and shoved against a table. From under my hood, I could tell I was in a kitchen area and several pairs of feet were moving about me. I heard shouting. Then somebody screamed out in agony. Every muscle in my body had clenched with terror.

My head was slammed onto the table and a guard whispered close by. Because of the hood – plus my tinnitus, following on from that train attack outside Illich – it was hard to make out the words. *Was he really asking me about football?* It certainly sounded like it.

'I can't hear,' I said, waiting to be smashed about the head.

Then a new voice called out in English. It was the other prisoner. 'He wants to know what team you support,' he yelled, before moaning in pain again. Judging by the noise, he was being beaten up against a wall. My thoughts tumbled; it was a weird request. But, as with the bloke who had wanted a selfie in the Prosecutor's office, I knew the smart play was to build another connection, no matter how fucked up the circumstances.

'West Ham,' I said, hopefully, praying the guard wasn't a Spurs or Millwall fan.

Big mistake. A rod was jammed into my kidneys and a charge of electricity crushed my spine. *The fuckers had a cattle prod!* My body stiffened and twitched. Then I collapsed in a heap. The guard crouched down and told me that Shakhtar Donetsk, a team that had previously played in the

Champions League, was the only acceptable answer from now on. As I was shunted into the back of a transporter vehicle, drooling and trembling with aftershocks, I consoled myself that I had at least tried to make friends. But I wasn't alone: I was being driven away with the other prisoner. The guards kept referring to him as *Morock*, or Moroccan, and when my mask was removed, I realised he was only a kid.

Once I'd arrived at the office and undergone the usual pretend paperwork, the Prosecutor read my charges from a page of legalese gobbledegook.

'You are charged with the crimes under Parts 20 and 34 of Article 323 of the People's Code of the Donetsk People's Republic,' he said, in Russian. 'You are charged with the following: "Approximately from December 2018 until April 2022, citizen of the United Kingdom Shaun Pinner . . ."'

As the bloke droned on, I wondered if he really knew what was happening in the war – if he had any clue about the death and mayhem in Ukraine.

'". . . in the wartime, being armed with firearms, took part in the preparation and conducting of hostilities against the armed forces of the Donetsk People's Republic for the purpose of forcibly seizing power and holding power in the territory of the Donetsk People's Republic . . ."'

I looked past him to the window, hoping to catch another peek at what was going on outside.

'". . . in violation of its constitution, as well as attempting to change the constitutional order of the Donetsk People's Republic by conducting terrorist acts, explosions, attacks from mortar, artillery, small arms; attacks on settlements, civilians, military personnel of the armed forces of the Donetsk People's Republic; intimidation of the civilian population who exercised their will during the 2014 referendum as a result of which the DPR was formed."'

I tuned out. The Prosecutor was going on and on. Finally he drew breath. 'You understand the contents of the accusation?' he said.

I didn't. My limited Russian meant the finer points of military law were beyond me and nobody was translating the charges. (This conversation was placed online and I watched it with subtitles once I'd been released.) Would it have really mattered, though? I was done for and arguing my case was pointless. I looked over at the Prosecutor.

'Do you understand the charges?' he said in English.

Nope. 'Pretty much,' I lied, wanting to get the day over and done with.

It was then explained that the penalty for these crimes, if convicted, was death.

Surprise, surprise, I thought glumly, trying not to show any emotion.

My defence statement was then read out, most of which I also couldn't understand, even though I'd supposedly said it. (Plot twist: *I hadn't.*) Eventually, I was taken away for another filmed chat with Andrey Rudenko. Once again, I was accused of being a trained killer with Azov and a Nazi. The routine was getting old.

The only way to stay sane in the face of such hostilities was to open up and talk to my cellmates once I'd been dropped back at the Black Site, and we soon learned that one way to take our minds off the relentless boredom of prison life was to discuss food. Oleg was tricky to communicate with because of his poor understanding of English, and my Russian didn't always cross over that well into Ukrainian – our jokes and the smaller details were often lost in translation. Dimitri, on the other hand, was becoming more and more of an ally. He came across as a good guy and he started talking fondly about his grandad, who lived off the land and cooked a mean suckling pig. Dimitri then chatted at length about the fine art of killing the animal swiftly, and humanely, before cutting it up to make sausages and ribs. But he also had a strong sweet tooth. Dimitri wouldn't shut up about his love for millionaire cake.

Going on about food while being close to starvation might sound like a form of torture to somebody who hasn't been in that position before. The reality was that it actually helped to distract my brain from the hurt of being deprived. Also, my taste buds were unemployed and after a fortnight of eating nothing but shitty bread it had become impossible to imagine any other flavours. That evening, as the three of us sat around listlessly, feeling bored, we decided to go on a virtual shopping tour around our favourite supermarkets. We talked about our grocery lists and what was being cooked for dinner. Dimitri described how he would prepare *syrniki*, beautiful Ukrainian pancakes that arrive loaded with cheese. As he talked, I could actually taste them. *And booze!* I'd never been one for picking apart the flavour profiles of a wine (as far as I was concerned, a white wine was a white wine), but after a long siege diet and a bread-heavy prison meal plan, I was suddenly able to describe all the components of a supermarket Chablis.

After a couple of hours, the emotional pressure of being cooped up, all while a brutal war was being waged outside, became incredibly oppressive and claustrophobic. I was suddenly all talked out. Chatting about food had become monotonous, but with too much time to think, I started to worry about Larysa, my family and my future. From time to time, I looked down at the tattoo on my chest, and thought of the good times with my wife. *I loved her so much.* Then I became fearful that I might never see her again. *This is not a good sign,* I thought. I knew the mind was an essential weapon in captivity, but it was also a fearsome enemy and if I couldn't control my thoughts they might very easily turn against me. I felt the emotional turmoil creeping into my heart and lungs. It tightened my chest and shortened my breath; my muscles in my shoulders, back and neck ached and contracted; my resolve felt close to crumbling.

These were the warning signs of an impending episode of depression and I'd experienced them before, during an emotional break-up with an ex. At the time, I'd learned to name the pain because I'd heard that some therapists worked with their clients on identifying and naming their difficult emotional experiences because it helped to detach them from whatever issues were going on. It was reckoned that by observing a problem externally, rather than living it, an emotional wound could be handled more effectively. I'd first used the technique when living in Bedford, after the failure of my first marriage. At that time I referred to the depressing moments as the 'Black Cloud' and I got pretty good at spotting the trigger points. If I was having a shitty day or found myself fretting about where I was heading in life, I made sure to tell the people around me. That way they could understand my moods – and me.

In the Black Site, I gave the new pain a different name, 'the Weight', and as my mood darkened I made a point of telling Dimitri and Oleg. 'I'm not good today, lads,' I said quietly. Together, we then attempted to lift the atmosphere with a series of jokes and stories. But I knew it was important to look out for the others too. The next morning, I watched as Dimitri curled up on the mattress with a sheet pulled over his head. I could tell from the shuddering in his shoulders that he was crying.

'Hey,' I said, putting my hand on his shoulder. 'What's up, mate?'

The guy looked distressed. 'I don't think I'm ever going to get out,' he said, sadly. 'All the people I love . . . They don't even know I'm here. They have probably written me off as dead. *My poor mother . . .*'

Dimitri was in the worst place: stuck in a life without hope. I'd been taught that the pain of separation could be enough to finish a prisoner off, so I tried to lift him.

'Don't worry, we'll get through this,' I said. 'Don't give up yet.'

To brighten the mood, I suggested that the three of us spend some time memorising each other's home phone numbers. The idea was that if one of us was released, or in the unlikely event that we were able to escape, our first call would be to the loved ones of every person we'd been banged up with. We then spent hours going over the digits, testing one another until the various combinations had become as familiar as our own birthdays or pin numbers. We might even have said them backwards at one point, just to increase the difficulty of the challenge.

'I promise to phone your wife if I get out before you,' said Oleg at the end of the exercise.

I think we must have killed half a day memorising and reciting, *memorising and reciting*, like kids studying their multiplication tables. Whether it was worth the effort or not was irrelevant. We had found a window of time in which it was possible to imagine a life beyond the Black Site.

16

I was off to the Prosecutor's office again.

By now the journey was becoming as familiar as a Sunday drive around my neighbourhood at home. Well, what was left of it. To keep my mind active, I made sure to study every turn and manoeuvre along the way – literally. *There are four right-hand turns; then the car travels along some major road, maybe a dual carriageway; this is followed by two left turns.* I paid attention to any strange details, like the way in which it always took about fifteen minutes to get to the location, but only ten to return. *So were we driving along a one-way system on the way there?* And if the radio was turned up, I made sure to listen out for any news about the war or Ukraine, hoping for an emotional boost, or something of interest for Dimitri and Oleg to chat about – anything to lift their day.

On this occasion, the route differed slightly towards the end, and once the fun and games had finished I was taken into a building where a guard sat me down forcefully. Then I heard a familiar voice. My flesh prickled with adrenaline and goosebumps. *It was Mr Balaclava.* Bad times were coming.

'Hello, Shaun. How are you today?'

Like you give a shit, mate. 'I'm fine,' I lied.

My hood was ripped off and I noticed another man standing in the room. Of all the monsters I'd encountered during captivity, he was the biggest and baddest-looking yet. The bloke was the size of a heavyweight boxer and must have carried at least twenty stone of beard, muscle and pent-up rage.

Christ, I thought. *He looks like a Wookiee.*

Mr Balaclava reached into his pocket. 'Would you like a cigarette? I apologise, they are only Russian brand.'

I reached out for one. 'To be honest, mate, if you'd said they were from Outer Mongolia, I'd have taken it.'

I wished back the gag immediately, but the response was surprising – *and weird.* Mr Balaclava folded up laughing. He then turned around to his colleague and repeated the joke. The ground seemed to shake. *Chewbacca was laughing, too.*

'Very good, Shaun,' said Mr Balaclava, settling himself. 'Very funny. Now, what is going to happen is this: shortly, a journalist called Roman Kosarev is going to come in and interview you. And you are going to cooperate, because if you don't –' he pointed a thumb to the big, walking carpet – 'this gentleman will make life very complicated for you.'

Mr Balaclava gestured for Kosarev and his film crew to come in. 'Oh, Shaun, one more thing,' he said casually, as if struck by an afterthought. 'Have you heard of the Red Cross in Mariupol?'

My antennae went up. *Surely everybody knew who the Red Cross were?*

'Yeah, I have.'

'What do you know about them?'

'They're an international organisation. Humanitarian. Their volunteers turn up in war zones to help people who are hurt, homeless—'

'Thank you, Shaun, but I don't want the details of *what* they are. I just want to know: do you know anything about the Red Cross *in Mariupol?*'

'Well, yeah,' I said.

He sighed. The Wookiee advanced towards me.

'And were they stationed there?' said Mr Balaclava.

Given that this information had been all over the internet as the war kicked off, I nodded. 'They help out in just about every war zone. But I think they left when the invasion started. It was too dangerous for them.'

Mr Balaclava and Chewbacca backed away, and Roman Kosarev, who had been waiting at the door, was ushered in. He had a notepad full of bollocks questions; his recorder was switched on; a cameraman was standing at his shoulder. But, as he sat down, he visibly recoiled. Either my appearance or my odour had offended him. Then, straight off the bat, he accused me of being a Nazi, and I noticed that he was speaking with a weird Californian twang, presumably to connect with any Putin fans in the West. I sighed. This was yet another show and I'd become tired of it. I was bored with being used as a propaganda tool. And I was angry – very angry. Not that I was going to reveal my emotions to the enemy or their client journalist friends. By kicking off or admitting how I really felt, I'd be playing into Russia's hands. Instead, I buttoned my lip and tried to think of happier times.

But they all seemed to be fading away.

A few days later, a man claiming to be the prison commander's right-hand man visited our cell. As we stood at the back wall, our hoods on, he asked if any of us had taken a shower in the past couple of weeks. I couldn't tell whether he was winding us up or not – it wasn't as if we'd been given en-suite facilities. My last proper shit-shower-and-shave must have been sometime before the war had kicked off and my pants were clinging to my thighs and arse cheeks like a second layer of skin.

'Er, no,' I said, nervously.

There was shouting in Russian. '*Vasylich is lying!* He hasn't taken them for a shower. They've just told me.'

Someone, presumably Vasylich, was in trouble.

Eventually, we were dragged away from the CCTV cameras. For the crime of answering truthfully, Vasylich, whoever he was, then had us beaten and the guards used their heavy boots, fists and truncheons to work over our legs, backs and arms. After a while, these more traditional forms of brutality must have become boring, because I was then thrown into a doorframe and kicked up a staircase. Then a voice ordered me to run forward at full speed.

'What do you mean?'

A fist clattered into my ribs. Somebody was yelling, 'Run, shithead!'

With my hood on, it was impossible to see what was in my path, but I jogged and then ran until, inevitably, I collided with a wall, face-first, and hit the deck hard. My vision blurred. Above me, the guards laughed and cracked jokes.

Once everyone had caught their breaths – our assailants and us – we were led upstairs to a dank and gloomy bathroom. Someone handed me a set of electric hair clippers.

'Shave your heads,' said a guard gruffly. 'Then shower. You have twenty minutes.'

He pointed to a tap in the wall. When I looked up, I noticed the showerhead and crossed my fingers that the water we were about to wash with was slightly less manky than the yellow liquid we'd been drinking. And then I saw the most horrifying feature of all. There was a mirror. Approaching it slowly, I gawped at the figure in the reflection. It was me, but in shadow form. I looked disfigured and unrecognisable. My skin had turned almost translucent and it was possible to track the sharp edges of my jawline, cheekbones and eye sockets. There was zero fat on me and my ribs were sticking out in neat little rows. *I looked like a fucking radiator.* After not seeing a mirror for months, the sight of my physical decline was a major shock.

Trying my best to mask the horror, I glanced at the others as they stepped forward and assessed their appearance. We all looked like shit. I stank something terrible, and my hair was long, matted and greasy. My breath was ripe too. Because I hadn't brushed my teeth for weeks, my molars had turned furry and my tongue was covered in a foul, yeasty gunk. I'd even attempted to scrape away the plaque from my gum line with my fingernails, which were also coated in filth. I was falling apart, not that there was any reason for the Russians to fret over my oral health or to take an interest in our personal hygiene.

Sadly, I ran the clippers over Dimitri's head and began to feel the onset of nerves. *Something was happening.* As several thick clumps of hair fell to the floor, I felt increasingly dehumanised and also a little scared. I sensed the three of us were about to be put on show yet again. *But for what?* And then I realised. During my last propaganda video, Kosarev had been offended by the sight and stink of me. *So that was why I'd been granted a DPR-style spa session!* Somebody had decided that my appearance was bad public relations.

These fuckers, always thinking of the optics, I thought, darkly.

When my hair had been shaved, I checked myself out in the mirror again, hoping for a miraculous transformation. I looked even worse. Oleg turned on the shower, which was pump-operated, and we took turns washing under a rush of surprisingly warm water. Then we dried, using our dirty clothes as makeshift towels. I did what I could to clean the wounds in my leg and wrist, but it was impossible. The stitches looked manky and the dressings were now pus-soaked and giving off a nasty whiff. I hoped they wouldn't become seriously infected, but without soap or antiseptic I had little chance of fixing the issue.

Knowing I shouldn't dwell on the negatives, I tried to get a laugh from the others. 'I'm like a brand-new man,' I said, pretending to spruce myself up at the sink. But it was all bollocks: I felt like crap. Then I reminded myself that a shower was definitely better than an electric shock to the ear, so I took the situation as a win. There wasn't time for anything else: the guards were ordering us out into the corridor for another beating. As the blows rained down on my body, I repeated the joke in my head. *Shaun, your pits and bits have been washed and you feel like a brand-new man.* I hoped that if I told the lie often enough, I might actually believe it.

Eventually, as we were led away, a guard instructed us to stand and stoop forward, so that we were bent over double. Then, one by one, the Black Mamba was released onto our shoulders. The heavy thud knocked the wind out of me and I dropped to my knees. As I gasped for air, I felt temporarily paralysed, as if my spine had been shattered and a lung had been punctured in the strike. But the pain wasn't going to break me. I wouldn't allow it.

Putting on a defiant face, I got to my feet and cracked a joke. 'Oh, I think you've fixed my dodgy disc,' I wheezed.

A few kicks to the ribs reminded me not to play the funny man. Dimitri, who had made the mistake of laughing, received the same treatment. When we were led back to our cell and the door had clanged shut, we both groaned and giggled, even though the laughing aggravated our bruised backs and shoulder blades.

This time, the pain was worth the laughs.

*

Boredom was the worst part of captivity, and it took every ounce of mental strength to stop my brain from caving in. The Weight was threatening to drag me down again. I fretted that my mobile phone had been discovered. I stressed about Larysa. Then I feared for my son. I wondered how he was coping in England.

How's he doing in his new job? I thought. *He's supposed to be having the time of his life, with everything ahead of him . . .*

Later that night, I even worried that I might never feel the sun on my face again or experience the crunch of sand beneath my feet during a beach stroll. In those moments, I did whatever it took to distract myself. I chatted to Dimitri; I tried my best to communicate with Oleg. But it was hard to shake the feeling that I was slowly losing everything that made me a human being and an individual. Every time I used the bucket, the swampy stink wafting up from my undercarriage turned my stomach, even after the shower. What I would have given for a bar of soap.

Emotionally, I was in a very dark place. Maybe it was the wash and a brief reminder of what self-care could feel like, but more than anything I wanted to take pride in my appearance again. A couple of days later, when I found a small stone in the corner of our cell, it felt like an epic discovery. Suddenly I had a makeshift nail file and I set about cutting down my gnarly toenails, using the pebble's rough surface to break and smooth the crusty edges, making sure to do my work quickly, so as not to attract the attention of anyone watching on CCTV. I worked on one toe for a minute or so. Then I put the stone away, returning to the effort once I'd felt enough time had passed. The process gave me a sense of purpose. It also created the idea that I was getting one over on the guards. I felt less like a tramp, but I made sure not to spend too much time on my fingers. They were on show in every propaganda video and I wanted to look like the absolute dregs. It was important my appearance reflected the reality of my existence. The world needed to know I was being treated like shit.

Whenever the death-metal soundtrack died down, I continued studying the rhythm of the prison. Although we couldn't see anything outside our cell, it was still possible to get a handle on what was happening just by listening. At first I believed that I'd found a clear sense of timing based on when the buzzers sounded. *Six in the morning; ten at night.* But after a while, the general prison activity around those timings seemed to shift. After a few weeks of captivity, the woman who dropped off our daily bread rations seemed to arrive much later than she had done at the beginning. It had also been possible to get a handle on the time of day based on the guards' shift patterns, which usually changed over at around eight in the morning. As the prison was running on a military schedule, these events were meant to happen like clockwork. So when the morning buzzer started going off *after* the guards had changed shift, I knew.

The bastards were changing the alarm settings to fuck with our heads.

If the music in the Black Site stopped for longer than a few minutes, it meant something was happening – either one of us was being taken away for a propaganda video, or somebody important, and possibly scary, had arrived at the prison. At those times, my ears pricked up because the moments of stillness often delivered a sense of where we were in the prison and what might be going on around us. Sometimes it was possible to hear a car or truck backing up nearby. That meant our cell was near an entrance of some kind. Occasionally, the sound of an engine cutting off was followed by a metallic clanging noise.

'That's the metal steps at the back of a prison van,' said Dimitri one morning. 'They're bringing more people in.'

He was right. Over the next few days, the clanging steps became a regular sound and we often heard the guards shouting and screaming German phrases, the kind used in old war films. *Achtung! Schnell!* The word *Nazi* was yelled a lot too, which meant that the Russians had captured more Ukrainian troops and Putin's bullshit narrative was still being taken as gospel among the DPR workforce. Our suspicions were later confirmed when we heard someone moving around in the cell next to ours. There was a small hole in our wall, near the ceiling, and the noise of footsteps, snoring and bloody violence often echoed into our tiny space. One of the guards even referred to the mystery resident as an 'Irish Pig'. Weirdly, it felt nice to have a next-door neighbour. But whenever I was tempted to call out to them or say hello, I thought better of it. Just the idea of being cracked in the spine by the Black Mamba gave me the fear.

I was called into a meeting at the Black Site with a character called Popov, who, if the Russians were to be believed, was acting as my social worker. After being banged up for around four weeks, it felt like a sick joke, but he had some news for me. Apparently, my captors had decided that I should be exchanged for the pro-Kremlin Ukrainian politician Viktor Medvedchuk – godfather to Putin's daughter – who had been placed under house arrest in Kyiv. Suddenly, I felt adrenalised, maybe even hopeful, though I sensed a sting in the tail was coming. Popov confirmed my fears by explaining that, for the swap to happen, it would be down to me to push the idea through several media outlets in the West. There was a caveat, however. Popov was adamant that the Donetsk People's Republic was a legitimate state and should be recognised as such by any media types I spoke to.

'Shaun, who are the best journalists for you to contact, to tell them of this plan?' he said.

I had to think fast. No way was the British government going to negotiate with people they presumably considered to be terrorists. I also suspected that such a deal would require the Ukrainian leadership to agree to Medvedchuk's release, rather than anyone in the UK. Then there was the fact that no British newspaper would validate the DPR as a legitimate state. But I had to give myself a lifeline. I wasn't sure if anyone was seeing the propaganda films that were being made, or if they were even being released. However, if it became common knowledge at home that I was being held hostage, some pressure might be applied for my release. In the end, I rattled off the names of a few prominent newspapers, making sure to mention their political preferences, before eventually recommending the *Sun*.

Popov looked interested. 'Why them?'

'Because the *Sun* appeals to a broad spectrum of people,' I said. 'I think some of the other papers might get a bit stuffy about what you're trying to say.'

Popov handed me a phone. 'Ring them. And don't forget to explain that the DPR have captured you and are holding you.'

I heard the British ring tone. Popov gestured at me. 'Oh, and Shaun? Don't talk about the conditions you are living under.'

I soon got through. Having convinced a receptionist that, yes, I was indeed Shaun Pinner and not some chancer or YouTube influencer looking to make a name for myself, I was passed over to a journalist on the *Sun* news desk.

'I'm in the Donetsk People's Republic in east Ukraine,' I said, doing my best to follow Popov's instructions. 'And I have a message for Boris Johnson.'

I heard the bloke calling people over to his desk, but pressed on.

'I wish to be placed on the prisoner exchange scheme and to be exchanged for Viktor Medvedchuk.'

The *Sun* journalist cut in. 'Shaun, are you OK? Is your life in danger?'

'I'm OK. I'm being treated well. I'm holding my weight at least.'

It was the closest I could get to revealing that I was slowly being starved to death without alerting Popov.

Frustratingly, the plan backfired. A few days later, I was taken back to Popov's office and this time the bloke looked furious. When he held up a phone and showed me the latest edition of the *Sun*, I understood why. I saw my photo. It had been placed underneath the headline 'Captured Brits forced by Russian troops to call for release of Putin's "Prince of Darkness".' Then I scanned the copy and my stomach knotted. Rather than running the text I'd been ordered to read under duress,[6] the story referred to me as being brave and focused on a quote from Medvedchuk's wife.

I, Oxana Marchenko, spouse of opposition politician, people's deputy of Ukraine Viktor Medvedchuk, address the relatives of captured citizens of Great Britain Aiden Aslin and Shaun Pinner.

---

6 The *Sun* later explained that they had decided not to run the staged interviews under advice from the British Foreign Office.

It is in your power to ask the PM of your country Boris Johnson to influence Ukrainian leadership and to achieve Aiden and Shaun's release by their exchange for . . . my husband Viktor Medvedchuk.

Popov snatched the phone back, presumably to stop me from reading any other news headlines or checking the latest horoscopes from Mystic Meg. 'Why do they say you are being brave, Shaun?' said Popov. 'What have you done to be a hero?'

Not expecting that I would have to deliver a crash course in media studies to the DPR's secret police, I did my best to explain. 'Well, you've got to understand that the papers in the UK are owned by different people, with different political positions,' I said. 'They respect different political parties and have different opinions on certain events – like this one.'

Popov was leaning forward. His mood seemed to have calmed. *He was learning*. And that, presumably, would please his masters.

I pressed ahead. 'The description of me will change from paper to paper. Another one might take a different view of me altogether.'

'What does your government think of this?' said Popov, waving the phone.

'What do you mean?'

'Well, why doesn't your government tell the newspapers what to write?'

I smiled. The bloke had no idea how the UK media operated. 'In the UK and the West generally, there's no major government control over the media,' I said. 'We have a free press. They can spin a story however they like.'

Popov snorted disbelievingly. He then waved for a guard to take me away. 'OK, Shaun. Thank you for the helpful information,' he said. 'We will be doing more of these media chats.'

He wasn't kidding. Shortly afterwards, I was ordered to contact Boris Johnson through the Department for Environment, Food and Rural Affairs (Defra), which I knew would be a total disaster. This thought was proved correct when I was eventually put through to Barbara on Defra's reception desk.

'Hello, Defra?' I said, trying to keep my voice straight. 'Can I speak to the prime minister, please?'

Barbara rightly tried to cut me off. She knew a dumb phone call when she heard one. 'I'm sorry I can't help you wi—'

I babbled. 'Look, I'm a hostage in the Donetsk People's Republic and I'm being ordered to get a message to Boris Johnson.'

There was an awkward silence on the other end of the line. Barbara must have been stumped. I pictured her at a desk in some drab, soulless office in Whitehall, surrounded by stationery, piles of never-ending paperwork and a mug of hot tea.

What I'd give to swap places right now . . .

'This is a bit above my pay grade,' she said eventually.

I didn't doubt that for a second. A hand came over my shoulder and slammed the phone down. Somebody standing behind me delivered a firm reminder that I needed to make the exchange happen. And that if I couldn't, I'd soon be going to court, in a trial that might end with me being executed.

There were zero good days in the Black Site, but weekends were the worst. *I hated them.* Mainly because I assumed that a lot of people in the UK were putting their feet up after a long week at work. Even with the national media being alerted to my situation, I worried about the idea that people in power were with their families and loved ones – *because that's what I'd be doing in their position* – rather than establishing how to free a POW like myself. The Black Site noticeably slowed down at the weekends too. On Fridays my now regular trip to the Prosecutor's office brought a little novelty factor, but on Saturdays and Sundays I knew I wasn't going to be speaking to Popov, Barbara from Defra or a tabloid journalist. Instead, I'd be stewing in my cell.

At random intervals during the week I was being forced to call all sorts of people that the Russians believed, hilariously, could help facilitate the Viktor Medvedchuk exchange. The unsurprising first choice was Volodymyr Zelenskiy, but also on the list, weirdly, was Princess Beatrice – the daughter of Prince Andrew. Not unexpectedly, these conversations were either cut short by a savvy switchboard receptionist or aborted in comical fashion. When I actually managed to get through to a UK government civil servant one morning, Popov's phone went off with a novelty ringtone, right as we were halfway through a conversation in which I'd claimed to be alone and acting of my own free will. The timing was almost comical. Popov then swore loudly in Russian.

'Er, is there someone there with you, Shaun?' asked the voice on the other end of the line.

Popov scowled as he switched his phone to silent.

'No, I – I'm alone,' I stammered, even though it was bloody obvious that I wasn't.

Meanwhile, my conversations with Mr Balaclava were becoming even more surreal, and as our talks relaxed, the two of us appeared to bond. I noticed that, over time, my interrogator had become less interested in the war and more fascinated by the cultural differences between Britain and Russia. Knowing that alliance-building in an incredibly hostile environment might eventually prove the difference between living and dying, I was more than happy to cultivate the relationship. (And I understood full well the concept of Stockholm syndrome, so I wasn't falling into that trap.) Then one day, Mr Balaclava gave me a short list of Russian film recommendations and I pretended to be interested, even though they all carried a heavy focus on Chechnya and their recent military encounters. (I didn't memorise a single title.) What it told me, though, was that the FSB hadn't yet hacked into my Netflix account. Had they done so, they would have learned that the new *Ghostbusters* movie was more my thing.

One downside to these trips was that Dimitri had started to suffer from serious FOMO. That might sound weird considering the scrutiny and humiliation I was sometimes being exposed to, but his minimal political value meant that Dimitri rarely left our three-by-two-metre space. The poor bloke was close to stir-crazy. If I picked up any news from the outside world, even something as trivial as the weather, Dimitri would treat it as top-class intelligence. To help lift his mood, I remained on the lookout for information that might be of interest. Whenever Popov presented me with a news article I'd appeared in, it was sometimes possible to read a couple of tiny snippets on the wider war. I knew where Dimitri's family lived and from what I could tell, the Russians hadn't yet swept into that part of the country. The information often gave him some relief, although it was slim pickings.

There were certain details I decided to keep secret, especially those rare occasions when somebody gave me a cup of tea at the Prosecutor's office. However, some things were harder to disguise than others. If I had managed to blag a cigarette, Dimitri had an uncanny knack for sniffing it out, usually before I'd sat back down in the cell.

The first time it happened, he looked at me sadly. 'You've been smoking,' he said.

Yeah. 'Sorry, mate . . .'

'What type of cigarette did they give you?'

'A Camel. Not my favourite.'

Dimitri fell back onto the mattress, closed his eyes and asked me to describe the smoke as it had filled my lungs. *Did it burn my throat on the way in?* He wanted to imagine the taste of tobacco as best he could. Eventually, he made a request. *Can you get me one next time?* Sadly, we both knew the DPR would never allow it, but I promised to try, if only to give him something to hold on to.

When it came to the subject of my potential release, it was hard to know what to say. When I'd first mentioned the exchange, Dimitri had been happy for me, but the sense of envy must have been crushing. Not wanting to add to his emotional turmoil, I made sure to temper any excitement I might have been feeling about the latest updates or developments. This also acted as a self-defence mechanism. Seeing as the Russians were still threatening me with a court case, plus a potential public execution, I didn't want to become overly optimistic either, and so if Dimitri ever stressed about the unknowns of his future, I pointed out that at least he wasn't going to be condemned to death by a kangaroo court.

To widen the fractures in our fragile union, the Black Site officials tried to play Dimitri, Oleg and me against one another. Whenever I returned from a propaganda meeting, I noticed that the portions of bread waiting for me were always much smaller than usual. The second or third time it happened, I couldn't help myself.

'Why is it every time I go away, I only get a little bit of bread?' I said, angrily.

Dimitri became defensive. 'The guards are doing it! We're not eating your bread.'

Sadly, because we were all embroiled in a brutal survival of the fittest, both scenarios were entirely plausible.

Judging by the noise, the Black Site had filled up, and other than the daily bread drop-offs and bucket changes, we didn't see much of the thugs who had battered us so frequently in previous weeks. Dimitri speculated that the facility was massively understaffed. He reckoned the Black Site employees were struggling to manage the growing number of POWs coming in as the war progressed. Given the reduced scrutiny upon us, the time had arrived to introduce myself to our new neighbour.

I stood on tiptoes to get closer to the hole in the wall. 'Oi, mate,' I whispered. 'What's your name?'

There was a beat. I heard footsteps shuffling closer. 'It's Paul. Paul Urey.'

'So what the fuck are you doing here?'

'I'm Red Cross, I got captured.'

So that's why Mr Balaclava had been so interested in the Red Cross! The Russians had obviously got their hooks into this chap and had wanted to confirm whether his backstory was legit or not. Seeing as I had mentioned that the Red Cross had long gone, there was a chance I might have dropped Paul in it. Either that or he was bullshitting me. I couldn't work out why he wouldn't have left with the rest of the organisation. *Something about this bloke's story wasn't adding up.*

'Are you lying?' I said. 'I thought you lot had pissed off when the invasion started.'

'No . . . *No.* Some of us stayed. Anyway, who are you?'

'Shaun. Shaun Pinner, I was with the Ukrainian Marines—'

'Fuck,' said Paul suddenly. 'Fuck. Fuck . . . *Fuck!*'

'What's up?'

There was a pause. 'I know exactly who *you* are. I've seen your mug all over the telly. I'm screwed, aren't I?'

I didn't have the heart to tell him what he should have known already.

I warned Paul that the only details we should be sharing were those already given up to Mr Balaclava. 'It's for your own safety,' I said. 'And ours.'

Paul explained how he had been captured by the DPR at a checkpoint near Zaporizhzhia at the end of April and that he was in there with another aid worker, Dylan Healy, though he was being held in a different cell. The DPR had accused them both of being mercenaries, before throwing them into the Black Site. A series of beatings and torture sessions had followed, but Paul was having a rougher time of it than most. While he was a couple of years younger than me, the bloke was in poor shape, overweight and a type 1 diabetic. That meant Paul needed regular doses of insulin, but because he couldn't speak Russian, communicating his medical situation had been impossible so far. Now he was physically fading.

'I can translate for you,' said Dimitri helpfully, perhaps hoping to find some sense of purpose by helping out another inmate.

'Yeah, he speaks Russian better than me,' I said. 'He can help.'

Then I turned back to Dimitri. 'Just for him, though,' I whispered. 'You don't want to become too useful in here. They'll never let you out.'

Paul had plenty of news regarding the wider war. Despite my fears of a nationwide collapse, Ukraine was sticking it to Russia's invading forces. I couldn't believe the country was still standing. That, in itself, felt like a massive psychological boost. But from what Paul was saying, a shitload of foreign fighters had come over the border to help with the scrap. Even better was the revelation that the *Moskva*, the flagship vessel in Russia's Black Sea fleet, had been sunk by an anti-ship cruise missile. This was possibly Russia's biggest naval loss in wartime for forty years. On hearing the news, Dimitri, Oleg and I fist-bumped quietly. *We were winning!* Then the Black Mamba rapped ominously on the door. One of the guards must have spotted us talking on camera.

'Shut up,' yelled a voice. 'And don't group together.'

We quietened down. But nothing was going to dampen our mood. Paul had dropped a positivity bomb. Everybody was feeling the good vibes.

'I saw your mum on the news,' he continued, once the guard had passed. 'You're famous now. Everyone's talking about how you're going to get swapped for some general or politician eventually.'

My head buzzed. The propaganda videos, plus those phone calls, had obviously made national news. Hopefully, deals were being made behind the scenes. Not wanting to add to Dimitri's woes, I changed the subject by explaining the Black Site's extensive list of dos and don'ts:

- Two buzzers go off – one to tell you to sleep, the other to wake you up.
- You can't kip during the day. And don't exercise in the cell.
- When the guards come into your cell, stand at the back of the room with your hood on and face the wall.
- Don't give the guards shit – no matter what they say or do.

But Paul didn't seem to be listening and I soon heard him snoring loudly through the walls.

Dimitri became edgy. 'No, Shaun,' he said. 'You have to tell him that this can't happen.'

I jumped up to the wall and did my best to wake Paul, knowing that his ribs were about to be pummelled if one of the guards caught him sleeping. 'Mate, wake up,' I said, as loudly as I could without alerting any sentries walking past.

Paul stirred. I heard him yawning.

'Don't fall asleep,' I said. 'If they come down angry, they'll beat the fuck out of you. Then they'll open our cell and we'll get the fuck beaten out of *us*.'

But I hadn't moved fast enough. Boots stomped down the corridor. They were gathering at Paul's door. A set of keys jangled in the lock. Then I heard screams as he was thrown at the walls and punched and kicked senseless.

'You Irish pig!' yelled one guard, over and over.

Feeling nauseous, I slumped on the mattress, head in my hands. Getting smashed up was bad enough. Hearing another person as they were being savagely beaten had become a harrowing side effect of life in the Black Site. It created a deep emotional trauma. When the thuds and grunts eventually came to an end and Paul was left whimpering on the floor, I tried to explain the consequences of his actions. But an hour or so later, he was snoring loudly and the sorry process began all over again. Then the guards took out their frustrations on us.

My guess was that a lot of Paul's problems were stemming from the fact that he wasn't militarily trained. He didn't understand the value of obeying orders to the letter and he certainly hadn't been schooled on the finer points of surviving in a POW situation. As a result, he was bound to make the same mistakes over and over again. Paul's situation also wasn't being helped by the fact that he was in medical danger. During my next interrogation a day or so later, I explained to Mr Balaclava that we had a prisoner near us who was in serious trouble.

'How do you know there is another English person in the cell next to you?' he said.

'Because the guards can't understand him and we've tried to translate.'

There was an awkward silence.

'He's having problems with his insulin,' I explained, hoping to dig myself out of a potential hole. 'Please can you get him a medic?'

Mr Balaclava grunted, which I took to be a positive sign, and later that night a doctor arrived to treat Paul. After he left, I was beaten by the guards for daring to mention that they'd required a translator. Apparently, it had made them look weak, but not that weak. The next day we were asked to translate for Paul yet again.

'If you don't help us, you will suffer,' yelled a guard.

We had been locked into a vicious circle of violence and helplessness.

Paul had been right. Talk of my exchange seemed to be gathering momentum inside the prison too. During yet another propaganda session, I was told, once again, how vital it was that I be swapped for Medvedchuk and my next task was to sell the same idea to the UK Foreign Office. In a video recording, I was forced to read from a script that addressed Boris Johnson and a long list of politicians. While I spoke, the thuggish journalist, Andrey Rudenko, did his best Phil Mitchell impression and loomed over me threateningly in his tacky leather jacket.

A cameraman yelled instructions: 'Tell them your life is in danger!' Then he pressed 'record'.

I ran through the words as best I could, but the script was a mess. Every sentence was clunky and I constantly stumbled over the words. The watching Russians weren't pleased with my efforts, least of all Mr Balaclava. Apparently, I'd not sounded scared enough. His eyes bored into me as I finished talking. He must have looked pretty angry underneath that mask.

'Listen, Shaun,' he said, ominously. 'You need to do better. *Much better.* It has to be authentic.'

'But that's the best I can do. I *am* scared . . .'

'Sell it harder next time . . . You know, I can add an element of realism by cutting off a finger or two if you'd prefer?'

I shook my head urgently. 'Yeah. There's no need for that. I'll give it another go.'

I threw myself into the role, imagining the pain as a bolt cutter chomped my pinkie in half.

'Mr Boris Johnson,' I said. 'Obviously, I'm Shaun Pinner.

'A lot's gone on over the last five or six weeks that I'm not fully aware of. Obviously, I understand that Mr Medvedchuk has been detained and we look to exchange myself, and Aiden Aslin, for Mr Medvedchuk.

'I would really appreciate your help in this matter and pushing this agenda. Myself, I've been treated well. Fully understand the situation that I'm in. We've been fed, watered, and that's all I can really say . . .'

My voice cracked with fear.

'I beg on my behalf, and Aiden Aslin's behalf, for you to help us in an exchange for Mr Medvedchuk.'

When the filming stopped, Mr Balaclava seemed satisfied.

'Perfect,' he said. 'Well done.'

I walked back to my cell and wriggled my fingers in relief. For now, everything was in one piece. Physically, at least.

18

In mid May, or thereabouts, Oleg was transferred to another facility. Having been taken away for an interview one morning, he was pushed back into our cell in the afternoon – wearing a brand-new set of clothes.

'I don't know whether I'm going for a trial or not,' he said as Dimitri translated. 'They said they might suspend my sentence, but nobody will explain what is happening to me.'

Oleg looked pretty freaked out.

He was taken away shortly afterwards and a new inmate showed up in his place the next day. It was *Morock*, the kid I'd met on the way to the Prosecutor's office. His name was Brahim and like me he'd been fighting with the First Battalion at Illich, but in the mortar division. Straight away, I warmed to him. Brahim was probably only twenty-one years old, but he seemed revved up on optimism and unfazed by our circumstances. I noticed that when Dimitri told him his story and how he dreaded a lifetime inside, Brahim refused to accept any negative chat.

'One hundred per cent, it's not going to happen like that,' he said. '*You're going home.*'

Brahim then explained how he suffered from ADHD, and that it had proved to be both a blessing and a curse. The positives could be found in his infectious spirit. He was forever cracking jokes, which helped to lift the mood, although it soon annoyed the guards. As we laughed together, the Black Mamba was smashed against the steel door of our cell.

'Stop laughing,' yelled a voice. 'Or I'll make you stop laughing.'

The negative side to Brahim's personality was that he wouldn't, or couldn't, stop yammering on, and as he careered from one subject to another without pausing, I knew he was going to drive me potty at some point. Even when the buzzer sounded that night, Brahim still chattered, though he at least lowered his voice. He finished the night by telling us that he spoke four languages, all of which he'd learned online, and before the war he'd been studying electromechanics.

Eventually, he calmed down, though not before he'd created some further drama by insisting on sleeping between Dimitri and me. For some reason, Brahim also refused to be separated from his prison-issued plastic hood. Whenever somebody rolled over in the night, the bag rustled noisily, waking up the group. Yet despite all this, Brahim's arrival felt like a breath of fresh air. Even Dimitri's gloomy mood was dissipating. For a while, the Weight fell from his shoulders.

I quickly realised that Brahim's occasionally annoying traits were massively outweighed by his infectious personality. That Friday, when we were taken to the Prosecutor's office, I noticed him doodling away on a piece of paper. When I looked over, Brahim had sketched an intricate technical drawing of a spaceship. It looked incredible.

I pointed to the design. 'Mate, what's that?'

'I draw these all the time,' said Brahim, shyly. 'I wanted to be a rocket scientist for a while, before the invasion kicked off.' Laughing, he then turned to the next page. 'But this one is better,' he said, pointing to a badly scrawled dick pic. Underneath, in big letters, Brahim had written the slogan 'Make love, not war'.

'Brahim, hide that one,' I laughed. 'Why have you done that?'

'Because there is always hope, Shaun,' he said. 'Don't forget it.'

Paul Urey had disappeared. We weren't sure whether the enemy had sent him, and the other NGO workers, deeper into Russia, or if something much darker was happening. We tried not to wallow in the negatives. Focusing on the issues we couldn't control wasn't going to help anybody, and before long the vacated cells in our corridor had been filled with more newly captured POWs. We heard the beatings and with them the screams and the pleas in different accents and languages.

Ni! Ni! Ni! Some of them were Ukrainian.

No! No! No! Others were British.

Go fuck yourself! One of them I knew.

The voice in the cell next to ours was undoubtedly that of a soldier called John Harding. *It had to be.* We had first met while fighting in Syria. A Falklands veteran and a very good combat medic, John was in his mid fifties at the time. He must have been close to sixty now, which didn't bode well, especially as he was bound to be on the receiving end of one or two pastings. Having been through the mill myself, and then watched the likes of Dimitri and Paul Urey as they were interviewed and beaten, I'd picked up on the pattern of play in the Black Site. The opening two weeks were all about shock; they were the worst. During that time, the most violence was inflicted and the interrogations were at their harshest. After that, the intensity tailed off, probably because the type of intelligence the Russian secret service were after, such as military positions and details about personnel and missions, was out of date by that point. From then on, if a prisoner kept his nose clean, he could expect a relatively easy ride. Though that in itself seemed bloody impossible.

I'd reached that point. As had Brahim and Dimitri. But John's arrival potentially placed me in the firing line again because he'd been in Moldova during that drunken weekend. *He had the* Happy Days *tattoo.* Aiden had it too, but his design had been done separately, several months later. This visible connection between us all had sometimes kept me up at night, as had my sunken mobile phone. But no one had yet connected the inked designs on Aiden's forearms to mine because we had been kept apart. There was a chance we were being interviewed by different people, too. I took further comfort when the DPR guards transporting us to and from the Prosecutor's office showed themselves to be a few cans short of a four-pack – I didn't expect any of them to make the connection either. But being so close to John suddenly opened up the possibility that someone might spot our ink and alert their superiors. If Mr Balaclava learned of the union between Aiden, John and me, I'd be electrocuted again, no doubt.

Judging by the insults being thrown his way, John had been accused of being an Azov soldier, as we all had. But the accusations sounded more pointed than before and were becoming increasingly aggressive. Whenever the guards entered his cell, John was screamed at for being a Nazi. He certainly took more beatings in his first few days than I had and that meant the enemy had something on him. Ironically, John was a totally different animal, ideologically and politically, to the manufactured Ukrainian right-wing aggressor conjured up by the Kremlin's propaganda machine. He was a patriotic lad, but very much on the left side of the voting spectrum. I recall him telling me that he was a staunch Labour man, though I'd generally avoided discussing politics with John in Syria. He had established himself as a handy debater, especially when it came to religion or politics. He liked to draw a person in and then intellectually rough them up. When he wasn't engaging in one-sided discussions, John liked reading poetry or reciting Shakespeare. Being a fly on the wall during one of his chats with Mr Balaclava would have been fascinating.

By the time John had got to Ukraine, he was a bit too old for the front-line stuff, so he ended up teaching combat-medic skills to the Azov National Guard before being transferred into the Marines like the rest of us. At the beginning, he schooled the troops on the basics of combat trauma medicine and how to deal with serious injuries. The higher-ups loved him because he was a former paratrooper with the British Army and had a wealth of experience. Later, while helping out in Ukraine, he saved the life of a commander whose legs had been blown off after stepping on a mine. Realising that his casualty was losing a dangerous amount of blood and fluids, John had attached a drip. The patient later described it as 'the best drink of his life', though he would need prosthetic limbs to walk again. Clearly, John loved working with the Ukrainian military. Like me, he enjoyed being an English *somebody* in a foreign country, and Mariupol felt like the perfect place to retire.

Though I was happy he was still alive, John's *Happy Days* tattoo had me worried. I feared a repeat of my first few interrogation sessions where I was stabbed and electrocuted. Because of that anxiety, it took me a few days to work up the courage to call out. The CCTV cameras were fitted with microphones; we had to assume they could pick up everything, though, granted, nobody had been attacked as we'd chatted to Paul Urey. On this occasion, the risks were much greater. If the Russian secret police eventually linked John to me – and decided that I was Azov too – any footage of us talking would only provide them with additional ammo, especially if the court case went ahead. Keeping my mouth shut, on the other hand, gave me plausible deniability.

In the end, I threw caution to the wind. 'John? *John Harding?*' I said, leaning up to the hole.

I heard John's feet as he shuffled closer. 'Yeah?'

I brought my voice down to a whisper. 'Mate, it's Shaun Pinner.'

'What?'

'*It's Shaun Pinner.*'

But John didn't respond. Then I remembered a sure fire way of making him laugh. Before I'd joined the Army, some Australian mates had given me the nickname 'Snowy'. At the time I'd bleached my hair blond and the moniker had then stuck with me throughout my military career. John had loved the gag and reminded me of it constantly.

'It's Shaun – *Snowy.*'

After a few seconds' silence, John spoke up. '*It's snowing?* What is this: some sort of fucking code?'

It was at that point I realised that John had been close to deaf while scrapping in Syria. Standing next to heavy artillery weaponry for forty-odd years will do that to a person. Getting bombed to pieces in Mariupol wouldn't have helped matters either.

'John, did you hear me?' I said again. But judging by the silence, it was clear that he hadn't.

I wanted to warn him of the Black Site rules. I wanted to tell him what to expect. I wanted him to know about the war and where Ukraine stood. And when the guards came in the next day and assaulted him so badly that he was left groaning and spluttering, I wanted to comfort him, and to tell him that everything was going to be OK. Even though I knew it probably wasn't.

The odds were being stacked against us. Even though there was a sense that the Russians needed POWs like Brahim, Aiden and me in order to secure the exchange of Viktor Medvedchuk, the Black Site had been designed in such a way that it crushed the spirits of anyone forced to exist within it, whether they were eventually being released or not. And there was no hiding place. Without a window, I went days without seeing daylight, which was bad enough. But the Russians also understood that a person's stomach acted as a second brain and that it could be used to destroy their emotional resolve. The food we were being given now felt like an act of violence in itself.

Living off nothing but bread and bacteria-riddled water for weeks was bad enough. The body needed plenty of liquid to digest just one loaf, and we were becoming dangerously dehydrated. After five weeks, even the act of going to the toilet felt like physical torture: I was shitting breeze blocks, and my guts cramped and went into spasm with every push. *But I wouldn't let it beat me.* I kept seeking out psychological wins and on those rare occasions when somebody offered me a ciggy at the Prosecutor's office, I took it as a massive gift. If I felt the sun on my hands while being transited from one place to another, I imagined a day at the seaside. The alternative was to go to a very bad place; to think, *I'm never getting out of here.* Dimitri would often fall into that trap, but I knew that a period of negative talk could easily become a self-fulfilling prophecy. Like Brahim, I was determined to shut it out.

Brahim also understood the value of small victories and we came up with some new methods of achieving them. Whenever we were driven to the Prosecutor's office, for example, we memorised the route to the Black Site's exit in the hope that if the opportunity to escape arrived we'd know exactly where to run. As soon as we were thrown back into our cells at the end of the day, we quietly debriefed on any new intelligence. Later, having realised that one of the guards hated us slightly less than the others, we did our best to befriend him. After a few days of chatting, he offered our cell a deal.

'If you sing the "Donbas Prayer", I'll get you a few extra slices of bread,' he said.

Knowing that the performance wasn't being filmed and wouldn't be used against us as propaganda in any way, we stood and gritted our teeth through the pro-Russian lyrics, which spoke about the sky being ablaze and of God being with Russia. When those victories arrived, and an extra portion of bread was pushed through the cell door, we celebrated as best we could. In what was becoming a war of attrition, it was the only control we had.

The small victories felt sweetest when the Russians were actively working to humiliate me. At some point towards the end of May, I was called to the Prosecutor's office for an interview with a woman who bore more than a striking resemblance to the prominent Russia Today editor and known 'face of propaganda' Margarita Simonyan. (Though I was never officially introduced to her.) Known to be a peddler of bullshit, she had been described by America's State

Department as someone who was 'adept at serving up lies as truth – and with a smile'. When I arrived, it was announced that she would be coordinating an interview through a series of pre-recorded questions on an iPad from the YouTuber Russell Bentley. Bentley was a pro-Putin American who also went by the nickname 'Texas'. If the rumours were to be believed, he had fought on the front lines with the DPR and was so entrenched in the community that he'd even been baptised in the Russian Orthodox Church.

Bentley certainly wasn't much of a media professional. As he spoke, using the woman who may or may not have been Margarita Simonyan as a conduit, he kept asking me questions that had clearly been written for Aiden. That led me to believe both of us were getting exactly the same treatment. Bentley later wanted to know about my family life and personal history.

'Have you done anything that could be considered good in your life?' he said, antagonistically. '*Anything at all?*'

What I would have given to punch him in the mouth, there and then. The same went for all of them. From time to time, the woman interjected with a question of her own, but as her English wasn't the best, she often relied on Popov, my caring, sharing social worker, to translate. It turned out that she was just as offensive as Bentley.

'Where did you get your tattoo?' she said, pointing to the *Happy Days* design on my arm.

Here we go, I thought. *She knows.* I then repeated the story of my time in Moldova and how I'd watched a World Cup game with mates. I told her about the drinking and the half-cut decision to get inked up. As I spoke, I noticed that the woman's mouth was contorting in disgust. She looked angry. Then she turned to Popov and spoke in Russian.

'The word you're looking for is *bullshit*,' he said, smiling.

'Yes, bullshit!' said the woman, staring at me. 'Your story is bullshit.'

I shrugged. I couldn't have cared less if a known Kremlin mouthpiece (or her lookalike) believed me or not. Her entire image had been built upon lies.

'Why would I bullshit you?' I said. 'What would that get me? I'm in prison already, maybe with a death sentence coming my way. It doesn't really make any odds to me.'

For a moment, the woman seemed lost for words. The corners of her mouth twitched with anger. 'Well, it's a horrible tattoo anyway,' she said, sounding like a ten-year-old brat.

The insults were for show. The aim was to justify Putin's invasion of Ukraine by presenting people like me as being inherently evil. Whenever my motives for supporting Ukraine were questioned, I repeated the same line that I'd given to Mr Balaclava, Popov and the Prosecutor: *I'm married to a Ukrainian woman. Ukraine is my home and I was defending it.* The fact that I was on show to an audience of millions on a channel that in all likelihood was under surveillance by British security services meant I had a platform. I raised my wounded wrist whenever possible. It wasn't likely to speed up my release, or any potential exchanges that were being discussed, but a screenshot or a headline might keep me in the public debate for a few days more. The more I was in the line of sight, the more my situation would be a talking point. If people were discussing me on the telly or in the papers, the pressure might increase on the individuals assessing my value in a prisoner swap.

The woman seemed to read my mind. 'How are you being treated?' she said.

There was no point in lying. I looked like a bag of shit. 'Well, I haven't eaten for two days . . .'

'Would you like a burger?'

Are you kidding? Not wanting to look a gift horse in the mouth, I nodded. 'Yes, please. And a ciggie too.'

Reticence wasn't going to get me anywhere. *If you don't ask, you don't get.*

A cigarette was thrown across the table. Somebody held up a lighter. I sucked in the tobacco. My lungs burned and the toasted, smoky flavour tingled in my mouth. Then from across my shoulder, a guard passed over a takeaway burger.

'That for me?' I said nervously, fearing yet another mind game.

Everybody nodded. They were trying to come across as benevolent hosts. 'Yes, Shaun – *enjoy.*'

I hadn't eaten meat for months. I tore at the wrapper and bit into the bun. *Bread. Beef. Cheese. Gherkins. Onions. Ketchup.* Oh my God, it tasted like heaven. Oil and fat dripped from my chin. Even though the burger was recently microwaved and still piping hot, I devoured the lot in under a minute, making sure to lick my fingers afterwards. I hadn't washed my hands with soap for ages, and my nails were covered in filth, but I didn't care. My taste buds had finally come back to life.

19

That cheeseburger had barely touched the sides and I wasn't anywhere close to feeling full. When well fed, well watered and militarily conditioned, I usually weighed around eighty-four to eighty-six kilos. But the exertion of fighting in a lengthy siege had taken its toll, as had surviving capture and torture, and living in my own shit for nearly fifty days. I couldn't have weighed any more than sixty-five kilos. Physically, I was still able to withstand the beatings that were occasionally dished out in our cell, but my greatest fear was that I would starve to death long before I was sent to trial. *Death by bread.* It wasn't the most glamorous way for a warrior to go out. If I was to eventually meet Dima at the Gates of Valhalla, I didn't fancy telling him that I'd been ended by a diet of *white sliced* and a Petri dish of waterborne bacteria.

'I can take the pastings,' I said to Brahim one morning. 'I can even take the electrocutions. But the lack of decent food is ripping my heart out.'

I yearned for the days of feeling grumpy at home about a lack of caffeine or sugar. I vowed never to turn 'hangry' again if I somehow escaped the Black Site.

Brahim was struggling too. But, unlike me, he was more inclined to open his mouth and complain. After returning from the Prosecutor's office one afternoon, he told me how he'd explained that we were being starved half to death. He'd then laid it on thick and told the Prosecutor it was unlikely we would live long enough to face trial. The way

Brahim told it, this news had come as a complete shock to those in charge, even though we'd assumed the abuse was being dished out at their request.

'They told me we were being transferred to another prison.'

'*What?*'

'Yeah, we're getting out of here,' he said, unable to contain his excitement. 'The Prosecutor was like, "OK, Brahim. We're going to move you, then."'

I didn't want to get my hopes up, especially not in front of Dimitri. 'When?' I whispered.

'He thinks a couple of days.'

The following morning I was sent to the Prosecutor's office to sign some more paperwork for the forthcoming legalities. In the same drab office, with its dark wood panelling and weird portraits of random Russian military figures, and surrounded by policemen, investigators and lawyers, I asked outright. *Can we move prisons?* A translator nervously relayed the request.

The Prosecutor nodded. 'Yes, next week you will go to a civilian prison,' he said.

My heart hammered. *Surely he was messing with me?*

'It's a place we put people before they go to trial,' he continued. 'Because the investigations into your activities have been concluded, there is no need for you to stay where you are.'

He clicked a document on his computer screen and I spotted a number of photographs taken from my social-media accounts. As the Prosecutor scrolled through them one by one, he studied me carefully.

'Besides, you don't even look like your social-media photos any more,' he said.

There were conditions, though. *There were always conditions.* Before being shunted out to the transit prison, I'd have to see a psychiatrist, so that my mental state could be assessed. It didn't take a genius to work out that mentally I was bloody well fucked, like most people being held captive. But protocol was protocol, and a couple of days later, Brahim and I were driven to a psychiatric hospital for what the Prosecutor had chillingly described as 'an evaluation'. The thought of my psyche being prodded and probed didn't exactly fill me with optimism. And thinking back to the kindly-looking old lady who had masqueraded as my translator several weeks earlier, part of me wondered if this was yet another ruse and I was being duped into giving up more information on my background and family life – stuff that might be used as leverage against me.

Having arrived at the institution, we were placed in a small cell with iron bars and a bench to sit on. Like everything, it felt newly put together. Probably because it hadn't been needed before the invasion. When I looked about the place, I realised we were in a corridor of small offices. People were walking about with folders and paperwork. Everyone looked very busy. *They must have had a rush on, what with all the POWs that were showing up.* Behind us was a window and outside I noticed a courtyard, which looked uncannily like the prison facility used in the movie *The Shawshank Redemption*. It had a concrete expanse that was some kind of recreation area and high walls with a ribbon of barbed wire running across the top. There was even an armed sentry post on each corner. If this was a psychiatric hospital, then some very dangerous people were being held here.

It wasn't long before I was called into the psychiatrist's office for what would be the first of two interviews. The first shrink was a fresh-faced man in his early thirties, and something about his appearance suggested that he was a military employee. His hair was cropped in the classic 'jarhead' style; he wore a fancy suit that accentuated a tall, slender frame, and I could easily see him in combat fatigues. He was efficient too. Before I had a chance to sit down, the shrink asked me one or two quick-fire questions about my personal life. He wanted to know about my family, my upbringing and whether I had a history of mental-health issues.

My internal dialogue snapped back with several imagined, snarky answers. *Only after I'd been banged up by you lot,* I thought, before deciding to stay quiet.

He gestured to my wrist. 'What did you do to yourself?'

'Look, I had a misunderstanding. A guard told me I was getting executed the next day, so I tried to kill myself in prison.'

'Yes, but why did you stab yourself there?'

'Like I said, it was a misunderstanding. They told me I was going to be killed. I didn't want to be killed. What would you do if a prison guard said they were going to slice your throat? I didn't want to go down that way. They were beating me up—'

'What did you expect was going to happen?' said the psychiatrist coldly. His bedside manner left a lot to be desired.

'And I was in isolation—'

'We were never going to kill you,' he snapped, becoming annoyed. 'Do you understand?'

I nodded.

'Well, not like that anyway,' he continued. 'But if you get sentenced to death, then that will change.' He looked at me carefully. 'Do you have any problems now?'

I shook my head. As he scribbled down a series of notes,

I took in the room. It was the size of a broom cupboard. There were no bookshelves or paintings on the wall. The psychiatrist sat at a cheap-looking desk with nothing more than a computer and a notepad. My mind ticked over. *Were they really going to move us to another prison, or was this yet another cruel form of torture?* I wouldn't put anything past these bastards.

Eventually he looked up. 'OK, everything is good here,' he said, gesturing to the door. 'You will speak to my colleague later.'

I stood up and was escorted back to the holding cell. When I arrived, another man was sitting across from me. I failed to recognise him at first because his head was bowed. He was a big dude; his dark hair had been shaved and his skin was grey and sallow. But on looking closer, I realised it was a familiar face. *Aiden Aslin!* Carefully, I called out to him. When Aiden looked up, he smiled.

'Where the fuck have you been?' I said, trying to make him laugh.

Aiden stood up and came closer. I could see that he was battered and bruised. '*Shaun?* You're still alive? Fucking hell, mate. They told me you were dead . . .'

That made sense. When Mr Balaclava had electrocuted me for not mentioning I'd previously worked as a trainer with Azov, he'd claimed that Aiden had thrown me under the bus. I'd always suspected the Russians might have tricked him into spilling some information on me.

'Are you OK?' I asked.

'Yeah. Better now. I was stabbed, but they've put me in a transit prison. It's not so bad. It's more like a normal prison. I'm not getting smashed about so much in there as I was before. And I'm getting fed—'

I couldn't believe it. '*What?* What are you eating?'

'Oh, just pasta and Grechka. There's tea in the morning and the evening, too.'

I fumed. What we would have given for *just* pasta, Grechka and a hot cuppa.

Aiden then told me he had been driven to the hospital and his prison was only a few minutes away. Then I noticed the empty sweet wrapper in his hand. *He was chewing.*

'What's that you've got there?' I said.

'Chocolate. Want one?'

Bloody hell: *did I?* 'Oh, mate, give it here,' I said. 'I haven't seen chocolate for months, let alone eaten any.'

When he handed one over, I inhaled it. The explosive, satisfying sugar rush felt like a taste of home.

After a few minutes, a guard led me into another broom-cupboard-sized room. Sitting at a table were the psychiatrist I had spoken to earlier and a furious-looking bald man with a grey moustache. In the middle sat a woman with immacu-lately groomed dark hair and an expensive designer suit. She was tanned and healthy. Put together, with their casual but pricey-looking outfits, the trio resembled a fucked-up ver-sion of the *Ugly Betty* cast. It was hard to take them seriously.

The woman cleared her throat and introduced the group as a panel of psychiatric experts. According to her, they would be determining my suitability for transfer from the Black Site and then trial. 'All of us will be making a determi-nation on your sanity,' she said. 'But I will have the final say.'

I raised my hand to ask a question. 'How will I be executed?'

The woman looked confused. 'What do you mean?'

'The punishment for my crimes is the death penalty, but nobody has explained how it will actually be done.'

'That is not going to happen,' she said. 'You'll be home in six months.' The woman seemed almost compassionate.

'Really?' I said, unsure of whether her claim was genuine.

'Yes, really. You'll go through trial, you'll be convicted, but they will send you home . . . *eventually.*'

Everything felt staged. My head was on fire. Someone was lying to me and I wasn't yet sure whether it was the officials in the Prosecutor's office or these psychiatrists. Emotionally, I was being pulled from pillar to post and I couldn't quite tell whether this was a deliberate tactic or if I was so tired and hungry that my brain couldn't comprehend the information being delivered. As I sat with the revelation, not wanting to get my hopes up, both men left the room and the woman opened the file in front of her. The atmosphere had changed. It was time to assess my mental state.

'Have you read Trotsky or any Russian literature?' she said.

Random. The question threw me off guard. 'No.'

She glared at me, almost in disbelief. 'Why haven't you?'

'It wasn't on our curriculum at school. And why would I want to anyway?' Then I remembered my potential transfer to a prison where there was *just* pasta, Grechka and daily brews. 'I don't hate Russians, by the way.'

'OK, good to know,' she said. 'But would you work for a black man?'

Now I was really confused. '*Eh?* What do you mean by that?'

'Would you accept being told what to do by a black man? As your line manager or commanding officer?'

I immediately understood what was taking place. The Russians were pushing our buttons. They wanted to see how we might react when presented with some of their uglier political positions – the ones that clashed with my liberal, Western values. What I wanted to do was to tell my interrogators to go fuck themselves. *But I couldn't.* If this woman was telling the truth, then I could expect to be released, maybe in six months. More than anything, I wanted to see my family again, but kicking off might place my potential freedom in jeopardy.

'Of course,' I said, trying to sound unfazed. 'My last boss was from India. I'm from London. It's a very multicultural city. And I don't care what country a person comes from. As long as they can do the job, that's the most important thing. But I don't understand—'

'What about a homosexual boss?' said the psychiatrist. 'Would you work for one of those?'

Before I had a chance to answer, she had interjected: 'We don't have gays in Russia, by the way. And we certainly don't like the way that your family values are structured. You're tearing it apart. The West is tearing it apart with all your gays, your lesbians and your street parades. You put it in everyone's faces. *We don't want that.*'

'Surely you have a gay community?' I said, not wanting to explain to her that my son was gay. I was very proud of his bravery. He had shown guts when coming out and now he was living the life that he'd wanted. No way did I want his name being dragged into what was already an ugly political debate.

'We don't have any gays in Russia,' she said again firmly.

The ignorance was staggering. Taking a second to compose myself, I said, 'I respect family values just like you.'

The session, unbelievably, took an even more surreal turn. The shrink then claimed that Russia had won World

War II single-handedly, and that the Allies had lost only 400,000 lives in the process. I started to argue, but thought better of it. *It's like banging your head against a brick wall,* I thought sadly as I was later led back to my holding cell, my piss boiling with rage. Aiden had already been led away and Brahim was now going through the same sorry process. I hoped he could find a way to manage his emotions. But when he was later escorted back to the cell, Brahim looked bemused and angry.

'You OK, mate?' I said.

'The psychiatrist is a real dick. She was trying to wind me up with all this racist nonsense, because I'm from Morocco. I wasn't going to fall for her shit.'

'So what happened?'

'I told her, "How can you talk to me like that?" Then I pretended to be massively offended. Really, I was just doing my best to piss her off.'

By the look of it, his tactic had worked. The lead psychiatrist, flanked by two men – one of whom was wearing a white coat – was now striding angrily down the corridor towards us.

I looked at Brahim. 'What did you do?' I whispered.

But he just shrugged his shoulders and looked away. The cell was unlocked and the woman stood in the doorway. Then she started shouting at Brahim in Russian.

'Whoa, what's happening?' I said, trying to diffuse the situation.

The shrink turned to me. 'And you would understand, being that much older than –' she pointed at Brahim – '*him.*'

After the rant had finished, she reached into her pocket. Instinctively, I leant back, fearing the worst. *Did she have a cattle prod or some weapon?* Instead, she pulled out a handful of Ferrero Rocher chocolates and dished them out to both of us.

'Good luck to you,' she said and walked away.

I couldn't decide if it was a sign of good things to come, or the kiss of death.

John Harding had moved closer to the wall. Finally, he was catching more and more of the information we were trying to give him. We explained the rules of the Black Site and what he could expect during his first weeks of interrogation. John was fearful that the punishments being dished out to him were more severe because he had been wearing Azov-style military fatigues during his capture. Every now and then he coughed and groaned. He reckoned that one guard had cracked him so hard with a body blow that his sternum had broken.

'Well, he should know,' whispered Brahim, sadly. 'He is a medic.'

As he spoke, John became increasingly agitated. 'They've said they're going to kill me.'

'Yeah. Well, join the club, mate,' I said. 'Just get through the next week or so and you'll be all right. It gets a bit easier after that.'

More and more prisoners were now flooding into the facility and not all of them were Ukrainian. John told me that he had been brought in with a Swedish soldier. As far as I was concerned, this was further evidence that the war effort was being taken to the Russians and that an increasing number of fighters from all over Europe were joining in the battle, but under our current circumstances it was impossible to get a clear picture of how the conflict was developing. I hoped that once we were transferred, there might be a way of gathering more intelligence on Ukraine's standing.

According to the guards, we were only a day or so away from being moved. But not twenty-four hours after our psychiatric evaluation, the Russians had one last inhumane task for us to complete. As part of their propaganda campaign, they had decided to take Brahim and me back into Mariupol, so that we could be filmed pointing to the various positions we'd operated from during the siege. I felt sick at the idea. My final memories of that place were utterly bleak, full of deathly imagery, gut-churning smells and a heavy sense of loss and death. I certainly didn't want to go back there, not while it was under Russian control. I hated the thought of seeing a Mariupol that was utterly unrecognisable, with my home and all my favourite places razed to the ground.

When we were shoved into the back of a car with the Prosecutor and driven into what was left of the city, the reality of Mariupol's situation was more horrific than anything I could have imagined. High-rise flats were now toppled. Vast expanses of housing had been flattened. Some shopping districts were still on fire. A favourite café of mine was now a pile of smouldering rubble. Then I wondered if I would ever get to sip coffee as a free man again. It was as if my good memories were being deliberately torched in a sadistic act.

We passed what was left of Port City, a modern, European-style shopping district with a cineplex and bowling alley. Larysa and I used to go there all the time. Now there was nothing left of it other than a one-foot-tall outline of bricks and ash. I wanted to cry. The only time I'd seen devastation on a similar scale was while serving in Bosnia, during the early 1990s, when it had been bombed to bits. In Mariupol, everything appeared equally post-apocalyptic, like a scene from the TV show *The Last of Us*, and at times I struggled to look. The Mariupol I'd loved was gone. The Russians had destroyed everything in a remorseless carpet-bombing campaign without any consideration for human life. I wondered how many innocent civilians had been slaughtered here. It must have been in the tens of thousands.

'Oh my God,' I whispered under my breath. 'I don't want to see any more.'

The Prosecutor turned around in his seat angrily. 'You have to see,' he said. '*You* did this. *Your* people caused this damage.'

There was nothing I could do or say to argue otherwise, not without experiencing terrible consequences. Russia and the DPR had taken gaslighting to an industrial level.

Eventually, we came to a position I recognised from the fighting. We were back at Illich, the place I'd left nearly seven weeks previously, and I spotted some of the shell scrapes Bear had helped dig with his 'borrowed' JCB. The skeleton of a building we had once slept in was also visible. *Somewhere around here, Dima had died.* The heavy thoughts wilted my shoulders and crushed my insides. Then another car pulled up and Aiden was hauled into the street, surrounded by several Russian journalists. Immediately, I noticed that the invited media weren't that interested in Brahim or me. *It was all about Aiden.*

As we were frogmarched to a variety of positions once occupied by Ukrainian Marines, he was grilled on what had happened at each one. Why we'd been brought along was a mystery – they didn't ask us any questions. But the relief I might have felt at not being degraded further was quickly replaced by fear. A group of around fifty heavily armed troops were eyeballing us angrily. Some of them had pulled up in armoured vehicles; others were crawling out of the steelworks like rats. Their kit was mismatched and patched together. With their huge beards and neck tattoos, they looked like East London hipster barbers, and most of them were wearing trainers rather than combat boots.

Russian-friendly Chechens.

'They hold Illich,' whispered one of the guards as we headed into the now-bombed-out steelworks. 'Don't drift off. Stay close or they will shoot you. And we won't come after you. Because they will shoot us too.'

Clearly, the DPR were as terrified of the Chechens as everyone else, even though both groups were scrapping for the same cause. *I could see why.* The gunmen watching our every move looked more like a gang of lawless pirates than a disciplined military unit. As I stepped forward, feeling the crunch of broken glass, shrapnel and bullet casings under my feet, my stomach tightened. We were outnumbered and dangerously exposed, and I feared that Brahim and I might be thrown to the wolves at any point. A DPR guard shoved me violently in the back. 'Move, faggot!' he yelled in a show of force. Then he called out to a Chechen fighter who looked to hold a position of power.

'We are on a patrol with some prisoners,' he yelled. 'We won't be long.'

The commander grunted and I was pushed again. The shove nearly sent me to my knees and I staggered past the Chechens with my head bowed, hoping not to make eye contact with anyone, feeling sick at the realisation that a mob of killers and torturers had taken over my hometown. Humiliation pulled at my heart; I felt the anger rising. And then instantly a wave of calm came over me. When I looked up, the sun was peeking out from behind the clouds. It was the first time I'd felt warmth on my face in weeks. When I sucked in a deep breath, I smelled flowers.

Summer was coming.

PART THREE

Hope

20

We'd nicknamed one guard 'Pohuy', a Ukrainian word that, when translated, became a phrase roughly equivalent to 'I don't give a fuck'. Or, if you were moving in polite company, '*Whatever*'. Mainly, it was a figurative shrug of the shoulders.

'Mate, it looks like you've put on a few pounds.'

Yeah? *Pohuy. I don't give a fuck.*

It also described one Black Site guard to a tee because he was a weed, no more than nine stone wet through, and an irrelevant piece of shit. Of all the thugs in the prison, Pohuy gave us the most grief. He pushed us around. He kicked us when we were down, usually after a bigger and more fearsome individual had done all the hard work. If you had been hooded and cuffed – and rendered even more physically vulnerable than usual – it was Pohuy who would slam you into a wall. He was a massive cliché: the bully's victim who grows up, gains power in adulthood and then wields his authority over anyone who displays weakness. *Bloody hell, I hated seeing his smug face.*

But all of that changed at the start of June.

One morning, Pohuy opened our cell door and pointed at me.

'Come here, Shaun Paedo.'

Then he pointed at Brahim. 'And you. *You're going.*'

This was it. Just as the Prosecutor had promised, we were finally leaving the Black Site and being transferred to another corrective facility. Once there, we would await trial and a potential death sentence. Or not, if the psychiatrist was to be believed. It was all so bloody confusing.

I grabbed my hood and turned to Dimitri. 'This is it, mate,' I said quietly. 'We're moving prisons.'

He looked sad. 'Shaun, please. Don't forget—'

The memorised phone numbers. 'I've got it. Your parents will be my first call.'

We stood in the corridor, our hoods on and our wrists cuffed. 'Move,' said another disembodied voice nearby, and I was shoved and kicked out of the building and led towards the doors of a prisoner transport vehicle. As I walked, the hood moved about my face and I briefly spotted the type of van I'd seen on the news, usually when a murderer or an organised-crime boss was being driven to the Old Bailey. The DPR were obviously taking no chances with their POWs.

Everything was changing so quickly. In the prison cell I'd shivered non-stop with the cold, even when wearing a T-shirt and hoodie, and my guess was that the temperature had been close to zero at times. But above ground it was a very different story. The sun was fierce and I rapidly overheated. Rivulets of sweat trickled down my cheeks, neck and back, and whenever I inhaled, the plastic hood stuck to my mouth. It soon became hard to breathe and I worried about suffocating before we'd even reached our next destination. Then I heard the van door sliding open and someone grunting and groaning ahead of me. It was Brahim and he was being loaded into the back of the vehicle. I was forced in next and from under my hood I realised we'd been jammed into one of several cages. Each one was fitted with a small wooden bench, big enough for three people.

More prisoners were brought into the truck, until eventually the door slid shut, the engine started up and we moved away. Immediately, the driver picked up speed and as we turned a corner, the POWs in the rear were thrown about like marbles in a tobacco tin. My face collided with Brahim's skull and I let out a loud groan. Up front, the guards bellowed with laughter.

Brahim nudged me in the ribs. 'Make like a starfish,' he said, enthusiastically. *Was he laughing too?*

'What do you mean?'

'Shoulders back, legs out . . . *Make like a starfish!*'

When I tipped my head sideways to look, I noticed that Brahim had extended his legs and was leaning back, his shoulders and toes pressing against either side of the cage for stability. I mirrored the position and for a while the shift in balance seemed to help. I had control. That is, until we next careered around a corner and I ricocheted off a couple of walls before landing in a heap on the floor. A guard banged on the rear of the driver's cabin.

'Fuck you, asshole!' he shouted.

I recognised the voice as Pohuy's and felt relief. *I'd hopefully never have to see that tosser ever again.*

After a bruising journey of around fifteen minutes, I was eventually pulled from the truck and led into what I assumed would be our new home from hell. Even with my hood on, I realised that as well as Brahim and myself, John Harding had also been transferred. I heard him groaning and coughing nearby as a guard fussed around us. My body tensed. It was a force of habit. While holed up in the Black Site, I'd regularly been forced into a series of stress positions, especially if we were being held in a waiting area or interview room. In those situations, my arms were usually raised and

I was ordered to hinge forward at the waist, which set me in an excruciating, crouching pose. As I stepped into this new facility, I instinctively contorted myself into a similar shape, only for a guard to place his hand on my shoulder.

'You can stand up straight in here,' he said. The tone was cold but calm.

Another guard unlocked my cuffs and reset my hands in front of me, at a considerably looser setting. As our hoods were taken off and our faces checked against passports, I noticed that we were being instructed to perform certain tasks – to step this way, to walk through that door – rather than being verbally or physically abused. But more striking was the building itself. I was reminded of the scene in the movie *The Wizard of Oz* and its famous cinematic shift from black and white to Technicolor. Yes, we were undoubtedly in a prison. There were guards with truncheons; I heard steel doors clanging shut and my hands were still cuffed, but there was a different atmosphere altogether. One guard even seemed to be smiling, albeit only slightly.

Finally, we were introduced to the Kurator – the most senior warden in the facility – and immediately I realised that our lives had taken a turn for the better. The man was in his late forties, around five foot nine, with a head of dark hair. Dressed in jeans and a shirt, he looked much more relaxed than anyone I'd encountered in the Black Site, a beer belly sagged over his belt and a large set of keys dangled from his hip.

'Good morning,' he said, looking me up and down. 'How are you?'

'I'm OK,' I said, nervously.

The Kurator smiled. 'Good. Well, you are in an MGB-run prison and you will be held here until your trial has concluded. Don't worry, you will be treated OK, but only as long as you obey the rules. If not, we will make life very hard for you.'

'What are the rules?'

The Kurator waved a hand dismissively. 'There are other prisoners in your cell. They will explain.'

I had no idea how to react. Compared to the Black Site, this place seemed to be another world altogether and part of me wondered if the Kurator had been incorrectly briefed on what we really were. *Perhaps he didn't know that some of us were potentially facing a death sentence?* Certainly, the treatment we were receiving was the kind usually reserved for minor, first-time offenders rather than soldiers accused of acting as mercenaries, terrorists and enemies of the state. Even so, we were all strip-searched and given the rubber-glove treatment, which felt painfully invasive. Then I was eventually led to a cell where John Harding and two other Ukrainian prisoners were sitting, at which point I started to feel even safer. There were four beds. I looked around for a CCTV camera, but there wasn't one. Instead the cell had a squat toilet and a TV, which seemed to be playing the state-sponsored local news. In one corner, there was even a kettle.

Fuck me, I thought. *Are we in the Donetsk Hilton?*

At the back of the room was a window that overlooked a courtyard a few levels down. I turned to John. 'What's down there?'

'It's a paddock,' said one of the other prisoners in the cell. 'We get to walk for one hour, every day.'

For the first time in months, my fight-or-flight response settled – but only slightly. Every muscle felt physically lighter. The heft in my shoulders and back seemed to be loosening. I wondered how long the sensation would last.

Then I nodded to my new cellmates. 'I'm Shaun,' I said.

The two men introduced themselves as Marko and Andriy. Of the two, Marko was the smaller – he was a wiry guy with shaved grey hair, grey stubble and dark brown eyes. Andriy towered over him. He was well over six feet tall and packed with muscle. His blond hair was also shaved and his face seemed set in a permanent scowl. He looked like a bruiser. I scanned both their physiques for any signs of abuse or malnutrition, but they looked to be in good shape. Marko then explained he was one of several acting head-men in the prison. Most of the time he served as a liaison between the inmates and the guards working across our wing, but his position of power also granted him access to the items most highly coveted by incarcerated men. Within moments of sitting down, Marko offered us both cigarettes. Then he suggested we talk over coffee. I looked around and wondered where Brahim was.

'You are in Makiivka,' he said. 'Or, as it's also known, the Western Corrective Prison, No. 97.'

Andriy stretched out on his bunk. 'Why are you helping them?' he said. He didn't sound happy.

'Because we are in prison together,' said Marko. 'That makes us the same.'

He reached for a box of unworn clothes that had been placed under his bed.

'Here. Take what you need. My wife brings in this stuff for me all the time, but I don't get to use it.'

Weirdly, his kindness unsettled me. We had been in Makiivka for less than an hour. I was still hardwired to hostility, but Marko had shown me more generosity in five minutes than I'd experienced in months. It was too much, too soon.

At some point he's going to want cash sent to someone, I thought, darkly. *Or something worse . . .*

'Listen, Marko, this is very kind, but I can't repay you,' I said.

He laughed. 'You don't have to. Honestly, this is stuff I won't need.'

He gestured to the walls and the cell door. 'It's not like I have a lot to dress up for.'

John and I rifled through the kit, picking out new T-shirts and a pair of sandals each. The fresh cotton felt like luxury, and, as I removed my damp, stinking top and changed, I wanted to cry. I stank. I was ill and broken. The Black Site had stripped so much humanity from my soul, shred by shred, that emotionally I had changed, having been thrown into a game of survival with my fellow POWs. But with one gesture from a stranger, I felt a little closer to the Old Me – the husband, dad and friend that had existed before the war. It wasn't much, but at least it was something. John was thankful too. His broken sternum was still a painful issue and he was now suffering from pneumonia. Bright green snot dripped from his nose and there was nothing to him but skin and bone. Slowly, he lowered himself onto a bunk with a loud groan.

I shook Marko's hand and thanked him for his generosity. 'How come you're in here, mate?' I asked. 'What's your story?'

He looked at me cautiously. 'You might not be feeling so thankful when I tell you.'

'Go on . . .'

'Well, under different circumstances, we might have been shooting at each other . . .' Marko drew in a deep breath. '*I was with the DPR.*'

My chest tightened. After my early experiences in the Prosecutor's office, my antennae had been set to Code Red. I was constantly on the lookout for potential sympathisers or spies and there was a chance Marko was both of those threats.

'So why are you banged up, then?' I asked, pointing to the warden outside our walls. 'These are your people, aren't they?'

'Well, yes and no,' said Marko, sadly. 'When Crimea was annexed by the Russians in 2014, I too wanted independence from Ukraine and Kyiv. I wanted Donetsk to be a republic, able to make its own choices. I had successful businesses in Donetsk. I was even a minister in the local government and joined the military for a while. But I never wanted to be ruled by the Russians. I wanted Donetsk to be ruled by Donetsk.'

'So what happened?'

'I fucked up,' said Marko, lowering his voice. 'We had a new mayor. A man called Denis Pushilin. You may have heard of him?'

I sighed. *Yeah, I'd heard of him.* Pushilin was a controversial figure within Ukrainian politics, having risen to power in 2018 when his predecessor, Alexander Zakharchenko was assassinated during a bomb attack. When an election was called later that year, Pushilin became the official leader of the Donetsk People's Republic, though neither the EU nor the USA recognised the results, which they claimed had broken the terms of the Minsk protocol. The then Ukrainian president, Petro Poroshenko, even claimed the voting process had been messed up by a Russian dirty-tricks campaign.

'We didn't have an election process!' said Marko. 'I put something online about Pushilin, basically saying, "We're not electing these people, the Russians are. This guy's a thug and he's an idiot, blah-blah-blah . . ." The next thing

I know, the MGB, *the secret police*, are at my fucking house. They gave me a four-year sentence, for treason or some other bullshit charge.'

I thought of Oleg and his prison stretch for daring to criticise Putin on social media. *Was he enjoying a little taste of freedom now? Or was he stuck in a facility like Makiivka?*

Marko reached under his bunk and pulled out a pen and a piece of paper. Then he started scribbling.

'Here, take my email address,' he said. 'When the war is over and we are free, contact me so we can talk properly on these things.'

'Why?' I said. The suggestion had thrown me.

'I want to show you that we are not all bad. *I am a good man.* As are a lot of us are in the DPR. Or, at least, they were. But war makes monsters out of decent people.'

He handed over the note. 'I want you to understand that.'

The guards delivered our first hot meal of the day. Then Marko warned me not to be fooled by Makiivka's benign appearance. *This was a very bad place.* Like John and myself, he'd spent some time in the Black Site and understood how the TV set, kettle and a diminished level of daily violence could create the impression that the Western Corrective Prison was some kind of upgrade. But the reality was that it housed a number of very dangerous people. Furthermore, we should fear most of them. Marko then explained how Makiivka usually acted as a holding cell for prisoners awaiting court hearings. Our arrival and the haste at which we were being processed had pushed many of them to the back of the line. Understandably, some of them were furious and looking for revenge, though the good news was that our status as Ukrainian POWs meant we'd been separated from the main population within the penal colony.

'There are guys in here who will kill you, given the chance,' said Marko. 'And not just because of who you are, but because they want to kill you for fun. It's a Russian-Ukrainian prison. The rules are a bit different down here.'

I shrugged off Marko's warnings about who might want to shiv me and concentrated on the food. It looked disgusting. In a previous life, I'd have felt decidedly unenthusiastic about a plastic plate of fish, bread and *kasha* – a gloopy, porridge-like grain. But those days were a distant memory. I was starving and dangerously malnourished, and even though everything was sloppy and over-salted, I didn't care. My fork became a blur as it moved from plate to mouth. I only slowed to breathe.

John tried to calm me down. 'Mate, take a few small bites,' he said. 'See how your body reacts.'

I glanced up, my gob full. 'Why? I'm fucking famished.'

'You haven't eaten properly for ages! Your guts aren't ready.'

Thinking back to how easily I'd handled the cheeseburger a couple of weeks earlier, I scoffed the lot down in minutes. And once the main course had been polished off, Marko offered up a dessert of chocolate and vitamins. I necked those too. Then I burped loudly. My tummy was full; I felt like a king.

The joy was short-lived. As Marko set up a match of after-dinner dominoes – in-house games were yet another benefit of acting as a prison headman – my stomach and bowels gurgled ominously. Then I recognised the symptoms of an oncoming explosive evacuation. My skin prickled and my adrenaline soared; saliva pooled in my mouth and my gag reflex trembled.

Oh, fuck, I thought. *Here we go.*

John was right. Everything I'd eaten had rebelled against my organs, but I was unsure at which end the kasha would make a violent return. I didn't have to wait long for the answer. Bile climbed in my throat. There was another powerful lurch in my guts.

'Lads, I'm sorry,' I moaned, diving towards the toilet, my belly cartwheeling. 'I should have listened—'

I projectile-puked into the hole in the ground. There was barely time to wipe my chin. As Marko looked on in horror, I wrestled with my trousers in a desperate attempt to squat before I soiled myself. Barely digested prison slop poured into the pit beneath me. Then I buried my head in my hands and whimpered.

The next twenty-four hours were a gastric hell. A medic visited our cell and I was diagnosed with dysentery, but between rounds of puking and shitting, I tried to adjust to my new surroundings. Thankfully, John was on the mend and did his best to foster prisoner relations by drinking coffee and chatting to Marko, though, like me, he was wary. Both of us had decided that we should play our cards cautiously.

When the TV came on, we watched the news together and Marko explained the various maps as they appeared on the broadcast. From what I could tell, Ukraine was still in the fight, but it was hard to know for sure given we were watching the Russians' take on current affairs. I applied a personal filter to everything. Any gains for the enemy were certain to be overblown; any wins for the Ukrainians would be downplayed.

It soon became clear that Marko hadn't been exaggerating: Makiivka *was* a bad place and every now and then I heard the familiar howl of physical violence. This time, however, the screams and pleas for mercy came from what sounded like prisoner-on-prisoner disputes, rather than warden-sanctioned torture. Even our discussions seemed to amplify the hostile atmosphere around us. Whenever a non-military prisoner passed by with a guard and overheard our conversations, their screamed threats echoed around the cells.

'Hey, English? *Fuck you!*'

I shivered at the thought of meeting someone with a murderous grudge, especially the real-life cannibal that Marko claimed was living somewhere on the wing.

'He's fine, but he was a very naughty boy. He will be in here for twenty-five years and his only regret was getting caught.'

The story got worse. In a sick twist of fate, Makiivka's very own Hannibal Lecter had been given a trustee role and performed some of the grunt work within the facility. He was often tasked with dishing out meals and cleaning the cells. 'Oh, you'll definitely meet him,' said Marko, cheerily. Elsewhere, another mass murderer performed haircuts for the inmates, though these were done with electric clippers. Scissors and razors were definitely not allowed. Finally, a prolific meth dealer had been placed in charge of cleaning the bed sheets and was acting as a warden for the shower unit. *The freaks are running the show,* I thought.

Despite these threats, Makiivka was still a million times better than the Black Site, and during our first two days we were allowed to sleep uninterrupted. Nobody minded if we spent the day chatting or playing games. And through our small window, it was even possible to experience a tiny slice of civilian life in the DPR. Just outside the prison was a bar where karaoke was a regular event. When the sun went down, we'd laugh and sing quietly as a drunk local attempted to croon their way through Robbie Williams's 'Angels', or some hit from Adele. Rather than acting as a reminder of what I was missing out on, the music brought me a little closer to home. I watched the bus stop in the street and the pavements as they filled with people going home from work. Whenever the sun dipped below the horizon and the sunflowers swayed in patches on the grass outside, I smiled. There had been times when I'd feared never seeing a sunset again.

Noticeably, the guards were a lot more pleasant than the bullies we'd encountered at the Black Site, like Pohuy. For the most part, they recognised that we were POWs and therefore an enemy of the state. But at the same time, they seemed weirdly interested in our well-being. That was probably because most of them weren't militarily trained, and hadn't been engaged in combat at any point. One female guard brought sweets to our cell. Another warden even gave me a slice of pizza so I could recover after the dysentery. I was later told that Makiivka had gathered an impressive reputation among our so-called defence lawyers as 'the best prison in Donetsk'. As with everything else that came from the Russian legal system, I took the news with a generous pinch of salt.

The relative good-time vibes were short-lived. As before, I was quickly strangled by boredom. Sleeping all day, though a treat at first, came to feel like a curse, and while Marko did his best to lift our spirits with his endless games of dominoes, I was desperate for a change of pace. When a warden called Misha next checked on how we were doing, I made a request.

'Have you got any English-language books for the inmates to read?'

Over a day or so, I had built an unusual rapport with Misha. I liked the bloke. He was thin, balding, with a kindly face and a good sense of humour. He spoke some English and liked learning new swear words; I loved sharing them, knowing that an inside connection might open me up to even more privileges.

Misha laughed. 'Sure,' he said. 'I'll see what I can do. What sort of books would you like?'

More than anything I wanted a Russian–English dictionary. During my time in the Black Site, I had listened keenly for any clues as to what was happening to us, but my Russian was limited. However, with a dictionary in the room, I'd be able to pick up on any words I hadn't yet learned, especially when the guards were chatting outside.

Not wanting to telegraph my motives, I pretended to think aloud.

'Honestly, mate, *anything*. I'd read the back of a cereal packet. I'm that bored. Or a bloody dictionary.'

I deliberately missed a beat. *Timing was everything.*

'You know, a dictionary might not be a bad idea,' I said. 'If I'm teaching you English swear words, it would be a great way of helping.'

Misha looked at me suspiciously and grunted. Then he slammed the hatch on our cell door.

Fuck, I thought, fearing the worst. *I've bloody overplayed my hand.*

But an hour later, the hatch opened again. *Misha had come back.* He was pushing a paperback into our cell. *It was a Russian–English dictionary.* I stared at the cover and smiled.

John looked over. 'What the fuck's that?'

'Something useful,' I said, scanning for words and phrases that might prove important as our trial approached.

Guilty.

Execution.

Transfer.

Life sentence.

And finally: *Home.*

The higher-ups at Makiivka soon changed their minds about our status as POWs with privileges. After a couple of days of sipping coffee with Marko and Andriy, it was decided that the Western POWs awaiting trial should be lumped in together, and John and I were soon shifted to the cells downstairs. Immediately, I feared the worst.

'Don't worry. You'll be fine,' said Marko, sensing my unease. 'You're not going to the penal floor with the bad people. That's in the basement.'

Still feeling weak from the dysentery, I shuffled down with my dictionary and was shocked to see we were rooming with Brahim, plus Paul Urey and Dylan Healy, and a Swedish bloke with a broken leg who introduced himself as Mathias Gustafsson. It was good to see everyone. I'd been worried that Paul and Dylan had been topped or sent somewhere even worse. Brahim was smiling too, which gave me a laugh. His verbal diarrhoea would come in handy for whenever the Weight kicked in.

After months of imprisonment, malnourishment and physical abuse, we were all in varying states of collapse, but Paul Urey was undoubtedly suffering the most. He was bruised all over and his face was a patchwork of cuts and abrasions. A lot of Paul's injuries were fresh, and as we settled into our new space, he explained how Mr Balaclava had accused him of operating as a spy, all because he'd once worked as a con-tractor in Afghanistan. It hadn't helped that he'd been caught holding two passports and that he'd lied about working for the Red Cross – as I'd suspected when we'd first met. Pleading his innocence was pointless and Mr Balaclava went to town on Paul's face and body for an hour or so. Dylan later told me that the screams had echoed through the prison.

As we swapped stories and information, Paul's lungs wheezed and rattled. A deep, rasping cough caused him to wince in pain. I wondered how he was going to endure a long stint inside.

By the sound of it, everyone had been put through the propaganda grind. Some of the lads had been forced to ring their local MPs; others were tasked with calling political and humanitarian groups such as the Environment Agency, the British Red Cross and even Plaid Cymru, the Welsh political party. No doubt Paul had drawn the short straw there, too.

'Yeah, they made me ring the director of Man City Football Club,' he groaned. 'Sheikh Mansour . . .'

From everyone's stories, it seemed that the DPR's angle of attack had become even more confused than before. Some of us were being gently cajoled into making phone calls and videos; others had been subjected to all-out hostility.

I would soon experience both approaches at once.

The Friday after being reunited with Paul, Dylan and Brahim, plus the Swede, I was driven away from Makiivka and informed by Popov the social worker that a POW like myself could, technically, be exchanged for just about any-body – even a Russian individual at the political level of Viktor Medvedchuk. I was then told that an exchange with Medvedchuk was all but confirmed because Volodymyr Zelenskiy had agreed to a swap, though I still needed to per-suade the UK government. My spirits rocketed. But when my first phone call of the day hit a brick wall, and a British civil servant made the point that it was Ukraine's war, not the UK's, Popov changed tack. He scowled at me menacingly.

'Your government doesn't want you,' he shouted. 'And if you can't make this happen, then the courts will make sure you're sentenced to death.'

Over twelve hours or so, I became a political football and the DPR's tactics flip-flopped with such regularity that it was hard to determine what their ideal endgame was. By the day's end, I was told that the only person not convinced by my exchange for Medvedchuk, strangely, was Vladimir Putin. The deal had collapsed at the final hour and I was once again threatened with execution. I felt deflated, and the abuse left me with the strange sense that, if I died, I'd end up leaving a rather weird mark on the world. As a kid, my geography teacher, Mr Negus, had pointed out that I wasn't the most academically inclined student in the school. 'Pinner, you're going to be a nobody,' he'd said one day, rather unkindly. But by being held as a bargaining chip in a high-profile game of political poker, I'd proved him wrong.

The most powerful leaders in the world know my name, I thought. *So fuck you, Mr Negus.*

In the background, momentum seemed to be building behind our trial. After my long day of cold-calling, I was called into a meeting at the prison with the Kurator. Behind him stood a woman with an Amy Winehouse-style beehive hairdo and a scowling lawyer. It was Friday night and they both looked as if they'd rather be anywhere else. I was then informed that my trial would begin the following week, as would Brahim's. Finally, after what felt like a lifetime of veiled threats, I was about to be put through the Russian legal machine, where I'd learn more about my immediate prospects. When the indictment papers were handed over and I glanced at the cover sheet, I noticed that Aiden's name was there too. *So he's being tried alongside us?* I thought. *This is nuts*. Then I was told that the judicial process would last no longer than a week, and at its conclusion I would either be sentenced to death or banished to some Russian hellhole, presumably for a lifetime of slave labour. So the psychiatrist I had spoken to was wrong.

'There's no way for you to get out of this,' said the Kurator, dramatically. 'This will bring karmic justice for Russia.'

I nodded and did my best impression of someone who gave a shit. *Pohuy*.

The other man leant in ominously. '*Sniper*,' he hissed.

But the Kurator hadn't finished. 'Even though, as a mercenary, you're not protected by the Geneva Convention, we're going to adhere to the Geneva Convention protocols—'

I snorted. The Geneva Convention had set out, among other things, the legal conditions in which prisoners of war could be held, and the types of treatment that could and could not be inflicted upon them. I doubted it regarded a firing squad or labour camp as an acceptable punishment.

'I'm not a mercenary,' I said.

'The courts will decide that.'

'Yeah? And where does electrocuting, stabbing and starving people half to death appear in the Geneva Convention?'

The Kurator looked at me blankly. He knew full well that my complaints would come to nothing, because I was being tried in a kangaroo court. We all were.

'Those things didn't happen,' he said, coldly.

And there was nothing anyone could do to argue otherwise.

Why were all the guards being so bloody reasonable?

The question had been bothering me all weekend. Sure, we weren't serial-killer dangerous, or criminals on the level of some lawless Ukrainian meth dealer, but we were confirmed enemy fighters in a bloody conflict. That made us a considerable threat. Weirdly, though, the attitude of the wardens at Makiivka – while not exactly generous – was still friendlier than anything we'd experienced in the Black Site. There were smiles and brief conversations. Some of them even seemed keen to highlight their more considered attitude towards the inmate community. 'When you get out, remember that I didn't beat you,' said one warden as he peered through our cell hatch. We were given three hot meals every day, and though the routine of fish, bread and kasha became very old, very quickly, I was regaining some of the weight that had fallen from my bones in recent months.

Then I realised. *It was all for show.*

Following Putin's invasion of Ukraine, Brahim and I were going to be the first foreign POWs on trial for made-up war crimes against Russia. The media scrutiny was bound to be intense. The courtroom would be filled with journalists, photographers and cameramen from Russian state TV. Through their bias, the events would be disseminated and edited by any number of Kremlin-approved stooges and client editors, and then dispatched around the world. If I shuffled into the first hearing like a cadaver, covered from head to toe in sores and scabs, the truth would be impossible to hide and an international outrage would follow. To head off such a PR disaster, and to spare the DPR's senior members from a potential war-crimes charge later on, I was being fattened up. I'd also realised that many of the guards in Makiivka were civilians working for a pay cheque rather than soldiers scrapping for a cause. Kicking in a POW's ribs for fun didn't carry that much appeal. They had families to go home to.

Despite my improving health, I was still a bag of shit. Fifty days of unrelenting cruelty in the Black Site had taken its toll and my body was visibly keeping the score. Frustratingly, the situation I'd found myself in was an outlier, because I'd been one of the early captives. Some of the other prisoners, like John, had been banged up in the Black Site for a considerably shorter amount of time than me. My guess was that I'd been captured at a moment when the POW facilities in Russia were still being organised and the system was grinding its gears. By the time John had been picked up, some semblance of order had been established and the Russian and DPR secret police were pushing people through the system more quickly, pausing only to electrocute, pummel or stab them when they felt the urge.

On Sunday night, I looked through the indictment documents given to me by the Kurator and seethed. Everything was a mess: my charge sheet had been headed with Aiden's name and the paperwork, which was written in English, was a series of interlinked, one-size-fits-all paragraphs, all of which had been transplanted from a previous court case. I also noticed that the offences I'd been charged with were wildly different from those that had been thrown at me by the Prosecutor's office back in April and my statements bore little resemblance to what had actually been said. In addition to the crimes of treason and mutiny against the DPR, it was being claimed that I had left the Azov regiment because of their 'right-wing views and nationalistic tendencies'. *What a load of bollocks.* I'd never seen any political posturing of that kind while I'd been there and I'd made a point of saying so. The entire document was a crock of shit.

Well, we haven't got a chance in hell, I thought, dropping the pages to the floor.

I said as much to Brahim. 'We're never getting out of this.'

This realisation was hardly surprising. At no point did I expect the Russians to offer me a fair legal fight, and I knew that if found guilty I could expect the death penalty. Still, the confirmation that we were battling a rigged system felt weirdly depressing. That weekend, neither Brahim nor I received any legal advice and when we woke first thing on Monday morning, a prison trustee – the once-prolific meth dealer – ordered us to get our clothes together.

'You're going to court,' he said, sternly.

'Yeah, I know that,' I groaned, pulling a T-shirt over my head. 'But when?'

The Ukrainian Walter White ordered us into the corridor. '*Now.*'

Everything was moving too fast. We eventually arrived at a courtroom in Donetsk and through my hood I heard the familiar crunch and grumble of exploding bombs in the distance. The war was getting ever closer. Once inside, we were put into a holding cell and made to stand for thirty minutes until an officious-looking man asked for our indictment papers. As we'd barely had time to dress that morning, Brahim hadn't thought to gather his together and the man looked bemused. He flicked through a file absent-mindedly, which felt particularly annoying given our lives were hanging in the balance, and we were ushered into a cage at the back of the courtroom. Aiden was sitting there too, dressed in a black hoodie and a pair of dark blue tracksuit bottoms.

'All right, mate, how are you doing?' I whispered.

He nodded glumly, but Aiden really didn't need to say much: he seemed terrified. His skin was pale. Dark rings circled his eyes. Aiden looked like a man in need of a good night's kip – or a cuddle.

Settling onto a wooden bench, I quickly assessed my surroundings. The courtroom was a space the size of a five-a-side football pitch. The decor was bland; the walls were a dirty white colour; the furniture was dark and cheap-looking. The place stank of bleach, mothballs and stale cigarettes. Opposite our cage, at the far end of the room, was a large desk where, presumably, the farcical legal figures presiding over this farcical trial would sit and make farcical notes. One side of the room was a seating gallery, a space that ordinarily would have been used for a jury of some kind, though I doubted we were being afforded such a luxury. More likely this would be used as a media bullpen for whenever our sentencing was announced.

I hadn't been to a trial of any kind before, but I was familiar with the set-up having watched the occasional episode of *Judge Judy*. Ahead of me were rows of desks. These were usually reserved for the lawyers and some of them were now walking around the room and staring at us. Then my stomach tightened. Standing at the doors were several guards from the Black Site. All were armed with truncheons, though, thankfully, neither Pohuy nor Captain Shovel Hands were amongst the mob.

Through the walls, the artillery shells were still audible nearby. Every now and then the lighting flickered and the fittings rattled. Each explosion created a murmur of alarm as the courtroom began to fill. I saw one or two people I recognised from our initial legal meetings, but there was no sign of the Prosecutor, Mr Balaclava or Popov. Several cameramen shuffled towards the cage and aimed their lenses at both the judge's desk and our faces. A small team of smartly dressed men and women leant over the growing media scrum and introduced themselves as our translators. Finally, a judge arrived and took his seat at the head table. He was bald, with a salt-and-pepper goatee beard, and was dressed in a dark black robe. His eyes drilled into us. I knew by the deep scowl that there would be no leniency in this courtroom. The judge was itching to hand down the death sentence.

Unlike the movies, there was no preamble – no introductions or grand statements to kick off proceedings. Instead, the judge announced that the charges against us would be read out. Then one of the translators asked if we would prefer one judge or three to preside over the court case.

I looked across at Brahim and Aiden uneasily. *What difference was it going to make?*

'What do you reckon?' I said. 'It might take them a while to find two more judges. That should kill some time . . .'

Brahim and Aiden nodded in agreement, but immediately another man and a woman, also dressed in the same dark robes as the judge, walked into the room. They had been waiting in an antechamber, ready to go.

I looked at Brahim and shook my head. 'Well, what are the odds of that? Two judges, all robed up, sitting next door. Very convenient . . .'

Brahim sighed. 'Yeah. *Funny that.*'

Then he chuckled to himself. 'I don't know, Shaun . . .'

'*What?*'

'Something tells me we might not get out of this.'

Now was not the time to laugh, but I couldn't help it. Across the room, the Black Site thugs stared. One of them seemed to be licking his lips at the thought of dishing out a kicking, for old time's sake. A cameraman, having realised that we were chatting to one another, shoved a microphone in front of the cage. Suddenly I felt horribly exposed. It was as if we'd been dropped into a goldfish bowl.

And then: '*Sssshhhhhhh . . .*'

The courtroom was hushed and a lawyer for the prosecution slowly read out the charges, my anger rising with every sentence. In addition to the accusations of treason and mutiny against the DPR, plus the trumped-up claim that we were mercenaries, we were also charged with being part of a criminal group and committing acts of terrorism. It was then claimed that these acts should warrant a greater punishment because they were premeditated – the prosecuting lawyer was arguing that the three of us had schemed to overthrow the DPR in advance of arriving in Ukraine, even though I'd only met Brahim in captivity and the DPR was a puppet state.

The lawyer turned to Aiden. 'Aslin was the instigator,' he said. 'The headhunter and the ringleader who brought everybody here to fight in an illegal war against Russia, during an attempt to take over the DPR.'

Aiden looked dumbstruck. Brahim turned to me and gawped: *What?* The idea that Aiden represented the brains behind an international network of mercenaries was mind-bending. For starters, we were all legitimate soldiers fighting for the Ukrainian armed forces, not soldiers of fortune, and while Aiden was a solid bloke, he was hardly considered a figure of influence. I had also outranked him; I'd been his commander when he'd helped us to guard the position in Pavlopil for several months. There was no way I'd have worked for him in a war zone, or taken on such a dangerous job, simply on his say so. *Not in a million years.* The accusation was so confusing.

Once Aiden's charges had been read out, similar accusations were levelled at Brahim and me. Finally, the lawyer held up a big folder, a dossier he claimed contained paperwork explaining the finer details of the Geneva Convention. Our alleged roles as mercenaries, he said, meant that we weren't protected by the protocols listed within. What a shock: the story had changed yet again.

After what felt like an age, the waffling finished. I noticed that an eerie silence had fallen over the room. The lawyers were conferring. *Something important was about to happen.*

Eventually the lead judge addressed the room in Russian. An interpreter repeated his question in English. *How do you plead: guilty, or not guilty?*

There was no point in playing along with their games. I was about to be sentenced for several crimes I hadn't committed. Inside, I was raging, so rather than giving the Russians what they wanted, I decided to go down with a fight. I leant close to Aiden and Brahim, and pretended to read my indictment papers.

'OK, so what do you want to do?' I whispered.

'I think we should plead not guilty,' said Aiden. 'We're not mercenaries or terrorists.'

Brahim looked confused. 'Not guilty!'

I tried to think tactically. 'I don't know, mate. I think we plead guilty to the lesser charges and not guilty to being terrorists and mercenaries. That way we might avoid the death sentence.'

We were so confused. None of us could make head or tail of the poorly written legalese that had been handed to us, and our defence lawyers weren't exactly helping. The court had assigned one to each of us, but they were out of earshot and gossiping around a desk. Eventually, the judge asked for our decisions. We rose and pleaded guilty to the accusations of treason and mutiny against the DPR. Then we made our protest.

'Not guilty,' said Aiden, to the charge of being a mercenary.

I repeated the plea, feeling defiant.

Finally, Brahim addressed the court. 'Not guilty.'

Calm turned to chaos. I heard gasps of disbelief, as if we'd committed some terrible act, and there were one or two angry shouts. The judges glared and called for order. I shouted out to the court. *Could we speak to our defence lawyers?*

The judge waved a hand dismissively. 'You have fifteen minutes,' he said grumpily.

My legal counsel approached the cage. Up close, I recognised her as the assistant to my original defence counsel – the DPR soldier from the Prosecutor's office. During our first meeting in April, I'd found it weird that he hadn't taken any notes. Instead, he'd instructed his assistant to do the grunt work – the woman staring at me now. *What was going on?*

She looked to the translator, wide-eyed.

'What did they say exactly?' she asked.

Then she stared at me. '*What did you say?*'

'We all said, "Not guilty,"' I explained.

'But you can't do that!'

I met the lawyer's gaze firmly. 'And why's that? This is a court case, isn't it? We don't have to go along with everything that's being said. *Especially as we're not guilty.* We're Ukrainian soldiers, not mercenaries.'

The defence lawyer seemed confused. She looked at her paperwork anxiously. 'Look, you're guilty,' she said, through the translator. 'So you have to say you're guilty. Use your head.'

'But I'm not,' I snapped, losing control of my boiling emotions. 'Listen to what I've just said: I'm. *Not*. Guilty.'

Behind her, a judge was ordering the camera crews to stop filming. The guards from the Black Site were shouting to the lawyers in Russian. Violence seemed to be nearby. My defence counsel spoke to the translator; the translator then shrugged and summarised the information as if it was just another day in the office. She looked distracted and bored.

'She says that if you want a lesser sentence, you'll have to say you're guilty. Otherwise you're getting the death penalty. She says she's trying to help you.'

I struggled to take in the details. *This had to be a trap.* Especially as zero attention had been paid to our legal well-being so far. Next to me, I heard Brahim talking to his lawyer intently. The exact same instructions were being delivered.

'Wait,' said Brahim. 'So if we plead guilty, you won't kill us?'

The other defence counsellor smiled. 'Yes! Exactly that. Have a moment to think about it.'

Brahim looked at me. 'What do you think?'

The lawyers were tapping their watches and telling us to hurry. Time was slipping away. The three of us huddled together and conferred. *Did we really have a choice?* The consequences of fighting our corner had been clearly established. If we told the truth: death. If we lied: life. But I was torn. The thought of rotting away in jail filled me with dread, and in some ways taking a bullet to the brain didn't seem like such a bad way to go – if that's how the DPR were conducting their execution business these days. Ultimately, though, by stalling and gaining time, there was a chance the three of us might outlive the war. If that happened we would, at some point, be pardoned and released. With almost exquisite timing, a bomb exploded somewhere nearby. For a second, the courtroom was plunged into darkness. There was a shriek. A voice yelled for calm.

When the lights flickered on again, we stood up.

'OK, we'll take the guilty plea,' I said, reluctantly.

Our defence lawyer smiled. Standing in front of the cage bars, phone raised, head cocked, she then took a selfie, her face a portrait of smugness. *This was a career-defining moment.* For us, it wasn't so great. We had been screwed and I seethed at the injustice of it all, but at least nobody was getting executed.

Brahim began muttering angrily. 'Fuck it. Fuck it. *Fuck it.*'

The trial was adjourned shortly afterwards. Though we'd only been going for a couple of hours, it had become clear that another almighty balls-up had taken place with our paperwork. From what we could tell, the documents being shared within the courtroom were just as poorly put together as our indictments. The wrong names had been inserted into the charge sheets; key bits of information were missing; and there was a strong sense that whoever had been overseeing the administrative process was in for a rough time. We were cuffed, pulled out of our cage and driven back to Makiivka. The case would resume the next day. As we were bundled into the back of our transporter, paparazzi-style photographers hustled and shoved.

In all the crazy, Brahim had become muddled. His hyper-activity had rocketed off the scale, probably due to the anxiety we were all feeling, and I noticed that during the trial he'd seemed unable to focus. Now he was bombarding me with questions, and of everything that had happened, he was most confused about Aiden, who had been asked to make a brief statement towards the end of the day.

'Why did he keep referring to the judge as "Your Highness?"' he asked. '*Your Highness this; Your Highness that.* What the fuck was all that about?'

I laughed. 'No, mate. He was saying, "Your Honour". It's how you refer to a judge in a court of law. Well, in the UK anyway.'

Given what we'd been through over the past six months, it was easy to forget that, really, Brahim was still a kid. When I next looked over at him, he was drawing a penis on his indictment papers.

Having returned to my cell, the mind games continued as the guards played roommate switcheroo yet again. Brahim and Dylan were moved to the space next door with another British POW called Andy Hill. I ignored the kerfuffle and tried to rest. A mental wobble was coming on and the Weight's emotional heft smothered my chest, ribs and shoulders. My heart was banging. I realised one of the many downsides of Makiivka was that I was being given way too much thinking time. In the Black Site I had been trapped by fear and I'd constantly worked to avoid the attentions of anyone in a position of power. But without that distraction, the brain was free to stew. My stresses and fears came crashing in.

I worried about how the news was being received outside Russia. *Did Larysa know what I was going through?*

I thought of my friends and family in the UK, and my dear old mum. *Was I going to see any of them again?*

Then I remembered the mates I'd lost during the siege, like Dima. *What would he say to me now?*

I consoled myself with the fact that a guilty plea had at least spared us from the death sentence.

'Maybe we'll get released if the war turns against Russia,' I said out loud to the room.

Going by the artillery blasts near the court, Ukraine's military forces were taking the fight to Donetsk.

'I'd rather get a bullet to the head,' said John bluntly. 'Fuck being banged up in a Russian cell for the rest of my life.'

'A lot could happen, mate.'

'Yeah?' he snorted. 'Like what?'

'Well, I'm hoping for a reduced term. Then we can work the rest out as we go. I don't want to die just yet. Not if there's a chance we might get exchanged.'

John shrugged and picked up the Russian–English dictionary. 'Well, good luck to you, boys,' he said, flicking through the pages, mouthing the big words. 'By the sound of it, the court case is a right Mickey Mouse affair. We're all going to get our turn at being played for idiots.'

John's pessimism was understandable, but no way was I giving in. Believing that the fight for freedom was in some way winnable was the only thing keeping me sane.

Tuesday was yet another waste of time. The Russians had spent the night rewriting our mismatched indictment paperwork and we were sent to the courtroom so that the correct documents could be handed out. There were more readings and more faffing, though I noticed that the correct names had been printed on the relevant folders this time, which was a massive improvement on the previous day's shitshow. Of course, nothing is ever perfect. Whenever a factual mistake was read out, I urged our defence lawyer to push back, but she barely bothered to leave the chair. Her work was done. She had the selfie to prove it.

The following day brought a considerable shift in mood and we were informed that the evidence proving our guilt was about to be presented. The court was packed and more media had arrived. As we waited in our cage at the back of the room, I noticed that nearly everyone in the building was carrying either a camera or a tape recorder of some kind. The propaganda videos I'd been forced to make had been an insight into the Russians' love for political theatre. Now Brahim, Aiden and I were about to take leading roles yet again. The media pack jostled for position around our holding cell and the judges' table.

'This is all a massive PR stunt,' I whispered to Brahim, using my indictment papers to cover my mouth.

I'd grown tired of the attention. I didn't want anyone to film or photograph what was being said between us. I felt just as enraged that we weren't being given the opportunity to talk or put our case forward. If I could take the stand, it might provide an opportunity to kick back in some way. But that was the last thing the Russians wanted. As the prosecuting lawyer spoke, I felt coiled up and degraded. My black T-shirt had been swapped for a lime-green polo shirt, presumably to create the impression that there was a walk-in wardrobe of clothes to choose from in prison. My head had also been shaved by Makiivka's murderous in-house barber. It was possible to see the veins pulsing in my temples.

And then the trial took a strange turn.

'We're going to bring in a witness,' said the prosecuting lawyer.

A murmur went around the courtroom. *A witness?* I'd seen another surname on my indictment papers, but I had no idea who it was and, looking up, I half expected to see Mr Balaclava, or one of the special-forces soldiers who had stabbed and shocked me during my flight from Mariupol. But the person walking into the courtroom was a woman. As she passed, I noticed her handcuffs and mismatched clothes.

Both were telltale signs of a POW. It was only when the woman turned to face us that I recognised her. *It was the medic I'd met during our evacuation.* I puffed out a sigh of relief. *She was still alive.* I had often wondered if she'd survived – and the other unarmed soldiers I'd had to leave behind. During several long dark nights of the soul in the Black Site, I'd been racked with guilt.

Did I make the right choice? I'd wondered, over and over. *Were those people still alive?* Looking at the medic now, I realised my decision had been spot on. Yeah, she was stuck in a DPR courtroom and was clearly being paraded about for propaganda. But at least she was in one piece. *And that gave her a fighting chance.* I hoped the men she'd been caring for in the gatehouse were somewhere safe – or better. I lifted myself up in the cage. I wanted to catch her eye, to acknowledge her; to let her know that whatever happened next, she was going to be OK. But the medic wouldn't look my way. The prosecuting lawyer had handed her a sheet of paper and her eyes were scanning the text – it was a prepared statement and a bad one. I could tell by the look on her face. *She was scared.*

Quietly the judge asked the medic a series of questions, only this time the translators weren't interpreting. Every now and then I recognised a sentence and made sure to alert Brahim and Aiden.

'When you met Pinner, was he an active shooter?' said the judge. 'Was he fighting against DPR soldiers?'

The medic nodded. *Yes, he was.* She had told the truth and reinforced the DPR's belief that I was a mercenary, but I didn't hold any ill will against her. Even if she had lied, or stuck up for me in some way, it wouldn't have made a blind bit of difference. We were all snared in a legal sham.

When the testimony came to an end, the medic looked visibly upset. She couldn't bring herself to glance up at the three of us at the back of the room, but if she had done, I'd have smiled at her. It felt important to show that there were no ill feelings. We all understood the game we'd been forced to play.

Our time was slipping away. As the day went on, I tried to speak and I occasionally gestured to the judges that I wanted to take the stand. Whenever I rose to my feet, a guard or my so-called defence lawyer ordered me to sit down. The fact that we were all part of a show was later reinforced when Brahim pointed to one of the assistant judges. He was slumped back in his chair, mouth open, head lolling. The bastard was asleep.

Oh, my God, I thought. *This is just a joke.*

Finally, I was asked a direct question. 'Shaun Pinner, are you a terrorist?' said the judge.

This was my moment. 'No, I'm not. I'm—'

'Really? Because in your indictment it says that Shaun Pinner is a UK terrorist and he is wanted by the UK Government.'

More lies upon lies. 'I'm not a UK terrorist,' I said. 'I'm not wanted in the UK. I've never done anything wrong in the UK.'

The judge wasn't having any of it. 'But you fought as a mercenary in Syria and the UK Government have accused you of being a terrorist.'

My fight-or-flight response detonated. Given I'd been caged there was no way of taking flight, so I opted for aggression. Standing up, I said, 'I can prove that I'm not a terrorist! Let me explain.'

The judge stared at me angrily. 'Sit down!' he yelled.

But I wasn't going to listen. I pointed at the prosecuting lawyer. 'I've already told him. I said to him I'd never done anything wrong. I can prove it. Give us a chance to prove it.'

I looked around the courtroom. Everyone was staring. A bank of cameras had swivelled towards me. I was making great television.

'I'm a terrorist in the UK, am I?' I shouted. 'Well, that's bollocks.'

I gestured to our defence lawyer to do something, but she had turned away and was shrugging to the court. Feeling totally helpless, I looked to the faces watching me.

'I'm never going to get out of this,' I said. 'I'm never going to go home. There's no defence, my lawyer won't even help me . . .'

Finally I lost my rag. 'I'm not a terrorist in the UK!' I shouted. 'It's a charge made up by Russia.'

The court exploded with shouts and gasps. Cameras flashed. *Click! Click! Click!* When I looked up, the sleeping judge had woken from his nap. His face was an angry shade of scarlet.

'Do you see any Russians in this room?' he yelled.

'What do you mean?'

'This is an independent DPR court. Do you see any Russians in this room?'

I looked at the crowd. My guess was that at least 50 per cent of them were Russian, especially among those journalists grifting for state-sponsored media outlets. Those that weren't Russian by birth were certainly sympathetic to Putin's political cause.

'Look,' I said. 'I'm pro-Ukrainian and nothing's going to change that. But I'm not a mercenary. I'm not a Nazi. I'm a Ukrainian Marine. I'm pro-Ukrainian . . .'

'Do you see any Russians?' shouted the judge again. The court was falling into chaos.

'I saw plenty in Mariupol,' I shouted over the growing kerfuffle. 'When they bombed the city and killed lots of innocent civilians.'

'*I meant in this courtroom!*'

'It's hard to tell,' I said. 'Just because I can't identify a Russian, it doesn't mean there isn't one here.'

The judge was trying to convince everyone watching – possibly even himself – that his DPR courtroom was beyond the Kremlin's influence. *Like anyone was going to believe that*. I thought back to my meetings in the Prosecutor's office weeks previously. There had been a framed portrait of Vladimir Putin hanging on the wall.

'But of course Russia's here,' I said. '*I know what this court is.*'

When I looked around, I realised both Aiden and Brahim were gawping at me. They looked terrified.

'What are you doing?' said Brahim.

I sat down. 'I don't know, mate. *Trying?*'

I was revved up. Though the situation was totally beyond my control, it felt good to push back a little. We were getting a guilty verdict, no matter what I said or did. Shouting was the closest I could get to regaining some sense of power.

'These people are idiots,' I sighed.

Then I dropped my head, hoping to shield my face from whoever was watching on the telly, hoping my photograph wasn't going to make it into the Russian papers the next morning. I was more exposed than ever before. I know Aiden felt the same. He seemed broken. For months the Russians, via the DPR, had used him as a PR mule, pulling him from propaganda video to staged interview. The process had dehumanised him, crushing any hope he'd held on to. But Brahim, while unsettled by my defiance, still brimmed with optimism.

'Don't worry, brother,' he whispered. 'At some point we're going home.'

The cogs of sham justice turned again. To add insult to injury, another prosecutor had arrived to argue that we should be considered for the death penalty after all, despite the fact that we'd pleaded guilty, as advised. Our defence lawyer gasped in shock and looked at us sorrowfully. I sighed, feeling convinced that this new claim was all part of the theatre and we were about to be locked up. Then some bastard would throw away the key.

But I was wrong, wrong, wrong.

The following day, the three of us were hooded and carted off to the courthouse for sentencing, and the enormity of our situation slapped me about the face. Having arrived, I realised we'd been taken to a different building and it was much bigger than the one in which we'd been tried. Dozens of photographers were waiting for us outside, as if Brad Pitt was making a surprise cameo appearance. *Click! Click! Click!* Cameras encircled us as we stepped into the street. *Click! Click! Click!* The crowd shoved and charged, as guards wearing camouflage uniforms and face masks forced us inside. *Click! Click! Click!* There must have been at least fifty people trying to take our photograph as we settled onto our seats in the cage. It was like being a newborn panda in the zoo.

The courtroom was huge, at least twice the size of the last, and hundreds of journalists and photographers shuffled around on the parquet floor in an attempt to get the definitive shot of our misery. *Click! Click! Click!* One bloke even pushed his phone under the bars to snatch a close-up. Four armed guards, holding 9 mm pistols, stood at the door of our cage. The mood was electric but ominous. When an important-looking TV crew was ushered towards our position, Brahim stared down their camera lens in defiance.

The gesture only drew more attention. *Click! Click! Click!* More photographers gathered at the bars; more journalists shouted questions. 'Fuck you,' said Brahim, repeating the statement to anyone that stepped towards him.

I was happy to have the heat taken off me. After the previous day's outburst, my aim was to play the Grey Man, and I'd become determined to sink into the shadows. Not standing out in any way was the new strategy, because drawing attention to myself would only cause problems once I'd been transferred to what I presumed would be a more permanent facility. Any inmates or wardens that recognised me would view me as a target, that's if I wasn't already one. Aiden, meanwhile, still looked forlorn. I had no idea how he was going to cope once we'd been sentenced to a lifetime inside.

There was banging from the judges' table. I heard shushing and pleas for silence. Slowly, the courtroom quietened. Our sentences were about to be passed down. I craned my neck so that I could watch the judges as they delivered their decisions, but I couldn't see past the mob of cameramen and journalists.

Then the lead judge began talking. 'Having committed actions against the constitutional order of the Donetsk People's Republic and attempted to overthrow the government by force, it is justified and objective to hand down the highest possible punishment . . .'

My skin prickled. *The highest possible punishment?* I thought, eyeballing our defence lawyer. *That can't be. We were promised.*

'. . . The death sentence.' He then explained we would be executed via a firing squad and that there were thirty days in which to appeal against his verdict. We had been fucked over.

There was shouting. People in the galleries pretended to be outraged.

No!

Oh my God!

I can't believe this!

The performance would have made a *Hollyoaks* actor wince. The media surrounded our cage and I backed away. But Brahim, still full of resistance, came alive. He smirked at the attention.

'It ain't going to happen,' he said, repeating the same sentence to the media that he'd said to me on countless occasions. 'We're going home at some point.'

Then he turned on the camera crews. 'Hi Mum,' he said, smiling. 'This is a sham process. I didn't do anything wrong.'

One reporter yelled out, 'You're a psycho!'

'Yeah?' snapped Brahim. 'I don't care. I don't recognise your laws or your court.'

Then I noticed all the microphones and tape recorders were being aimed at Aiden. As had been the case throughout our depressing PR trip to Mariupol, he was once again the centre of attention and everybody wanted his opinion on the verdict. The poor bloke seemed haunted, distant and completely different from the fighter I'd known before the invasion. I wanted to see if he was OK, but Aiden looked lost.

'I was hoping the sentence would be a lot fairer,' he said to the journalists gathering at the cage door. 'Especially judging the circumstances by which I helped the investigation and also because I surrendered to the Donetsk People's Republic. I wish it could be different. But God would be the one that would judge me when the time comes.'

Secretly, I was thankful the spotlight was on him rather than me. I'd been degraded enough. Turning my face away from the crowd, I tried to sneak out of shot, but it was impossible. The cameras edged closer. If I hadn't been bound at the wrists, I'd have swatted them away – forget playing the Grey Man, I was that angry. Only a mug would have expected a fair trial from the DPR, but I still felt cheated. The Russians had obviously leant on the court to deliver a show, and the idea that we would be spared execution by pleading guilty was yet another lie.

We were screwed. And I only had thirty days to save myself from a bullet to the brain.

23

My head was a mess. Everything had changed for the worst.

Bloody hell, I thought. *I'm on death row now.*

As we left the courtroom, my so-called defence lawyer made repeated assertions that an appeal was possible. *But surely that was going to be rigged too?* I ranted and raved with Brahim as we bounced around in the back of the transport vehicle, our hands cuffed, our heads hooded, our tempers rising. The *fucking* Russians. The *fucking* DPR. And Vladimir *fucking* Putin. I was so tightly wound with rage that I could have ripped through the plastic loops binding my wrists together, no problem, though I'd probably have taken a beating from the driver at the other end of the journey. Still: *fuck the lot of them.* All I could think about was the court's chilling verdict: death by firing squad. My only way out now was a prisoner exchange.

Shuffling back to the cells, I tried to lift what was becoming a perilously heavy mood and reminded myself that the trial had been a sham; that any number of political forces in the West were probably feeling outraged at our treatment; and that the resulting media attention on my case might speed up the outstanding negotiation points in a prisoner-swap deal. There was also the forthcoming referendum to consider. If the people of Donetsk voted in favour of official Russian control, the death sentence would be abolished and I'd be left with a lengthy prison sentence. I refocused. Considering these upsides was bloody important: I had thirty days to buy some time and change the narrative. But dwelling on the negatives would only cause me to spiral.

One way of keeping my head straight was to help the others around me. At some point, the likes of John, Paul, Mathias and Dylan would have to endure the same nightmarish scenario as me. John and Mathias were facing identical offences and would probably be forced into pleading guilty too, even though they were technically Ukrainian Marines, not mercenaries. But Paul and Dylan were in a stickier position. They had been working for an NGO, and without official military identification the Russians were still struggling to verify their previous work histories. As a consequence, Mr Balaclava remained adamant that Paul was a spy. Dylan, meanwhile, had been left upended by a recent interrogation in which a series of photographs were laid out on the table in front of him. Snapped by an FSB spy, they were images of his family walking about their home town in the UK. The implication was clear: cooperate and confess to our bullshit charges, or we'll strike the ones you love. Not surprisingly, the threat had rattled him. It had rattled all of us.

I thought there was a chance of helping the lads avoid the death sentence because I had come to realise that our case had been a series of missed opportunities. The facts: we had been tried in what was a Russian-controlled court where the administrative arm of the enemy was highly conscious of any negative PR. Putin had become involved in a complex propaganda campaign and was desperate to present Russia as the hero in a war of good versus evil. Our regular meals in Makiivka were evidence of that – they hadn't wanted us to look so close to death in front of the media. It's also why we'd barely been allowed to speak during the hearings. (Apart from Aiden's forced testimony and my rogue outburst.) My instincts now told me that they were fearful of one of us telling the truth on live TV. Annoyingly, there had still been one or two opportunities to speak out about the catalogue of abuses we'd suffered – and we'd blown them.

But now I was feeling more clued up.

'Whatever happens, you're going to be pushed into pleading guilty,' I told John, Mathias and Paul later that night. 'But if you can alert the court that you've been mistreated, the media might pick up on it. It's the last thing the DPR and the Russians want.'

My feeling was that if someone could blurt out that we'd been coerced into giving false statements through physical beatings and electrocutions, and that we had been starved close to death in an off-the-grid Russian black site, it might cause enough of a public embarrassment to slow or even derail the trial.

Really, time was the only thing any of us had left. We had to delay, delay, delay, and then delay some more, until hopefully the conflict broke in Ukraine's favour or the Donetsk referendum went the way of Russia. By the following morning, we all felt a little better about pushing back against a corrupt legal system. While we were undoubtedly underdogs, the idea that we could kick up a fuss at least created the impression that we were grabbing back control. In our heads, we were taking the war to the enemy.

Certain circumstances were in our favour too. One advantage of being cooped up in Makiivka was its more relaxed attitude towards the residents. We were allowed a daily hour of recreation time, when we'd gather in the small outdoor paddocks, which had been fitted with a pull-up bar and a park bench. I immediately noticed that the space ran adjacent to our corridor and was walled off into several five-by-five-metre squares – we were usually shoved into the one closest to our cell. Because of the prison's shoddy design, the asbestos roof covering each paddock was much higher than the walls. That meant we could talk with the inmates either side of us. Carefully, quietly, we spread word to the other prisoners about the Russians' legal tactics and our plans to outsmart them.

Brahim then went a step further. A couple of days later, he told me that his sister had paid for a Donetsk lawyer to organise an appeal. Unbelievably, the DPR had agreed to the idea. I was not entirely sure how the set-up would work, but Brahim was pretty certain of a positive outcome. The lawyer was even allowed to visit him in Makiivka to provide counsel and following their first meeting, Brahim seemed more energised than usual. The lawyer had known all about our situation and explained how the charges against us didn't stack up. He was also confident that Brahim could get away from the death penalty. By extension, the rest of us could too.

'He thinks we can fight this,' said Brahim. 'Shaun, I told you: we are going to get out of here.'

Nobody liked hearing the words *I told you so*. But on this occasion I was happy to take the hit.

By July, Brahim's lawyer had become a key source of information. He smuggled in letters from the family, which included updates on how the war was going. By the sound of it, Ukraine was still fighting back with considerable force, and its troops were edging ever closer to Donetsk. Around the same time, both Brahim and myself had received legal letters confirming our death sentences. Conveniently, everything had been translated into English and, somewhere in the small print, our protections as prisoners were listed under the Donetsk Code of Practice. As I scanned the text, I felt lifted. My hunch had been correct. Our legal rights had been violated, without doubt – the paperwork confirmed as much – and while it was too late for me to make a difference, if the others could push this point during their upcoming proceedings, there was some hope for a postponement. As we made the most of our daily exercise breaks, relaying these updates to the prisoners around us, it was hard not to feel a growing sense of optimism. *Maybe there was a way out of this after all?*

A high point soon arrived when Brahim's lawyer was allowed to bring a food parcel to the facility. It was packed with coffee, cured meats and sausages, sweets, chocolate and cigarettes. A bribe then ensured that any passing guards would turn a blind eye as the contraband was distributed. A party vibe hit the cells. The delivery was an instant morale-booster and I immediately sparked up a ciggie and drew in the sharp burn of tobacco; the chocolate, though a cheap Ukrainian brand, tasted like the work of a master confectioner; and eating cured meat for the first time in God knows how long gave me goosebumps. I took care to chew everything slowly. No way did I want a repeat of my *Exorcist*-style projectile-vomiting episode.

Most exciting of all was the coffee. The last cup I'd drunk had been during my first two days in Makiivka. Since then, I'd tasted nothing but manky water and piss-weak tea. Now, with a bag of instant granules, the time had come to crank myself up on caffeine, though there was one hitch. While a water pipe had been fitted in the cell, it only worked inter-mittently – we'd been told that a bomb had destroyed the local canals feeding into the prison. As a result, our water source was unpredictable. When the main supply did come on, the liquid arrived in small drips and was as yellow as the stuff we'd been forced to drink in the Black Site. The upside was that our cell had a makeshift kettle – a rudimentary element that boiled any waterborne bacteria when dropped into a full saucepan.

As the cell quietened down after the excitement of our evening feast, I pointed to the pot on the floor. 'Let's get that coffee going,' I said.

It took an age for the water to bubble up, but the wait was worthwhile. The coffee tasted wonderfully bitter. Even better, a few sachets of sugar had been stuffed into the food parcel. I tipped one into my cup and the next sip was even more delicious – a rush of sugar and caffeine burned through me, and I wanted to bounce off the walls. Everybody clinked cups. *It was time to plan again.*

As the days ticked by, there was an increasing confidence that an effective blow could be landed in the courts, which was reassuring given there seemed to be very little news on our appeal. Whenever the guards did their rounds, we'd ask for updates or timelines, but the response was always the same. There would be an apologetic shake of the head, a shrug and some mumbled excuse.

'No. Not today. Maybe tomorrow.'

The suspense was killing us.

The waiting could have been worse, though. At least nobody was getting beaten in Makiivka and the conditions were fairly manageable. Thanks to Brahim, we had a steady supply of cigarettes and coffee, and our immediate surroundings were comfortable enough, especially when set against the horrors of our previous home. The beds, while wedged together, were clean and we were allowed to wash the sheets in a prison laundry room.

There was also access to the showers, though using them had its difficulties. The units were on the lowest level, but were operated from several floors up. Once under the showerhead, I would have to shout at the top of my lungs before a rush of icy cold liquid poured from the ceiling. It was also a risky business because, on that level, the killers and the rapists were all around me – and even in their cells some of them were more terrifying than a Grad attack.

We knew that the Ukrainian inmates were still enraged that we'd jumped the judicial queue, despite the fact some of us had received the death sentence. Whenever I was moved around the prison facility under armed guard, the voices screaming out from the other cells were unsettling.

'Go to fuck, you English faggot!'

'You'll be dead soon!'

'We will fucking kill you . . . *for the DPR!*'

Not everyone had been hardwired to hate, though, and one or two inmates tried to communicate with me civilly as I walked to the showers or laundry room. This was mainly out of curiosity. A lot of them hadn't met an English person before, and it was the same with the friendlier guards, who enjoyed discussing British culture and our views on politics, sport and even music. For a lot of them it was the first time they'd spoken to a person outside Russia, or Russian-controlled Ukraine, and they wanted to know if we lived up to the propaganda. I sometimes got the impression that they felt a little duped for believing the negative, Kremlin-instigated narrative. They realised we weren't anywhere near as bad as our portrayal in the media.

This growing connection soon paid off and we were given pencils and paper to write with. One guard had also brought in an old wooden draughts board and half a set of pieces. We supplemented the missing parts with bottle tops before turning the game into a chess set by marking each disc with a symbol to denote the various figures. ('K' for king, 'P' for pawn, 'R' for rook and so on.) These contests helped to pass the time. What the guards didn't know was that we were also using the paper to orchestrate our legal defence by making a series of notes. Any updates, ideas or instructions were thrown over the paddock walls and shared along the corridor.

But then our judicial war suffered its first heavy defeat.

One afternoon, following yet another legal meeting, Brahim returned to our cell in a state. 'The lawyer says he can't help us any more,' he said.

I sat up. 'Why not?'

'He told me, "I don't think I'm going to be able to fight this." Then he mentioned there was pressure being put on him and it was coming straight from the very top.'

I was devastated. The lawyer's updates from the outside world had proved invaluable. 'What the bloody hell does he mean by that?' I said.

Brahim looked at me seriously. '*Putin*. Apparently he won't accept that we're *not* mercenaries, so it's unlikely we're going to win any kind of outright appeal. The good news is that the lawyer thinks we still might get our charges reduced, but now he's freaking out. He's worried they're going to put him in the same cell as us.'

It now seemed more imperative than ever to engineer a prisoner exchange. Maybe I was deluding myself, but I remained optimistic about our chances, mainly because the

Makiivka staff seemed so interested in the personal well-being of all the POWs. In addition to our daily meals, we were often given painkillers and medication for any serious bumps and bruises we might have suffered in the Black Site. When I asked why anyone from the prison should give a toss about our comfort – in what was, essentially, a hard-core prison, filled with cannibals, meth dealers and enemy combatants – it was explained that everyone had been ordered to keep us safe.

'It causes no end of problems for us if a prisoner of war dies in here,' said a guard we'd nicknamed Davidoff, because of his choice of cigarettes. 'So we don't want you to be murdered.'

He smiled. 'In fact, it would be much better for me if you were shot outside.'

As he walked away, laughing, I reinterpreted his cold-hearted appraisal and found a positive to cling on to.

So you're saying there's a chance.

24

I was on the move again, this time into a cell with Dylan and Andy. The three of us were shoved in a space next door to Paul, Mathias, John and Brahim, and I soon got to know Andy pretty well. He'd been captured and sent into the Black Site in April where his arm had been broken during a serious beating. The Russians had then inserted metal pins into the bones to help him recover, but the procedure was still causing him some irritation. Not that Andy was getting too much sympathy from the lads. When Brahim first noticed the steel rods protruding from his infected limb, he cheekily nicknamed him 'Chandelier Arm'.

Once settled in with my new cell mates, I realised I'd become an unofficial senior figure within the group, mainly due to my age and combat experience. For the younger lads with the Ukrainian Marines, like Brahim, I acted as a sounding board on how to handle the prison guards. During my SERE training, I'd been taught all sorts of techniques for building a rapport with the people responsible for feeding, watering and not killing us. For those lads without military training, like Dylan and Paul, I tried to provide psychological support, so they could manage the challenges of being banged up with no end date in sight.

It became important to shield this mentorship position from the guards. If anyone learned of my role as a teacher/counsellor/morale booster, they'd probably separate me from the group. But as far as they were concerned, I was the sociable war dog – a salty but harmless military veteran with way too many stories to share. This homespun appearance was deliberately deceptive. I knew exactly what I was doing and, like an old-school football manager, I adapted to the personalities around me. It was important to know which of the POWs required an arm around the shoulder during tough times. It seemed equally vital to understand who would benefit most from a motivational boot up the arse.

Andy fell into the latter category. During our first week together, he fretted constantly about his family. He feared getting the death sentence and often became tearful at the thought of never seeing his kids again. It did my head in and I eventually decided to buck him up with a few hard truths.

'Stop crying,' I said. 'I don't want to hear you feeling sorry for yourself.'

'What do you mean?' he snapped back, angrily.

'Well, you weren't exactly thinking of the kids when you first signed up to fight, so why start now? Dwelling on the situation is only going to make things worse for you.'

The funny thing was, I wanted to get emotional. I wanted to pour my heart out. And I wanted to dream and talk about Larysa, and our time together. But I knew that reliving those happy times and mourning our separation would put me in a very dangerous place. Instead I held it together and Andy took my advice with a scowl, but it had a positive impact. The next time I looked over he was studying our shared Russian–English dictionary. Whenever the guards passed nearby, he did his best to track their conversations.

Meanwhile, the Ukrainian bombs drew nearer and became more frequent. At night they rumbled away in the background like an advancing thunderstorm, and by watching from our window I soon realised that the DPR's military forces had gathered tightly around the prison. They were tooled up with heavy artillery – which made the prison a legitimate target. There was now a growing chance the facility might get struck in an attack. This understanding came with a mixture of emotions: on the one hand, a rocket assault might kill everyone in the prison; on the other, it could breach the compound walls and allow the POWs to escape in the chaos. The odds of a direct hit were slim, and at times it felt like I was willing on my own death, but at least it was something.

When a shell later landed nearby, the explosion blew rocks and debris into the cell and everybody cheered. 'That's from a tank,' coughed Andy. '*Definitely a tank*. And that shell could have only landed about eighty metres away. The Ukrainians are closing in.'

I jumped up and danced around the room. 'Come on!' I shouted, pulling Dylan to his feet. '*Come on!*'

Minutes later, another bomb blast rocked the ground. 'There's another one,' said Andy, noting the distance at fifty metres. 'Getting closer.'

'It's going to come, mate,' I laughed. 'It's going to happen.'

Suddenly, there was a rap on the door. The viewing hatch sprang open. 'What are you doing in there?' shouted a voice.

I sat down on my bed like a scolded kid. 'Nothing,' I called back cheerily, hopeful that at some point I'd be free from this hell.

One evening, I asked Dylan how he felt about his forthcoming court case. 'What do you reckon?' I said, refilling my coffee. 'Pushing back against the judge and all that.'

'I don't know,' he said. 'It feels like we're going to get screwed over no matter what we do.'

I nodded. I respected Dylan; he was a nice bloke. Like Brahim, he was in his early twenties, though that's where the similarities ended. Dylan hadn't been military trained. As he told the story of his capture alongside Paul, I realised he'd had an even rougher go of it than me. After the initial round of beatings, interrogations and electric shocks, he'd been moved into an isolation cell away from Paul, and from there the torture had intensified.

'They fucking waterboarded me,' he said angrily, sipping his coffee. 'They stuck a rag in my mouth and whenever I didn't give them the answer they wanted, they poured water on me, till I started choking. Did you get the same?'

'No. *Thank fuck.*'

Dylan shook his head. 'Yeah, Paul said the same thing. Bloody hell, it was just me, then. Though I don't know why. They used to wake me up in the middle of the night and beat the shit out of me.'

He rubbed his side. 'They've definitely broken some ribs. But I didn't cry or beg. What good would that do? It wasn't like I was going to change the situation.'

Like all of us, Dylan looked haunted. His skin was white; his eyes were bloodshot.

'What do you think they wanted?' I said.

'They wanted to know if I was a spy, which I'm not, but how could I prove it? They also wanted to know how we'd got behind their lines.'

He leant forward. 'Do you really think we can get out of this death sentence?'

I nodded. 'Maybe,' I said, refilling my coffee cup. 'Who knows? But your best shot is to slow the trial down.'

'It's easier said than done though, isn't it?' said Dylan.

'Yeah. They'll try to shut you up in court. You'll be at

the back, in a cell, but every now and then you'll get asked a question.'

'Like what?'

I sighed, remembering the accusations that had been thrown at us. 'Like *why* you're a mercenary, rather than *if*,' I said. 'I was confused by it all. We were the first on trial, so we had no idea what to expect. If I'd known then what I know now, I'd have used the media to say we'd been mistreated and that our testimonies were made-up bollocks.'

Dylan sat back. He was taking it all in. 'Well, I'm going to be sentenced to death anyway,' he said, eventually. 'I might as well go out with a bang.'

Over the several hours, we devised a playbook of strategies on what to say in court and how to say it, refilling our five-litre bottle of water whenever the taps came on before loading up on coffee. I wanted to make sure that Dylan knew exactly what to expect in his trial. By the time the sun had come up, we were knackered but happy. Slowly but surely, our brief for sticking it to the enemy was taking shape.

Life had become incredibly monotonous by that stage. The propaganda merry-go-round and my judicial proceedings had come to an end, and I was bored. Of the Brits in Makiivka, only the ones still standing trial were being taken away for legal meetings. Meanwhile, Brahim and I had been left alone for weeks, with zero clues as to what was happening with our respective appeals. (I also had no idea what Aiden was being subjected to, because he was in another building altogether.) To pass the time I fantasised about how we were going to escape should a rocket strike Makiivka. On the good days, I visualised our reactions as the bomb blew through the building; I pictured myself running to freedom through the prison corridors with the others. On the bad days, I saw our escape falling flat, especially as I had no idea how we would get the likes of John, Mathias or Paul away, given their injuries.

In general, though, the morale in our space remained high. Between us, we were developing a strong connection, much of it built on optimism, dark humour and a shared belief that we had become involved in a POW effort to match the Boy's-Own escapades from *The Great Escape*. This idea was ramped up when Andy and Dylan were given a date for their court case, which meant we could put our cobbled-together legal defences into action. The Kurator announced that they would be tried on 15 August, alongside John, Mathias and a Croatian soldier called Vjekoslav Prebeg. The news sharpened everyone's minds and our intelligence-gathering went on unabated.

Meanwhile, the enemy were inadvertently helping our cause. In addition to the Russian–English dictionary, Davidoff had decided to ease our boredom with a couple of books – one dog-eared Harry Potter novel and a copy of F. Scott Fitzgerald's literary classic *The Great Gatsby*. We passed both titles between us in what became an emotionally turbulent game of swapsies. I soon realised that reading about a child wizard was fine because it allowed me to escape into a fantasy story. But delving into the fictional, hedonistic world of Gatsby and his opulent parties sometimes felt a little masochistic. With each chapter, the FOMO increased and my brain caved in a little. Given the choice, my imagination was happier in Hogwarts.

Of all the titles within our threadbare library, the dictionary was still the most popular, and by now everyone had taken on the responsibility of learning new words and phrases. We spent hours poring over the terms to listen out for. *Exchange* was important. So too was *Handover* and *Swap*. 'If any of you hear those words, give me a shout,' I told the others. I wanted to know if anything was changing around us – for better or worse – in case we had to alter our legal strategy. We took turns listening at the door, and one afternoon, while I was taking an afternoon nap, Dylan shook me awake.

'I've heard it!' he said, excitedly.

'Heard what?'

'*The word.* The guards are outside in the paddock talking about an exchange.'

I jumped up, keeping a lid on my excitement as we crept cautiously towards the window. Slowly I picked up the thread of a conversation. Two, maybe three guards were chatting outside. *One of them was Davidoff.* And then I recognised a single word in the middle of a jumbled sentence. *Swap.* I looked at Dylan and nodded. *He'd been right.* The guards were discussing a deal of some kind.

'... I've had it for six years ... Now everything is fucked ...'

I looked at the others and shrugged. *Well, this isn't making any sense.* I felt confused and reached for the dictionary. *What the hell are they talking about?*

Then I recognised several words from my Russian language classes. *Car. Wanted. Garage.*

Shaking my head sadly, I stepped away from the window.

'So?' whispered Dylan. 'Are we getting out of here or what?' He was staring at me.

'No, mate,' I said, trying to see the funny side. 'By the sound of it, one of these pricks is selling his car at the local garage. Good call, though: you picked up on what was being said.'

Dylan looked gutted.

'Don't worry about it,' I said, trying to lift his spirits. 'You recognised the word, and that's the most important thing for now. At some point, it'll be relevant to us.'

Sometimes it felt as if global events were conspiring against us, too. Early in July, a guard knocked on our cell door to deliver the news that Boris Johnson had resigned as UK prime minister in June, and the information briefly deflated us. Boris had been a champion for Ukraine. A number of soldiers had taken to him because of his unwavering support for our military cause, and he was someone that we hoped might secure our release in the future. With him suddenly out of the picture, there was a good chance that any gathered momentum would be lost.

'What the fuck's going on at home?' asked Dylan, once the guard had walked away.

'I don't know, mate,' I said. 'It might not even be true. But if it is, you can bet we're not in the newspapers any more. And that isn't a good thing.'

Dylan sat up. 'Why?'

'Because nobody's going to be talking about *us* any more, they're going to be talking about Boris. If we're not in the public conversation, there won't be any pressure on the people in charge to get anything done.'

Andy had been taking in the news from his corner of the cell. 'We can't believe anything they tell us,' he said eventually. 'For weeks the Russians have been saying they're taking Ukraine. Now we can hear our tanks bombing the shit out of them.'

'So what do we do?' said Dylan.

'Keep believing,' I said. 'Somebody somewhere is fighting for us and talking about us. *Maybe that somebody's going to get us out of here.*'

*

Hell broke loose a week later. One morning, the lads still awaiting trial were unexpectedly taken to the Prosecutor's office for the signing of several judicial documents. Once everyone had returned to the cells, I was told that Paul had caused a fair amount of trouble during his processing and had been badly beaten. Apparently, the Prosecutor had asked a series of questions but Paul clammed up and refused to say anything other than to demand cigarettes. 'I want a fag,' he said. 'Give me a fag.' Paul made the same request over and over, until eventually the Prosecutor snapped.

'Paul, this is very serious!' he shouted. 'You have to listen to the questions being put to you.'

He pushed a stack of forms across the desk. 'Your life depends on you signing these as well . . .'

But Paul wouldn't budge.

The drama escalated. Paul couldn't, or wouldn't, accept the severity of his position. I knew he'd been making a nuisance of himself in Makiivka and had angered a prison medic who had been helping him with his diabetes medication. But by doubling down and annoying the Prosecutor he was only adding to his growing reputation as a troublemaker. When the session came to an end, word of Paul's behaviour made it to some of the guards in the building. Among them were several soldiers from the front line who were best described as being battle-hardened and angry. Enraged, they then spent forty-five minutes beating the shit out of Paul in a separate room and Dylan and Andy had heard the screaming from several doors away. By the time Paul returned to Makiivka, he was a mess – his face had been bludgeoned and his body resembled a bag of broken biscuits. The others had taken some lumps too. Andy's face was badly swollen, and Mathias's injured leg had been repeatedly kicked and was now re-broken.

The fallout was huge. For starters, this off-the-books beating hadn't been approved by the Kurator, who understood better than anyone that any accusations of prisoner abuse would result in a war trial, and that he would be the first suspect in line – that's if the conflict turned in Ukraine's favour. When a medical officer checked Paul's injuries, it was announced that an investigation would be taking place as the DPR attempted to cover their arses. But none of this was helping Paul. For two days, I listened as he coughed and choked in the cell next door. It was horrific. At times it sounded as if his lungs were going to come up.

The following Sunday, the corridor was sent for its daily recreation hour and, as always, we exchanged intelligence and told jokes between the cells. Unusually, Paul had stayed in bed. He'd been complaining of serious pains in his abdomen and wasn't feeling well. The symptoms of his diabetes had been causing him some trouble too, but there wasn't anything we could do without help from the prison medics – and they hadn't been available that afternoon. Then, as we filed back to our cells, I heard shouting in the space next door.

'We need a doctor!'

'Quick! He's not breathing.'

I looked at Andy and Dylan. It didn't take a genius to work out what had happened. Paul had been found dead in his bunk.

When the guards arrived there was more yelling as John, Mathias and Brahim were taken away to another cell. I sat on my bunk and groaned. *Paul was the first of us to die.* The realisation was totally demoralising.

'There will be an investigation into this,' shouted another voice. It sounded like the Kurator.

Makiivka was immediately locked down and as the news rippled through the facility, there seemed to be a noticeable change in mood. Some of the guards became edgy and I remembered Davidoff's comment from a couple of weeks previously. *It causes no end of problems for us if a prisoner of war dies.* I wondered what those problems might look like in Makiivka. But I wouldn't have to wait long for my answer.

Shortly after Paul's passing, I heard Misha, the guard, talking on his mobile outside our cell. After he'd given me the dictionary during my first day or so in Makiivka, he had continued to show an interest in our well-being. Among the inmates he was known as someone who generally treated the well-behaved prisoners with respect. When the bombs landed nearby he often popped his head into the cells to check on our welfare, but more than anything he liked to swear at us in English.

Judging by the conversation, Misha was in trouble. Sadly for him, Paul had died on his shift and the Kurator was taking an interest in his activities that day. Misha seemed pretty stressed about how the interrogations might go.

'The FSB are coming,' he said, nervously.

It was the first time I'd heard anyone mention that name in Makiivka. According to the judge in my trial, the DPR was beyond Kremlin rule, though everyone knew that had been a joke. I thought of Mr Balaclava and tensed.

Misha carried on talking into his phone. 'They want to investigate Paul Urey's death. They think it is because of me.'

I felt sorry for him. Sure, he was a member of the enemy, and under different circumstances – in the trenches, or while defending Mariupol – I might have shot him, given half the chance. But inside Makiivka, under a different set of rules, he struck me as an OK bloke. Whenever Misha came to our cell, he wanted to swap jokes with the British lads. If ever we became too rowdy, he teased us about our prison sentences. 'Why are you making chuckles?' he would laugh, darkly. 'You will be dying soon.' Unsure of whether he was being serious or messing around, I did my best to fake outrage, hoping to remain on his good side.

In the corridor, Misha let out a sigh and walked away. Because of Paul's death, his demeanour had visibly shifted, and all because he'd been in the wrong place at the wrong time. He would soon be scrutinised by the most terrifying individuals on Putin's authoritarian payroll, the same people who had beaten, stabbed and electrocuted me. I understood his anxiety. If Misha wasn't able to convince the FSB of his innocence, he'd be tortured, as I'd been. He might even be 'disappeared' in a convenient accident. *Would Mr Balaclava be involved?* I wouldn't have traded places with Misha, not for another five minutes of freedom.

Paul's body wasn't moved for two days and it was hard to know what to say or do. At times we shouted out macabre jokes and traded in gallows humour to stop everyone from freaking out. Somebody asked if Paul wanted a cigarette; we said our goodnights to him as we fell asleep. It felt weird that there was a cellmate lying dead on the other side of our wall and nobody was doing anything about it. The mood was bleak.

There was a certain level of anger and frustration too. I raged about the guards responsible for beating Paul. *I mean, why bother?* He had been an easy target: out of shape, unwell and vulnerable. There was nothing to be gained by assaulting him. But I also felt weirdly annoyed at Paul for not understanding the severity of his situation.

'Why couldn't he have played the game?' I said, eventually.

'What do you mean?' asked one of the other lads.

'I mean: *Paul, keep your mouth shut, mate*. Don't make yourself a target. He spent a lot of time winding up the people you're not supposed to wind up.'

'But he wasn't military-trained. How was he supposed—'

'That doesn't matter,' I said. 'We gave him enough warnings. We told him what to do.'

Then I remembered Paul was not three feet away. Instantly I felt a pang of guilt. 'I wanted him to have his day in court,' I said. 'I wanted him to push back against the Russians.'

His death felt like such a waste.

The guards in Makiivka were equally angry about Paul's death, though this was mainly because their workload had increased as a result. We were soon visited by another medic, who took statements from anyone who had seen or spoken to Paul in the previous forty-eight hours.

'This is not right,' she said, over and over, as I explained how Paul had been assaulted at the Prosecutor's office.

She then asked if Misha had been in close contact with Paul at any point that day. I shook my head. *No. Not a chance.*

The medic stared at me. 'Are you sure?' she said.

I nodded. *Very.*

When she left, a part of me wondered if I'd succumbed to a form of Stockholm syndrome, the famous psychological condition in which a hostage, or prisoner, feels empathy, or even affection, for their kidnapper, or captor. I reassured myself that I was in good shape emotionally. Yeah, Misha was DPR, but in Makiivka, he'd been fair to us and I wouldn't have wished the treatment I'd experienced in the Black Site on anyone. More importantly, it felt like the right thing to do. So much of my humanity had been stripped away, first by war and then by incarceration, that it seemed important to stick to the truth. I didn't want another piece of me to die.

Once the medic's investigations had been concluded, and Paul's body was removed, the Russians declared to the world that his death was a result of natural causes. To hammer the story home, the Kremlin's media machine then moved into action and later that week, my old mate Roman Kosarev arrived outside our cell to film yet another fictional news piece. As we listened to his nonsense about how Paul had died due to underlying health conditions rather than the result of yet another horrific beating, the lads took turns to cough during the recording. Someone shouted out the word 'Bullshit' between splutters, like a naughty schoolkid acting up at the back of the classroom. One by one, we followed suit.

Bullshit.

Bollocks.

Wankers.

Eventually, a guard told us to pipe down and the camera crew were moved on.

At the next recreation break, I called out to John over the wall. 'This is mad,' I said. 'Wonder how Misha's getting on?'

There was a pause. 'Who cares?' replied John, eventually. 'It's not like there's any nice ones in here.'

'He seems all right, though—'

I heard a derisory snort. 'Yeah, whatever, Snowy,' he shouted. 'You tell yourself that. There's not one I wouldn't shoot in the face.'

Paul's cellmates were shifted along the corridor to another space around four doors down. To placate them, the Kurator placed a TV in their cell, believing the likes of

John and Brahim would feel calmed by a stream of shitty, subtitled films and some Kremlin-sponsored news reports. But the TV soon became a tool every bit as useful as the Russian–English dictionary. With a few twists of the aerial, they were able to tune in to the women's football and the Ukrainian news, and the mood lifted considerably. Their reports, relayed during our daily paddock breaks, told us that Zelenskiy's advancing forces were only a few kilometres away and the conflict was swinging in their favour. Instantly, we felt galvanised. The first time Ukraine's leader popped up on the telly, wearing his famous green T-shirt, Brahim had apparently stood up and pointed.

'*Our* president,' he said, his chest puffed out.

I laughed at the story. Brahim was a proud Moroccan – albeit one serving with the Ukrainian armed forces – but I got his point. Zelenskiy was a beacon of hope for every POW in Makiivka, regardless of their nationality. In the face of some unbelievable pressure, he'd stood up to Russia's military might by deploying tactical savvy and some forceful and imaginative propaganda. *Maybe we could do the same.* I also had several solid reasons for supporting him: I'd spent nearly five years with the Ukrainian military; I was married to a Ukrainian; I loved the bones of Ukraine. *I was indoctrinated.* At no point did I think Zelenskiy would abandon us or his country. When a Russian guard came to our cell a few days later and told us that Zelenskiy had fled Ukraine for London, we saw the story for what it was. *Grade-A bollocks.* The bloke was laughed out of the room. A quick twist of the telly aerial soon confirmed everyone's faith. Zelenskiy was still in Ukraine, fighting the good fight.

And so were we.

*

Emotionally, 15 August was a day of mixed emotions in Makiivka. During the morning, Dylan, Andy and the others were hooded, cuffed and taken for trial. For the first time in months I was alone, and the realisation felt terrifying. Without another person to talk to – *or talk at* – a depressing sense of isolation swallowed me whole. I was as frightened and lost as I had been during those first few days in the Black Site. My mind twisted wildly. One lonely hour became two and then three, and before long I was in a weird, doomy headspace where everything seemed jumbled and unstable, with nothing tangible to cling on to for support.

The news at home wasn't helping. A number of Ukrainian TV channels were reporting that Britain was in a right muddle, especially following the news of Boris Johnson's departure. At first I thought about Mum, then I wondered how Larysa was doing and I quickly spiralled from there. My thoughts lurched through the siege of Mariupol in a series of memories and unresolved trauma that had been waiting to strike from the shadows. The stink, cold and hunger came back to me in waves. Grief followed soon after and I saw Dima. Then I stressed about my team-mates, like Bear, and wondered whether they were alive and safe or rotting in a cell like mine. *What was going to happen to us?* Finally I thought about Paul Urey and broke down in tears. My body shook with emotion, as if some pressure valve had been released. I'd worked so hard to stay strong in front of the other lads that I hadn't allowed myself to vent in any way. Now every negative thought was coming out of me at once, and in floods.

The day dragged by. Dylan and Andy had been gone for ages and I started to fear for their safety. Given what was happening in the war, I considered the possibility that Putin had intensified his violent rampage and was now topping guilty prisoners on the spot. My mind flashed back to that awful day when we'd been informed the Russians intended to execute us. I saw flashbulbs popping. I heard the mock cries of outrage from the lawyers. I felt my rage increasing at the lies and the political theatre. I prayed the lads were sticking to our plan and telling the court about how they had been beaten, starved and coerced into falsifying statements. *They had to mention Paul's death, too.* It was their only chance of avoiding a fatal charge.

I tried to sleep. The day was slipping away; shadows were lengthening outside. The karaoke bar had opened across the street and someone was butchering Robbie Williams's 'Angels' again. I pulled a sheet around my ears and tried to muffle the wailing, but I was soon distracted by a kerfuffle outside the door. Someone was jangling a set of keys and shuffling their feet. A prison guard spoke loudly.

'*Go inside. Slowly.*'

The lock turned and the cell door opened. Andy and Dylan stepped inside. When the door slammed shut behind them, they both smiled.

'A result?' I asked.

Andy nodded. 'Yeah,' he said, laughing excitedly. 'We got a month and a half recess. *Fifty days.*'

'All of you?' I said.

'All of us.'

Bloody hell. I did the maths. A pause of that length would probably take them up to October, and though I couldn't be sure, there was a chance the referendum might have been decided by then. The right outcome there would then spare us all from the death sentence. Andy and Dylan were buzzing and their good mood was contagious. A win for them was like a win for all. Finally, we had something to celebrate.

'So, what happened?' I said.

'We went in there and did everything as planned,' said Andy. 'When they asked how we wanted to plead, Mathias said, "Actually, we were tortured. There was an investigation into one of our friends who had died. And we've been starved and forced to make statements that aren't true." The place went crazy. They told the TV cameras to stop filming. Then the judges and the lawyers got together . . .'

'We didn't know what the fuck was going on,' said Dylan. He was grinning broadly.

'Then what?' I said.

'Then they postponed the trial,' said Andy. 'They're talking about conducting an investigation.'

He threw air quotes around the word *investigation*. 'We've bought ourselves some more time, mate.'

He leant down to our makeshift kettle and turned on the power. 'We just pushed back the Russians thanks to a plan built on shitty instant coffee.'

The Weight lifted from my shoulders. Finally, it seemed as if we might be winning.

Despite our first legal victory, the following few weeks dragged by uneventfully. Misha returned to Makiivka, but his attitude towards us was noticeably different – the joking had come to an end; there was no more swearing in English. Elsewhere, my thirty-day appeal process expired without the Prosecutor calling either Brahim or me to his office, and every time we asked the wardens for an update, the response was the same as before: *Not today; maybe tomorrow.* We were caught in a state of flux. By early September, Ukraine's forces hadn't yet reclaimed occupied Donetsk and the referendum was still to be held. I was living through a succession of hellish Groundhog Days and had become increasingly disorientated and overwhelmed. I reassured myself that time meant hope; no news was good news and all that. But under the conditions, I also feared for my long-term mental health. In a mild panic, part of me even wondered if I was hallucinating.

I had good reason. One morning in bed, as the guards strolled by on their patrols, I was convinced they were discussing our release, just as Andy had believed previously. This time, though, the details were more pointed. 'They're going soon,' said a voice outside our door. I sat bolt upright. *They're going soon.* This was the news we'd been waiting for. And once the others had woken up, I shared the details.

'This is it,' I said, excitedly. 'I'm a hundred per cent sure of it.'

We talked emotionally about how our lives would change once we'd made it home, and I imagined being reunited with Larysa, but as the days passed and nothing happened, I wondered if a cruel mind game had been played on us. I became paranoid that the guards were deliberately making comments as they walked by. Andy and Dylan soon started to take the piss out of my story, and for a while I stressed over a more worrying truth: that the entire episode had been a mental wobble.

If that was the case, I wouldn't have been surprised. Life as a prisoner of war was a weird blend of boredom and bewilderment. The days were a grind, but at the same time certain world events were impacting on my life in a way that felt totally surreal. At the beginning of September a guard cannonballed past the paddocks on a recreation break. He was making comments and laughing. He seemed to be gloating about something as he walked our way.

'This doesn't sound good,' said Andy, looking worried. 'Do you think Ukraine has surrendered?'

Then he came to us. 'Your Queen is dead,' said the guard. 'The Queen is dead!'

He giggled and pointed, presumably in the hope that one of us might break down at the announcement. At first, I felt spun out. On top of Boris Johnson resigning and the news Liz Truss had taken over, the UK sounded like a right shitshow. *Now we'd lost the bloody Queen too?* I imagined the scenes at home, the newspaper headlines and the sense of loss. The country's figurehead was gone and I worried that the information might shatter our morale in some way – not only mine, but the other Brits too. So far, we had done well to stand strong in the face of psychological manipulation, and while I wasn't sure how the other inmates in the prison felt about the Royal Family, or if it was even a matter of importance in the grand scheme of things, I sensed that another destabilising event in the UK might upend our mental resolve. One of the things holding everyone together was the idea that Britain was unchanged. She had been keeping calm and carrying on in our absence.

And now, all of a sudden, she wasn't.

My concerns were put to rest almost instantly. From down the recreation yard I heard more talking. It was John, and at first it was hard to grasp what was being said, probably because it was a phrase I hadn't heard in my lifetime. Then another voice chimed in, and another. I caught different accents, British, Swedish, American: everyone was saying the same thing.

God save the King!

The voices bounced along the paddocks.

God save the King!

The volume grew louder and louder, as one by one the prisoners realised what was happening. *We were under attack.* The Russians had wanted to pile on the misery and break our spirits. But we were standing firm.

God save the King! God save the King! God save the King!

The guard stared back at us, uncertain of what to do next. We weren't responding as he'd hoped and his emotional assault had backfired. Eventually he walked away, his tail between his legs, and our spirits lifted. Turning collective grief into a defiant show of force suddenly felt like the biggest small victory of all.

Her Majesty would have been chuffed.

Then everything happened all at once.

The first sign that change was in the offing came from beneath us, in the subterranean wing of the penal colony, where the prison's scariest inmates were housed. It was a hellhole down there. Every day a raid took place where the murderers and rapists were forced to stand outside their cell doors as the guards ransacked their spaces, tipping up the bedding and searching every corner and loose brick for drug stashes and makeshift weapons. Anyone discovered with contraband was punished severely, and the prisoners downstairs were sometimes banned from sitting for days at a time.

Every day they threw abuse at us for jumping the judicial queue. Then they screamed at the guards. Ordinarily they would have been housed on a higher level, where it was warmer and there was a little outside space, but we had pinched that privilege too.

The verbal exchanges ran like clockwork. A prisoner would begin yelling, 'When are you moving us?'

The guard on duty often responded with a dismissive comment. 'There's no room, you're stuck on the bottom floor.'

'Why are all the mercenaries up on the second floor, living normally, and we're all down here, living in shit?'

'Well, there's no room.'

'When are they going?'

'I don't fucking know.'

And so on, and so on . . . *Until the mood changed.*

I barely paid attention as a familiar voice shouted out the same old question. He sounded big, his timbre felt huge, and his throat was raw with anger and hate. I imagined the words belonged to a brutal killer and winced.

'When are we going upstairs?'

Here we go again, I thought. *The same old bollocks.*

'Soon,' said the guard, and my attention sharpened. The sun was filtering into the cell through our tiny window. It could only have been around 6 a.m. and Andy and Dylan were still sleeping soundly. Instantly, I was up and out of my bunk and listening at the cell door. The conversation from downstairs was muffled, and it arrived in fragments, but I could make out the important details.

'About time,' shouted the inmate. 'When are they fucking off?'

'Next week,' said the guard.

I called out to the others to wake up. I wanted someone else to hear it. Having made the mistake of lifting everyone's hopes a couple of weeks previously, I needed one other person to hear what might be the first confirmation of our release. *Were we really getting out of occupied Ukraine?*

I nudged Andy first. He stirred grumpily.

'Mate, what the fuck do you want?'

I put my fingers to my lips. 'Listen.'

He sat up, rubbing the crumbs from his eyes. I gave Dylan a kick too. He rolled over and glared.

'I need you to hear this,' I said.

'Hear what?' yawned Dylan.

'I've just heard a guard telling the prisoners downstairs that they're being transferred up here next and that—'

'Yeah? And why is that happening?' said Andy, propping himself up on an elbow. 'Don't tell me: we're getting out?'

Fair point. I understood his scepticism. My recent track record on picking up intelligence regarding our release wasn't exactly impressive, and the slow realisation that my previous information was wide of the mark had been a massive downer. Nobody wanted their hopes raised unnecessarily, not for a second time. The comedown was just too painful.

Dylan rolled over in his bunk. 'Fuck off, Shaun,' he said. 'I'm tired.'

'Look, I think we're going to get exchanged or released,' I said, trying not to sound desperate or crazy. 'I just heard two people chatting and one of them was a guard. Yeah, I must have been half asleep or whatever, but the talk was that it's happening next week.'

'Where are we now?' said Andy.

'Saturday.'

'Saturday. So that means it could be as early as Monday, or as long as another week away.' He pulled his covers around his head. 'We'll soon find out then, won't we?'

I felt high. For the next thirty-six hours I imagined being back on British soil, or somewhere in Ukraine with Larysa. The time seemed to drag by. But by Monday night, nothing had happened. Meanwhile, the activity in our wing ground to a halt – nobody was being taken away for filming or questioning. The following afternoon, Dylan began to poke at me.

'So I guess it must have been another dream then, eh?' he said, smiling.

I shrugged. 'Yeah. Maybe. *I don't know.* I could have sworn I'd heard it.'

'Or maybe you *wanted* to hear it,' said Andy, trying to sound supportive. 'Don't beat yourself up, mate. It's a human response in a shitty situation.'

I felt bruised by the incident, and slightly unnerved that I might have imagined the entire thing. But I wasn't yet out of hope. The timeline was intact. There were five more days in which we could be released.

And then the next day, in the afternoon, everything changed once more. Our cell door crashed open. A guard stepped inside. He was ordering us to pack up our things – our clothes, the home-made chessboard, *The Great Gatsby* and the Harry Potter books.

Was this it? 'Why?' I asked, hoping for the best and mentally preparing for the worst.

'Because you're going on a long journey.'

We looked at each other. 'What's happening?' said Andy.

The guard gestured for us to hurry. 'You're packing up. I think you might be going home.'

My heart jackhammered. Every part of my body became light, as if I was floating above myself and viewing the scene as a witness rather than a participant. *I was going home . . . Wasn't I?*

The three of us were marched along the corridor, down a flight of stairs and into a holding cell. I looked around for any sign of the others. *Were John and Brahim being released too?* I wondered whether the same thing was happening to Mathias and Vjekoslav, or the Americans that had recently been brought inside. Then my mind reached for the dream scenario: that the war was over; that Ukraine had pushed the Russians back to their borders; that Ukraine was free of violence.

I forced myself to stay calm, because there was also a chance that we were being moved to somewhere much worse, or more worrying, that the order had come to execute us ahead of schedule, and the grisly work was to be conducted off the books. I felt flushed; a wave of nausea hit me. When the door opened and John, Brahim, Mathias, Vjekoslav and the Americans joined us in the holding cell, everyone seemed to be of the same mind. We were stunned. Some of the lads were close to tears with joy; those that weren't looked terrified.

Dylan nudged me in the ribs. 'Fucking hell, mate, you were right,' he said.

'I think so. But let's not get too excited, eh?'

After what felt like an age, we were hooded and escorted out of the prison and into a car park. By twisting my neck and looking underneath the hood, I could pick out various details. A Kamaz lorry, an army personnel carrier with a heavy fabric outer shell, had pulled up and the loading hatch was open. This, clearly, was our vehicle out of Makiivka. But standing around it were several bulky-looking guards and they were all dressed in instantly recognisable uniforms. A rush of panic crackled through me. Though I couldn't identify anyone by face, they were wardens from the Black Site, and as they gathered around us threateningly I felt the Makiivka guards nudging the group forward. *We're going back to that place,* I thought. *Or we're being killed.* There was no way of avoiding whatever was coming next.

'Show us your possessions,' shouted a man who was probably the most senior thug within the group.

We lifted up our books, clothes and other bits and pieces. Everything was taken away and dumped by the side of the road. Then the binding began. I heard the familiar ripping and tearing sound as my hands were bound crudely in front of me with masking tape. The circulation in my wrists was soon cut off and my fingers throbbed and tingled. At the Black Site, this procedure was often the preamble to a beating or an electrocution. Something bad was coming and every muscle in my body tensed as I was hauled onto the truck bed. My head was smashed into the steel frame and I heard laughter. Then something warm and wet dripped down my face and the bitter metallic tang of blood filled my mouth. My head had been split open.

I heard heavy breathing nearby. A guard was whispering in my ear. 'We have a nice Russian surprise for you . . . *faggot.*'

I was dead. My gut told me that when the hood was

next lifted, I would be staring into a shallow grave, with a loaded rifle jammed into the back of my skull and a crowd of Russian soldiers crowing and pointing at me. I wanted to puke. Freedom had felt like a very real possibility just minutes earlier. Now we were being carted away like cattle to an abattoir.

We were loaded into the vehicle. I heard thuds and groans as the prisoners were shoved to the floor, until eventually we were lined up like a human caterpillar. The Black Site guards punched and kicked us together and the tangle of limbs soon became excruciatingly painful. Though I couldn't see much, it wasn't hard to imagine the scene around me. We had been crudely linked together. I was sitting in someone's lap; their thighs trembled beneath me. Another prisoner had been seated on top of my crossed legs and my arms were then yanked up and looped over their head. With my shins pinned down by the full weight of another human body, the ligaments in my knees felt set to snap. I leant forward and whispered to the man in front. 'Who's that?'

'Shaun? It's John.'

John wasn't the biggest, but already my calf muscles were cramping and my thighs burned. Then suddenly, the pain intensified.

I groaned. 'What the fuck is that?'

John was breathing hard. 'It's Mathias. He's in my fucking lap.'

The Swede was a man mountain, around six foot five and the size of an old phone box. Wherever we were going and however long it was going to take us to get there, the ride was set to be painful. There were more groans and sighs around me. Everybody was close to breaking point.

'Shut up!' shouted one of the guards. 'Or it will get much more painful for you.'

The Kamaz's engine choked and grumbled. As we pulled away, every vibration in its rickety suspension placed more pressure on my muscles and joints. I felt heartbroken. I still couldn't believe that our brief taste of freedom had been snatched away.

You idiot, Shaun, I thought. *You should know how these people work by now.*

As the truck turned a corner at high speed, the pile of men collided and crushed together. In the shouting, I heard Ukrainian voices. There must have been some local POWs travelling with us too. And at the front of the bus, the Black Site guards laughed their heads off.

After twenty minutes, we pulled over and another body was thrown on board. When the truck rumbled away again, a voice muttered at the back of the bus. *It's Aiden.* The name was passed down to the front like a children's game of whispers.

That's Aiden?
They've brought Aiden on board.
Aiden's here . . .

The then familiar emotional tug of war returned: I felt pleased that Aiden was still alive, but also fearful for what he was about to be put through. As I sat, sweating in the autumnal heat, my body clenching with cramp, more blood trickled down my face and pooled in the bottom of the bag. The only way to slow the red drip was to lick my lips from time to time. The taste of salt and iron soon caused my stomach to turn. *Fuck me: this is hell on earth.* But everyone was in extreme pain, and at one point there was a disturbance at the back of the bus. A man was yelling as the human caterpillar wriggled anxiously.

'He needs help!' shouted a voice.

People were talking loudly as a wave of confusion rippled through the truck. Something bad had happened, but it was impossible to tell what exactly, or to which prisoner.

'Dylan's blacking out in my lap,' shouted another voice. It sounded like Andy. 'He's having an asthma attack . . .'

My thoughts naturally went to Paul and his brutal ending. *Was it happening again?* The idea of losing yet another mate filled me with dread, especially as the Russians would probably force us to sit with the corpse for the remainder of the journey, or dump him on the side of the road like a bag of rubbish.

I heard Dylan groaning. He sounded nearby. 'I can't hold on, boys,' he coughed. 'I can't breathe.'

'Hang in there, mate,' I whispered.

An awful silence of several seconds followed. 'Is he still alive?' I shouted, my head turning from side to side in a desperate attempt to get eyes on the situation.

'Yeah.' said Andy. 'He passed out for a bit, but I think he's OK now. He's moving . . .'

I sucked in a sigh of relief. Then I wondered if we were reaching the point where blacking out and dying in the back of a Russian truck might eventually turn out to be a blessing in disguise.

The guards toyed with us for hours. At intervals, they pulled over to the side of the road, and through the gap at the bottom of my hood it was possible to spot their movements between the slats in the truck's fabric shell. Sometimes they stopped for cigarettes and toilet breaks. On other occasions, they seemed to be swapping shifts and there were one or two changes in driving personnel. With every stop my body braced for pain and I was more convinced that one of two things was happening: I was about to be executed or tortured. I wasn't entirely sure which option was preferable.

As day turned into night, the Western prisoners were separated from the Ukrainian captives and linked together in a different vehicle, where the conditions were no less miserable. I wondered where the executions would happen. In my darkest thoughts, part of me imagined that we were being transported even deeper into Russia, where we might be paraded in Moscow before the firing squads did their work. If there was one small crumb of comfort, it was that we had been driving far too long for us to be heading to the Black Site. I'd rather have died than gone back there.

Then somebody begged the driver to pull over so the prisoners could piss on the side of the road.

'No,' laughed the guard. 'You will have to do it where you're sitting!'

Everyone groaned. Our bladders had knotted, and I readied myself for the acrid stink of warm urine, but it never came.

John came closest, though. 'I really need to go,' he moaned. 'I feel like my stomach is about to burst.'

I leant forward. 'Think carefully,' I said. 'If we ever get out of this, you'll be known as the man who pissed on me.'

John moaned grumpily and managed to hold himself. That in itself felt like an impressive act of resilience.

I dozed off briefly and awoke to notice the flicker of streetlights on the road outside. More and more people were moaning in agony. John in particular was coming undone. Every bump or turn in the journey brought a yelp of pain as his broken sternum and bulging bladder jarred and rattled. Another American prisoner near me was complaining about a nasty head injury he'd suffered. From what he was saying, one of the Black Site guards had sadistically taped his hood too tightly around his head with masking tape. After several hours of being bashed around on the back of the truck, the circulation in his face had been cut off.

'My head is swollen,' he moaned. 'I can't see. I think I'm going blind . . .'

I wondered how much more my body could take. The pain of being crushed by two men was not so great that I was going to black out in a few moments of blessed relief. Nor was it so mild that I could shut it out with mental strength alone. Instead I had to suck up the pain and push through. And all around me was the soundtrack of suffering.

Eventually, we pulled over again and I briefly caught a flash of daylight. It had been around mid-afternoon when we'd departed from Makiivka. We were now well into the next morning. The Kamaz engine stilled and I heard a whining noise that sounded strangely familiar, like something from another life. Carefully, I tipped my head to one side, hoping to get a better listen from underneath the plastic hood. Then I heard the jets of an aeroplane. An aircraft was passing overhead. We must have stopped at an airport. *Were they selling us to another country?* I ran through a list of Russia-friendly destinations. China. Brazil. South Africa. *Bloody hell, North Korea.* I was all out of hope. During my first few days at the Black Site, the thought of being sold to Russian-friendly Chechens had scared the shit out of me. This felt so much worse.

I was dragged from the truck and taken into a building. A set of automatic doors slid open and as I shuffled forward I saw military boots walking alongside me. My heart was somewhere around my Adam's apple. I heard the blood swishing in my ears. I'd been so discombobulated by the journey that even breathing felt like a laboured effort – something that needed careful thought rather than an unthinking process. We were lined up against a wall and when I looked down, I noticed the floor was tiled and shiny. *Oh fuck. Was I in a wet room?* I jerked my head to get a clearer view of our surroundings, frantically looking for a drain hole, hoping that a firing squad wasn't waiting somewhere nearby.

And when the hood was yanked away and I looked up, blinking at the harsh lights, my world seemed upside down.

Several men in civilian clothing fussed around me. As my eyes adjusted to the glare of strip lighting, I realised my fears had been misguided and we were being held in a private air terminal. There were several rows of plastic chairs set along a wall, plus a water cooler and a check-in desk. The clock read 9:30 a.m. It was several months since I'd physically read the time and the sight of something so bloody normal threw me into a loop. *Were we actually going home?* Everyone from the truck was being escorted inside and from top to bottom we looked like shit – banged about, broken down and close to falling apart. But of the group, the American I'd heard suffering in the Kamaz was in the worst shape. His head had ballooned, his eyes were bulging and the skin on his temples and forehead was turning a funny yellow colour. From a distance he looked like Homer Simpson. As a doctor carefully checked his condition, the American moaned softly.

'I can't see,' he said. 'Help me. I can't see.'

Alongside him, John had doubled over in pain and was clutching his chest. When I felt for the cut on my skull, the skin was crusted with dry blood. In the grand scheme of things, I'd got off lightly.

A medic flashed a torch at my eyes. 'What have you done to your head?'

I flinched. 'We were thrown into the back of a truck,' I said cautiously, unsure of exactly who I was talking to. 'Where are we?'

The man wrote down some notes. 'At the airport in Rostov. Don't worry, you are safe. We are from Saudi Arabia …'

Safe? I couldn't allow myself to believe that, not when the Black Site guards were somewhere nearby. Rostov was deep into Russian territory proper, which suggested our immediate future was delicately balanced, but when I checked the Saudis' security detail and realised the Black Site boneheads had been replaced by three military policemen, I allowed myself a little sigh of relief. They certainly seemed a lot friendlier than our previous carers. Some were even helping the medics as they carried out their checks. I saw Mathias being carefully escorted to the toilet.

'So who are you?' I said.

The man smiled. 'I'm a doctor. You are in good hands.'

I looked him over for any signs of who, or what, he was working for, but there was nothing in the way of badges, insignia or even a name tag. Eventually my photograph was taken. Another doctor asked me a few basic questions. *What is your name? How old are you?* And finally: *Are you allergic to any medicines?* Then I was told to go to the toilet. John, Andy, Aiden and everyone else seemed to be receiving a similar level of treatment. I turned around and caught Dylan's eye, who now looked recovered from his asthma attack. *What the fuck was going on?* He shrugged. Nobody had the wherewithal to guess. We'd been so scared that it was hard to know what was real and what wasn't.

Eventually a single-decker bus pulled up outside the terminal. 'Everybody up!' shouted a voice and the group, previously a painfully constructed human caterpillar, was gently arranged into a civilised line and duckwalked towards the bus. Once inside, we were instructed to kneel. Finally, when the transporter had made its brief spin around the airport runway, we were duckwalked outside again. With my hands on my head, I couldn't get a good look at what was going on around me, but our destination seemed to be a fancy-looking private plane. Its fuselage was short and sleek. But the tail was unmarked, and other than a couple of Arabic words on the door, there was no clue as to the identity of its owners. When I stepped on board, a security guard pointed me towards a La-Z-Boy-style seat at the back of the plane. I smelled the luxurious whiff of leather and freshly cleaned upholstery. That made for a nice change. The overwhelming aroma of the past day had been BO.

My head seemed to swivel and I looked left and right, and then left and right again, in a manic risk assessment. But the reaction was out of habit more than anything: I'd become paranoid. *Get yourself together, mate,* I thought. According to the medic, we were now safe. Certainly our new surroundings suggested we'd been escorted away from immediate danger. Unless I was imagining things, the Western prisoners from Makiivka were being embarked on a Kim Kardashian-style jet, looking more like competition winners on an all-expenses paid jolly to Disneyland than POWs. *Surely we weren't being flown to North Korea now?*

There were stewardesses. I watched the captain beaming at his dishevelled passengers, all of whom were sitting down in a nervous silence. And at the centre of it all was a man in his fifties. He was slim, with greying hair. He had a neatly trimmed beard and gentle blue eyes. He was also wearing a perfectly tailored suit, but he seemed to exude an extra layer of power to everyone else. This was amplified further by the small but muscular security man by his side. I recognised him as the type generally employed to neutralise

315

an approaching assailant without blinking. The Important Man was a big deal.

After a second or two I experienced a flicker of recognition. I nudged Andy, who was sitting in the row ahead. 'Hey, that bloke don't half look like the Chelsea owner . . . *What's his name?*'

Andy stared at me in disbelief. 'Roman Abramovich?'

'Yeah. *Him.* He looks like Roman Abramovich!'

Andy stared at the Important Man and snorted. 'You're tripping, mate. What the fuck is Roman Abramovich going to be doing out here? It's the middle of September. The football season's started.'

Fair point. My observational powers hadn't been the best in recent weeks. I'd even been disorientated at the sight of a wall clock. I closed my eyes and settled into the chair, reclining the seat and fiddling with the footrest. I couldn't remember the last time I'd experienced such luxury. But the Important Man was in my head. *Who was he?* Half-opening my eyes again, I noticed that a PA was fussing around him. The woman carried a dossier that bulged with paperwork and she seemed to be filling him in on the details of our flight. *Who were these people?* Then I overheard their conversation. The Important Man and his PA were talking in English, and one sentence sucked the air out of my lungs.

'We're just waiting for confirmation of the people at the other end.'

The people at the other end? This was it. *We were being exchanged.*

The plane's jet engines whined. I sank deeper into the seat and squeezed my eyes shut, fearing yet another false dawn. To distract myself, I focused on the activity outside. I looked for the Black Site guards – to make sure they weren't boarding the plane for one final beating. I searched for someone who might direct the plane away from the runway – to confirm that, yes, we were actually taking off. And I looked out for any enemy military personnel or activity – an indication that a political change of heart had taken place and we were about to be whisked back to Makiivka. Eventually, an attendant sealed the plane doors. Somebody handed me a bottle of water. Then a man I recognised as one of the doctors from the terminal stood in front of us. He had an announcement to make.

'Gentlemen, you're not officially free until we're away from Russian airspace,' he said calmly. 'But you're free. A deal has been struck to broker your release.'

There was yelling and cheering. I felt overwhelmed with relief. I folded over in my chair, my head in my hands, and wept. I thought of Larysa and my son. I imagined hugging my mum. I dreamed of England. Bloody hell: *Steak and chips*.

Slowly, the plane taxied down the runway and climbed into the sky.

We were on our way.

Everything felt so weird because everything seemed so *normal*.

Another man in a suit sat next to me and offered up a cigarette. I'd been so conditioned to fear rule-breaking that I very nearly jumped out of my seat.

'Mate, I'm on a plane!' I said, startled.

The bloke smiled. 'No, you're fine,' he said in broken English, handing over a fag. 'Just don't tell the pilot. Though after what has happened, I don't think anyone would really mind.'

For the next hour or so, I asked for so many cigarettes that he ended up giving me the packet.

A flight attendant brought out hot shawarma. We were given more medical checks on the plane. This was followed by a round of cakes. Remembering back to my projectile-vomiting episode on that first day in Makiivka, I reassured myself that I'd at least have a luxurious toilet to chuck up into if my tummy turned into a washing machine. We eventually learned that we were being taken to Saudi Arabia. After that, we were to be flown home and reunited with our families. Every snippet of good news brought a flood of tears. After all the pain, suffering and violence, I couldn't believe that something nice was happening to me. Every act of kindness felt otherworldly. Finally, we were given phones and told to message our loved ones. Just the thought of contacting Larysa put me into a spin.

'I'm free,' I wrote in a text. 'I'm coming home.'

From behind me, I felt movement. The Important Man's assistant had come over to talk.

'What is your name?' she asked, gently.

'Shaun.'

'Shaun, I'm Steph.'

She raised her hand apologetically. 'No offence, but when I saw you, you guys looked like crap.'

I tried not to laugh. *No shit.* 'Well, it's been a journey to get here,' I said, explaining my time at Pavlopil with the Ukrainian Marines, our retreat to Mariupol and that brutal siege, and our eventual withdrawal from the city as the Russians had rumbled in behind us. The fighting felt like a lifetime away. I told her about my capture, my torture at the hands of the Russian special forces and my introduction to Mr Balaclava. Finally, I detailed the court case, our death sentence and the homespun legal defence that, when it had finally come to fruition, felt like an Olympic gold medal win.

Steph shook her head in disbelief. 'Oh, my God,' she said eventually. 'I can't imagine what you must have been through.'

I excused myself and went to the toilet. When I returned, the Important Man was sharing a joke with John. And as he laughed, I leant back and caught his eye. He nodded and brought me into the conversation.

'I've got to get this off my chest,' I said, nervously. 'And I'm sure you must get this all the time, but . . . you really look like Roman Abramovich.'

The Important Man laughed. And I knew by his smile that I'd been right. 'Well, that's because I am Roman Abramovich,' he said, reaching out to shake my hand.

'I can't believe this: what are *you* doing here?'

Steph tapped me on the arm. 'Mr Abramovich has helped to broker your release . . .'

Composing myself, I looked across at Andy, who was staring. He mouthed the words, 'Is it him?'

I nodded. Andy shook his head and gawped over my shoulder. 'Bloody. *Hell.*' he said.

There was more laughter. When I turned back, John was messing around cracking jokes. 'Why couldn't you have bought West Ham rather than Chelsea?' he shouted.

Abramovich laughed. 'Because Chelsea is closer to my house.'

The mood had turned delirious. Our pilot was soon making the descent into Riyadh, and as we fastened our seatbelts, Steph explained the next phase in our release. Once processed on Saudi soil, we were to be taken to a hospital, where our various injuries and conditions would be assessed and treated. From what I could tell, Crown Prince Mohammed bin Salman of Saudi Arabia was footing our medical bills.

Plus the cost of the five-star hotel we'd be staying in for the next couple of days.

Steph leant over. 'Shaun, you seem to be the responsible one, or the oldest one. You might want to think about how you handle all this attention.'

After everything we'd been through, I guessed that one or two UK tabloids were being alerted to our return. But I really couldn't have cared less. After facing down the FSB, being interviewed by a journalist was going to be a doddle.

'Yeah, we'll have to do a few chats and some photos, won't we?' I said.

Steph smiled. 'Well, not exactly. You've caught the world's attention. Everyone wants to speak to you.'

I felt a slight panic coming on. '*Everyone?* We've done nothing,' I said, almost defensively. 'We've been banged up since April, so none of us have a clue about what's going on. How many people are you expecting us to talk to?'

Steph scrolled through her phone. She showed me the image of a Japanese newspaper. A photo of Aiden, John and me had been positioned on the front page. *This is you.* She showed me another. *And this is you.* And another. *You're in this one, too* . . . With each cover story, Steph named the country. *Thailand. Great Britain. America. India* . . . Our tale was being told all over the world.

I thought back to Mr Negus and his snarky comments during Geography. My head couldn't comprehend what was happening. In the space of twenty-four hours I'd awoken in a cell, been bound and beaten on what I'd assumed was the final journey before my execution, and then handed over to the now-former chairman of Chelsea Football Club and his rich Saudi Arabian associates. I felt disorientated. Even our destination was alien. I had never been to Saudi before.

I really had no idea what to expect. I wondered whether I'd be allowed to drink a pint of ice-cold lager at the hotel, because that was what I wanted more than anything.

The same mood had gripped us all. When we eventually stepped off the plane and onto the runway, I noticed Aiden walking beside me on the tarmac. He seemed wired, like a gazelle on a savannah, checking for some unseen predator. Recognising his paranoia, I called out.

'Aiden. *Mate*. Relax. It's going to be OK.'

But Aiden couldn't shake the feeling that something was off. His footsteps quickened. He almost broke into a jog. I grabbed him by the shoulder.

'Aiden, it's OK,' I said, trying to reassure him. 'We're safe.'

'Are you sure?'

I laughed. 'Yes. A hundred per cent,' I said. 'We're on the front page of every paper and website in the bloody world. No one can hurt you now.'

EPILOGUE

What was normal anyway?

Nothing could have prepared me for those initial moments of real freedom when, for the first time in several months, I was alone and allowed to do whatever the hell I wanted. Everything seemed new and invigorating, and I became locked in a permanent state of Beginner's Mind – a Buddhist concept in which a person looks at the world as if experiencing it for the very first time. The shampoo in the hotel felt weird. The bedding in the hotel felt weird. The carpet in the hotel felt weird. The experience was turbulent and brilliant all at once.

During my first week in England, the surreal nature of what I was going through continued and daily events that had previously seemed mundane and insignificant were now vibrant and more exciting than ever before. Watching a game of football on the telly – *amazing!* Picking up a newspaper in a café – *incredible!* Ordering a Chinese takeaway – *mind-blowing!* A hug from my mum, a cold pint in the local pub, a walk with the family dog: these events, though they had always been enjoyable, were suddenly so much more real and more important. I was learning to fully appreciate the people and places around me; I became determined to take nothing and no one for granted. Life had changed.

Physically, I was shot. I had lost a horrific amount of weight and my body was broken and vulnerable. Being dangerously malnourished for so long had left some serious scars and I spent the first week coughing uncontrollably. My thigh still throbbed from the knife wound and my bones had become brittle and rickety. Once I was in a position to scoff food more regularly, the urge to turn into a right greedy-guts became overwhelming. So I worked on bulking up – I had a pretty good excuse after all – and packed on so much timber that a doctor later commented that my new-found nutritional drive might push me close to a diabetic state. That was the wake-up call I'd needed.

Mentally, I was in a different place too. Gluing my fragmented life back together would take time, but I seemed remarkably OK considering. Yeah, I was undoubtedly sad. But I seemed to be in a place where I could accept my experience without any outbreaks of irrational anger or crushing depression. There were times when I'd mourn the people stolen from me by war. I felt anger at the way I'd been treated in the Black Site and the DPR courts, too. But at no point did my emotions feel overwhelming or uncontrollable. Having previously experienced the pain of a failed marriage, I'd learned how the mind could darken during moments of trauma. I wondered whether a certain amount of groundwork had already been laid for the fallout from imprisonment.

Importantly, I knew how to respect my emotions – the light ones and the dark. My brain had been subjected to a seismic level of hurt, and yet I was able to go to the supermarket, hang about with mates and watch a film without too much reaction. Despite being physically tortured and mentally abused, I hadn't become cold or closed off from the people living in my immediate orbit. When painful memories resurfaced – such as Dima's death or my brutal treatment under Mr Balaclava's watch – I wept. A counsellor later told me that I was crying at the appropriate times.

He also warned me to keep an eye out for any slow-moving symptoms of PTSD or serious depression.

Much of my stabilisation was rooted in a new sense of purpose. After returning to the UK, I was immediately asked to share my POW experiences with a raft of NATO-affiliated organisations. Apparently, as the most recent survivor from a modern POW camp – and a SERE-trained soldier – I was something of an unusual asset and my story became a case study for soldiers and other personnel learning to manage the pitfalls of potential capture. I retold anecdotes on how I handled the stress of torture and interrogation. Then I watched as people took notes and nodded approvingly. When I explained how I'd managed to carefully release information under duress, my stories became colourful and timely talking points. Every meeting was rewarding. While the experiences were still fresh in my mind, I was invited to speak to soldiers and senior officers in Norway, Denmark, the UK and Sweden. My attitude: if retelling the story was going to help a future POW, then the travelling was worth it.

In the background, I developed an appetite for justice. I would have to wait several weeks before finally being reunited with Larysa. She didn't have an English visa and though the British Foreign Office were working hard to speed up the process, it would take an age before she was allowed to enter the UK. We spoke for hours every day. In the meantime, I kept myself busy. I set up a VPN and scoured through Russian social media in an attempt to track down the people who had tortured me in the Black Site. Popov, my social worker, had been located. The cheeky bastard had become a spokesperson for the DPR. By checking a number of known Russian propaganda websites, I also found several videos filmed at the Black Site. Masochistically,

I looked for the footage of my electrocution – I felt weird knowing that it was out there. But the search also allowed me to identify some of the people who had inflicted their abuse upon me. Several of them were stupid enough to post public comments and I was then able to pass on their profiles to war-crime investigators working in the UK.

Every now and then a snippet of good news filtered through. I was invited into the *Good Morning Britain* studios and later received word that President Zelenskiy was awarding me with a third-class Order of Courage medal for my 'selfless acts in the defence and sovereignty of Ukraine'. Then, one morning, an attaché from the Ukrainian Embassy texted me a newspaper article with an update on what had been happening in the conflict. Apparently, the judge responsible for my death sentence had been seriously injured in an orchestrated hit.

I scanned the story and clicked on the accompanying photograph. The judge's face appeared and I recognised him straight away. *The bastard was at death's door.* A huge rush of anger and adrenaline hit me.

'Fucking hell. Karma is real,' I wrote.

'Yes, karma,' said the attaché. 'And the Ukrainian special forces.'

He then added two smiley emojis.

When I wasn't looking for members of the DPR online, I was contacting the families of soldiers I'd known, the ones that had died in battle. I also spoke to any parents wanting information on the sons I'd met in prison. I called Dimitri's mum and updated her on his whereabouts. I wrote letters to Dima's dad. I even messaged one of the injured lads I'd had to leave behind in the gatehouse outside of Mariupol. He contacted me on Facebook with a nice note. 'So glad you're alive,' he said, before reassuring me I'd done the right thing at the time and explaining that some of the people I'd encountered that day were safe and well, and had been exchanged before me. One of them, tragically, was later killed in a Russian prison. They hadn't been spared from the Russian mind games, though. While being held, an interrogator had told them I'd been executed.

Even though Ukraine is a big country, its community is very tightly knit and I realised that everyone was taking an interest in the whereabouts of their soldiers in an act of national mourning. I was soon bombarded with photos of lads who had been declared missing in action. And every picture arrived with a request for information. *Have you seen my son? Was my brother in prison with you? Do you have any information on my father's friend?* Most of the time, the faces were strangers. On one or two occasions, I knew the person but had no idea of their whereabouts. The worst messages came from those who had been informed that someone they knew was dead. They wanted to know if a mistake had been made and they'd instead been sent to Makiivka, or the Black Site, without anyone realising.

Confirming the bad news was heartbreaking but unavoidable, because I felt compelled to help. Bringing closure to those people cut adrift by war was important, especially as I'd been given a second chance. When I was released on 22 September, it marked the start of a different era, though the date was already important: it was the day Larysa and I had married; my birthday, and that of my mum, were around the same time, too. But shortly after being flown back to England, I discovered that, by being liberated, I was living a miraculous new life. I became determined to celebrate the event with every passing year.

And, finally, I was reunited with Larysa.

We met at Heathrow Airport and cried. In all the time I'd spent at home, this was the closest I'd come to really breaking down. During those long stretches in a Russian POW camp, I'd feared not seeing her again. But even when the last scraps of humanity were being stripped away from me – while I was being beaten and abused in the Black Site – I did everything I could to keep Larysa in my memory. I looked at our shared tattoo and heard her voice willing me on to live. I remembered her shouts telling me to fight. Her spirit pushed me to survive. She never faded from view.

As we hugged and sobbed, the human traffic of a busy airport swirled around us. Then Larysa handed over a silver wedding band. It was a replica of the one stolen from me in the Black Site.

'I noticed it had gone in the photos,' she said, pushing the ring onto my finger.

We kissed again and I held her close. 'I love you so much,' I said, not believing that I could actually say those words to her in person.

In prison, I'd been surrounded by so much hurt and hate that, at times, the likelihood of us being reunited had seemed out of reach. Even imagining Larysa's touch had brought pain because I feared it not happening. Now I wanted to savour every second.

I held on to her hand and didn't let go for hours.

ACKNOWLEDGEMENTS

At the time of writing, it has only been several months since my release, which has been somewhat of a surreal experience. On one of my first days back, my mum asked me what I was doing standing in the garden barefooted, in light drizzle, apparently staring into the sky on what was a very English day. All I remember is looking at the sun and the clouds, feeling the grass on my feet and the wind in my face, while thinking how new everything seemed. I could see, feel and smell everything all at once. It was overwhelming.

I have probably given my mum and family some serious headaches over the years with my sense for adventure and a curiosity to see what's behind the door or on the other side of the wall. The death of my father, John, at an early age, possibly gave me the drive and ambition I have today. But on reflection, his passing also helped me to deal with death itself — it wasn't alien to me and I had experienced it in the worst way. As hard as that event was, it was my mum who gave me the resilience and strength to handle the knocks life throws at you. Her calls for me to, 'Get off that computer' made me look at life in the military and shaped my future. As did my granddad, John Lumm, whose stories, pictures and a love for old war films put me on the path to military life. I would listen to his stories of that era, as a sergeant in the Middlesex Regiment during World War 2, and as a machine gun instructor who used to work on the buses in London.

Also, a big thank you to Lyndon, my stepdad. My sister Cassandra, whose unwavering support helped to keep people informed with the limited knowledge at her disposal, and to my son, Evan. I'm sorry to this day I missed some of your most important events over the last five years, but some fights can't be ignored. I'm here for them now.

My thanks also to Tony Giddings, my friend for thirty-plus years since our days as privates in the Royal Anglian Regiment. He inspired me in many ways to fight and keep fighting. *Be safe in Ukraine, brother.* My business partner and friend, Sean Lee, who helped me get to Ukraine. To the Royal Anglian Regiment who offered a financial donation to my wife and supported her through my detainment. To my brothers of the Royal Anglian Regiment and my closer friends in the 1st Battalion (Vikings): you are family. You all defended me when Russia tried to push the mercenary narrative, and sent me updates and news when I really needed it the most. You also maintained radio silence while every journalist was sniffing around trying to get a story. It would be unfair to single anybody out, but I am truly grateful.

I'd like to shout out to Chris Garrett (Swampy), who guided us all in the early days in mine awareness, and really kick-started my love for all things Ukraine. Denis Šeler and Tom — my mentor. Kvat Azov (National Guard) a sniper/reconnaissance platoon commander who unfortunately lost his life in Mariupol with his team, some of whom attended my wedding. Mars, Indian, Fish, Royce, Oysteri, Juice and many more — you will be truly missed too.

There's also the historic 36th Marine Brigade, 1st battalion of the Ukrainian Marines who had the faith and patience to accept me into their fold, in particular our Air Assault Company who so valiantly defended our positions in Mariupol. Out of those heroes I'd like to mention Captain Rudenko, the company commander 2020, and Captain Serhii Stratichuk (Bear) whose amazing leadership as our platoon commander saved many lives. He will be my friend always. To Kovalenko, we survived your first contact, brother, and you did good, glad to see you reunited with your family. Lt. Zip, Ivanov and my close friends Yarik and Dima who paid the ultimate sacrifice, I will never forget you all, together with all those that are still stuck in captivity and unable to be reunited with their families. The piano recital in the school at Sartana is etched on my brain forever. *Until Valhalla, brother.*

A mention must go to Boris Johnson, Liz Truss and the British Foreign Office who worked for my release, in particular, the crisis team who kept my family informed of the unfolding events, sometimes daily. I don't want to mention the individuals by name but you know who you are. My local MP, Richard Fuller, who raised the issue in Parliament and worked with my family continually. *The Sun* newspaper who repeatedly answered my calls while I was captive. Thank you for looking after us on our return. I must also say thanks to Hostage International who offered fantastic support, and my case worker who still looks in on me from time to time.

I would like to give special thanks to the people that had an influence in the exchange process, the full details of which I may never understand. President Zelenskiy and his team in Ukraine who also recognised our sacrifices and named me as a recipient of the Order of Courage, 3rd Class for 'selfless acts in the defence and sovereignty of Ukraine'; Crown Prince Mohammed bin Salman for his hospitality and medical treatment in Riyadh; Roman Abramovich and his team who gave us some good PR advice before we were introduced to the media.

Also special thanks to Colonel Richard Kemp C.B.E. who visited me on my return. If it weren't for him this book probably wouldn't have been written. Generally concerned with my well-being, he listened to the story I had to tell and gave me the confidence that it was a story worth telling. For that I am hugely grateful. Rory Scarfe, my agent at The Blair Partnership, for his direction and support. And writer Matt Allen, whose unique ability to put himself in a room with me during those dark times and draw out those emotions is truly a talent. To Rowland White and all the team at Michael Joseph and Penguin Random House who coached me through a new chapter of my life, if you pardon the pun. Their careful handling of such a sensitive subject made the process very easy and, at times, therapeutic.

This work is also dedicated to all my fellow prisoners at Makivka 97, John (God Save the King) Harding, Mathias (The Swede) Gustafsson, Sadoun (Morrock) Brahim, Dylan Healy, Andy (Chandelier Arm) Hill, Alex (Alabama) Drueke and Andy (Huuuungh) Huynh and my very good friend Vjekoslav (Grouch) Prebeg. Also to Paul Urey who was lost tragically in captivity. Thank you for trusting me to tell our story, I hope I've done you all proud. You are the best team ever. We picked each other up when we were down with a brand of humour that was second to none. You're real fighters all of you. And, of course, to Aiden Aslin: thanks for the Post-It note explaining that my wife was OK. I'm so glad to see you reunited with Dianne.

Lastly, and most importantly, to Larysa, the inspiration for the title, *Live. Fight. Survive.* There aren't enough words to express my gratitude and thanks to my wife, who under immense pressure managed to hold everything together. Not only did she deal with the invasion, me, the media, Russian propaganda, and the Ukrainian authorities, but she also held down a job and found us a new home while living out of a string of hotels on the retreat back from the east of the country with two cats. Larysa has now lost two homes and many friends to Russian invasions. She is the definition of the Ukrainian fighting spirit and the proudest Ukrainian. A resilient humanitarian and environmentalist, she continues to support Ukraine until this war is over.

Those words 'Live', 'Fight' and 'Survive' echoed through me throughout my incarceration and came to me at a time when I needed to hear them the most. They reaffirmed my one goal. *To get home.* Looking to the future, I hope I can provide Larysa with the love and support she truly deserves because she is my hero.

Glory to Ukraine!
Shaun (Sniper Cook) Pinner, 2023

Published by Lonely Planet Global Limited
CRN 554153
6th edition – July 2023
ISBN 978 1 83869 726 6
© Lonely Planet 2023 Photographs © as indicated 2023
10 9 8 7 6 5 4 3 2 1
Printed in China

MIX
Paper from
responsible sources
FSC™ C021741
www.fsc.org

THIS BOOK

Design Development
Marc Backwell

Content Development
Mark Jones, Sandie
Kestell, Anne Mason,
Joana Taborda

Cartography
Katerina Pavkova

Cartography Development
Darren O'Connell,
Piers Pickard,
Chris Zeiher

Series Development Leadership
Sandie Kestell

Production Development
Fergal Condon,
Sandie Kestell

Commissioning Editor
James Smart

Production Editor
Claire Rourke

Book Designer
Clara Monitto

Cartographer
Mark Griffiths

Production Development
Marc Backwell

Assisting Editors
Anne Mulvaney, Melanie
Dankel, Clare Healy,
Brana Vladisavljevic

Cover Researcher
Gwen Cotter

Thanks
Gwen Cotter, Esteban
Fernandez

Learn to sail the waters of the Kingsbury Estuary (p98) at Salcombe.

Discover more about the legend of King Arthur at Tintagel Castle (p178).